Communication Breakdowns

Communication Breakdowns

THEATRE, PERFORMANCE, ROCK MUSIC AND SOME OTHER WELSH ASSEMBLIES

RUTH SHADE

UNIVERSITY OF WALES PRESS
CARDIFF
2004

British Library Cataloguing-in-Publication Data.
A catalogue record for this book is available from the British Library.

ISBN 0–7083–1761–8

Published with the financial support of the Arts Council of Wales

The right of Ruth Shade to be identified as author of this work has been asserted by her in accordance with sections 77 and 78 of the Copyright, Designs and Patents Act 1988.

Typeset at University of Wales Press
Printed in Great Britain by Dinefwr Press, Llandybïe

Contents

List of Illustrations

(Between pages 82 and 83)

1. The Stereophonics in front of Cwmaman Institute, 1997, just before they released their first album

2. The Coliseum Theatre, Trecynon, Aberdare, 2002

3. The front of the Cwmaman Institute, 2002, Cwmaman, Cynon Valley

4. The Little Theatre, Gadlys, Aberdare, 2002

5. The Phoenix Players in *The Merchant of Venice* on the stage of the Coliseum, Aberdare, *circa* 1970/71

6. The Parc and Dare Theatre, Treorchy, Rhondda, 2002

7. Ferndale Band Club, Rhondda, 2002

8. Llwynypia Workingmen's Club, Rhondda, 2002

9. Canolfan Rhys Arts Centre, Penrhys, Rhondda, 2002

10. Soar Ffrwdamos Centre (a former chapel), Penygraig, Rhondda, 2002

11. Judges Hall, Trealaw, Rhondda, 2002

12. Spectacle Theatre company in Dic Edwards's *Over Milkwood*, 1999

13. The Muni Arts Centre, Pontypridd, 2002

14. Rhondda Cynon Taff Community Arts

15. The Pontypridd Community Play, 1992, *Valley of the Kings*

Acknowledgements

When I embarked on the doctoral research out of which this book project has grown one academic asked whether I really thought there was enough Welsh theatre to warrant a thesis on the subject. Even more doubt was expressed when it was realized that I was intending to investigate English-language theatre in Wales. To say that this field of research is treated dismissively by the academy would be an understatement and I have frequently been urged to turn my attentions to subject matter which has more 'status'. I have persisted with my investigations for the simple reason that the material absorbs me and has done since I was four years old, standing in the playground opposite the Coliseum, Aberdare, and wondering what theatre was for. I am still trying to answer that question.

I am especially indebted to Susan Jenkins, Director of the University of Wales Press, for showing an early interest in the material. I am also particularly grateful to Duncan Campbell and Ceinwen Jones of UWP for their support and patience. I owe a particular debt of gratitude to John Barnie and Keith Morris, both of whom were instrumental in publishing my work in *Planet* and on the Theatre in Wales website, where some of the material in this book has previously appeared in different versions. In the early stages of my research, Phil Clark of the Sherman Theatre and Professor Mike Pearson, then of Brith Gof, provided significant encouragement and food for thought. I am grateful to the following for their contributions: Strinda Davies from RCT arts development team, David Newland of VAM and ACW, Ian Roberts of the Cwmaman Institute, John Prior of ACW, Lynfa Protheroe of VAM and Iwan Williams of ACW. My colleague, and tame philosopher, Dr Kevin Magill has been unfailingly supportive. My thanks are due to Joy and Paul Rosser, both of whom work with RCT Community Arts, and to the staff of Spectacle, Valleys Kids, Canolfan Rhys and all the organizations throughout the Valleys who responded to my requests for information. The rock musicians I have had discussions with have been especially helpful. I am grateful to Professor Ioan Williams and Dr James Stredder, who offered many valuable comments on the original Ph.D. thesis, and to the University of Wolverhampton Research Committee for providing funding to enable me to have some time to work on the book. Many people have helped me during the long process of writing – first the Ph.D. thesis; and then the book which, while based in part on the thesis, is different. All errors, however, are my own.

My husband, Dr Michael Dixon, and my mother, Dinah Griffiths, have made a vital contribution to my personal support system. Above all, I'd like to thank all those Valleys audiences, unholy congregations and riotous assemblies who inspired me in the first place. This book is dedicated to the mavericks, punks and dissenters who produce the best performances – in Wales and everywhere.

Ruth Shade
July 2003

List of Abbreviations

ACE	Arts Council of England
ACGB	Arts Council of Great Britain
ACW	Arts Council of Wales
ARL	Aberdare Reference Library
BDL	British Drama League
CEMA	Council for the Encouragement of Music and the Arts
CVBC	Cynon Valley Borough Council
ENSA	Entertainments National Service Association
NAW	The National Assembly for Wales
NWR	*New Welsh Review*
OCLW	*Oxford Companion to the Literature of Wales*
ONS	Office of National Statistics
RCT	Rhondda Cynon Taff
SEWO	South East Wales Office (WAC)
TiE	Theatre-in-Education
TYP	Theatre for Young People
VAM	Valleys Arts Marketing
VAW	Voluntary Arts Wales
WAC	Welsh Arts Council
WAPA	Wales Association for the Performing Arts
WNO	Welsh National Opera

Introduction

During the 1970s, a Welsh theatre company was working in a secure hospital for those with long-term, often severe, psychological disorders. The company performed a version of the folk tale, 'Leda and the Swan'. Many of the patients, some of whom had been institutionalized for years, seemed uninterested in the performance. They maintained interior dialogues, looked elsewhere and babbled. At the end of the performance, one elderly man, who had stayed silent since his admission to the institution forty years previously, walked up to the actor who had played the swan and said: 'I saw a swan once.'

This story encapsulates what is most important about theatre. In that instance, the elements, which include a non-theatre venue and a non-paying, involuntary audience, amounted to an inauspicious circumstance. Despite being shorn of the traditional appurtenances of theatre, this theatrical event contains a rare depth of effectiveness produced by a special, albeit limited, relationship between performer and audience. It seems to me that the whole point of theatre is to make such connections between performers and audiences, to enable an association to develop through the material and the way in which it is delivered.

Yet contemporary theatre seems to do this only sporadically. Instead, so much theatre offers pre-prepared product which audiences (merely) consume. They go to the theatre to see actors, as seen on TV or film; or because the play has received media coverage; or because the company has been acclaimed. Theatre is bought in the same way as goods in a supermarket: it is an artefact which is purchased and consumed. Hence, the audience has nothing to do with the process of theatre: it does not shape it or influence it, which detaches the audience from the source of theatre production.

The problem of theatre is that it has to take its place alongside cinema, television, radio, CDs, computer games, the internet, and so on. We are a less congregative culture in some respects: there is increasing use of mobile phones and emails in place of direct contact, although that picture is complicated by the popularity of, say, dance culture, festivals and live football, where the congregational aspect of the activities is crucial. Theatre practitioners have, therefore, to devise methods of producing theatre that acknowledge the ways in which relationships between 'artists' and audiences have been fundamentally altered by technology. By this, I do not mean the practice, common during the 1990s, of theatre companies incorporating video and film into live performance. What I am referring to is the need to recognize how the interface between the arts and audiences is being changed – by the internet, for instance. The fact that the public can access information and cultural practices directly impacts on its perception of how relationships ought to work. The move, slow but inexorable, is towards greater audience involvement in the processes of 'art'; and theatre will find itself looking very 'last century' if it does not reinvent itself with this in mind.

Conversely, though, theatre's live immediacy serves as a counterpoint to the digital age; so the simplicity of the 'Leda' piece of theatre described at the beginning is arguably more powerful than hi-tech performances because its plainness shocks us into engagement. The reason for this is that, while other art-forms can work effectively as products, theatre rarely does. Thus the drive to make theatre more consumable is counter-productive; because all that does is increase the gap between audience and performer. The purpose of this book is to explain why that gap is particularly critical to theatre/performance in Wales and why, moreover, the nature of that gap is such that it stands as a metaphor for theatre internationally.

The imperative for such a book now is prompted by the changing cultural and political position of Wales during the last decade and the need to find a way of documenting that social history. It is a narrative without a conclusion, for the situation is ongoing and constantly· developing. The book is written against a dramatic background occasioned by, first, the establishment of political independence through the National Assembly for Wales and, secondly, the maelstrom caused by the Arts Council of Wales's publication of a theatre strategy.

The third element of the background is the cultural reconfiguration of Wales during the 1990s. In the last few years of the twentieth century, Wales, or 'Cymru' in Welsh, became 'cool'. Welsh bands like the Manic Street Preachers, the Stereophonics and Catatonia enjoyed international success, while older performers Tom Jones and Shirley Bassey found their careers revitalized. Welsh actors also came to the fore. The 1990s was the decade when Anthony Hopkins won a Hollywood Oscar, Rhys Ifans's performance in the film *Notting Hill* was widely acclaimed, and Catherine Zeta Jones rose to prominence through her film career and then married one of the world's most famous film stars, Michael Douglas, for good measure. Additionally, Welsh actors featured in major TV roles in *EastEnders* and *This Life*. Elsewhere, Howard Marks cultivated a notable career as a writer and cult figure. There were 'Welsh' films: *Twin Town, Human Traffic, House of America*. Clothes designer Julien MacDonald was eminent in his field. Athlete Colin Jackson was successful. The Millennium Stadium was opened in time for Wales to host the Rugby World Cup and, a few months later, was the venue for the Manic Street Preachers concert, attended by some 60,000, on the eve of the new millennium.

Wales seemed to have come a long way from the perception, expressed by the character of Dr Fagan in Evelyn Waugh's *Decline and Fall*, that 'almost all the disasters of English history' could be traced to the 'influence of Wales'. It was possible to be Welsh and not be regarded as a hick. Welsh accents, which used to be considered a hindrance – until relatively recently, few Welsh actors achieved international fame with a Welsh accent: Richard Burton was a notable exception (who, moreover, celebrated his Welshness when it was very 'uncool' to be Welsh) – became chic. Being Welsh used to be a mere minor detail. There were eminent Welsh musicians, for instance. But the fact that they were Welsh was not usually foregrounded: Amen Corner, Dave Edmunds, Man, Budgie and Badfinger were all successful at various points, but their Welshness was viewed as irrelevant. (Paradoxically, there were those whose Welshness suddenly became 'available' to them, when it was fashionable to be Welsh, who had previously put some distance between themselves and Wales.)

'Cool Cymru', however, focused predominantly on the young Welsh, and the term had probably lost most of its currency by 1 January 2000. But Welsh theatre never seemed to be a part of 'the cool'. This is perhaps a good thing in that one of the problems of hype is that whilst it propels its targets towards fame, it also hastens antipathy towards them. Already, critics are disparaging towards Welsh rock music. In contrast, Welsh theatre, having never been iconized, is not passé. Of course, Welsh rock music was not, in any case, a genre and the bands themselves had less in common than the British media sometimes supposed. But the outside attention probably did not harm the Welsh music scene and nor was it deleterious to the Welsh who, even if it was in a limited and short-term way, at least derived some benefit. Nevertheless, Welsh theatre seems to have benefited less than other performance forms; and, as a 'brand', it has an image problem. We should not see this as a failure. Indeed, I want to go further and argue, sacrilegiously, that what Welsh theatre needs to do is become more inward-looking, more parochial, more populist. These terms are anathema to many Welsh theatre practitioners and analysts. But this is because they use them improperly. What I am talking about in this book is the need for a radical parochialism which is profoundly oppositional to consumerist approaches to theatre/performance and which challenges the whole basis on which the dominant thinking about theatre in Wales, and in the UK as a whole, is founded.

From an outside perspective, though, the reader might well wonder what the point is of producing a book on Welsh theatre. After all, even taking into account the diaspora of first-generation emigrants, there are only about five million Welsh in the UK and, of those, perhaps fewer than a million have an interest in theatre. The prevailing attitude to Welsh theatre seems to be that it is too familiar to be inherently interesting for its foreignness and too undistinguished for it to merit discrete inclusion in the canon of British excellence. Moreover, theatre from Wales has not been legitimized by authentic suffering. Welsh cultural disenfranchisement is difficult to substantiate without bona fide victim status: the Welsh are not black; they do not have cultural practices which have been suppressed by an authoritarian regime; and they have not been occupied or shot at. Worse, they are regarded by some to have been the junior partner of the English imperialist project. In any case, they are as near like the English as makes no difference. What, then, is their problem?

One problem is that Wales has some serious social conditions that are not experienced to the same degree in England. For instance, according to the Chief Medical Officer for Wales's (CMOW) report *Health in Wales* (2001–2002), life expectancy rates are lower in Wales than in England (and the highest mortality rates are in the Valleys, in Merthyr Tydfil). The CMOW's Annual Report, included in the *British Medical Journal* in January 1999, stated that 'health indicators for Wales are worse . . . than corresponding figures for England'. In 1995, the average weekly household income in Wales was the lowest of all the UK regions (source: ONS, *Regional Trends 31*, 1996). The Statistical Directorate for Wales's *Comparative Indicators 2000* (figures based on 1998) show that, in comparison with England (and Scotland), more people in Wales are without qualifications, have long-term illnesses, the employment rate is lower, and more income comes from social security benefits. The evidence of data and statistics contained within a range of publications (like *Social Trends*, *Regional Trends*, *Cultural Trends* and *British Social Attitudes*, along with reports published by the Joseph Rowntree and Calouste Gulbenkian Foundations and the Office of National Statistics) supports the idea that Wales is differently configured politically, socially, economically and culturally from England.

This is not to say that Wales and England are monolithic, homogeneous entities: Wales contains pockets of the well-off and the bourgeoisie; and England has areas of dense privation. I am not arguing in favour of absolutes. What I have to say in this book about performance practices might well be applicable to parts of England where there are significant disenfranchised constituencies, or communities who consider themselves to be 'excluded' or differentiated in some way, to Scotland, Northern Ireland and the Republic of Ireland, and also to particular regions outside the UK, like Brittany, the Basque territories and Catalonia (French and Spanish), where issues of identity and the role of perceived marginalized constituencies within larger nations are of interest.

There are tendencies and shifts of emphasis within Wales which have not, perhaps, been sufficiently acknowledged as differentiating. Theatre is not floating free of all this: the lived experience – the houses people live in, the friends they have, the food they eat, their sociocultural attitudes – is fundamental to performance practices. But whilst there is indeed a multiplicity of performance practices, they are often unrecorded, undocumented and uncelebrated. The south Wales Valleys, for instance, contain the highest concentration of Welsh population and the lowest percentage of Welsh speakers. Despite the relative size of this constituency, it is a relatively silent culture. Yet the south Wales Valleys are extraordinarily distinctive and although they are comparable, in some ways, to greater Glasgow and Dublin, their cultural practices are comparatively under-explored.

This book uses the south Wales Valleys as a means of locating and exploring certain key issues: namely, those connected to coercive ideas about what (ideal) theatre is, the relationship between politics and performance, the conundrum of community theatre, the role of theatre practice in marginalized regions, the significance of class to theatre, the predicament of small nations, the problem of a system of arts subsidy which, in my opinion, often foists inappropriate, external theatre product on indigenous audiences, and the discrepancy between formal structures and organic performance traditions.

The book's structure moves from the small to the bigger picture to show how nineteenth- and twentieth-century performance practices in a small, Welsh, Valleys' town contain within them an explanation for the limited success of the grand British project of state subsidy of the arts in achieving its original objectives. Hence, the first chapter provides an account of how Aberdare changed from being the 'Athens of Wales' during the nineteenth century to a place which is virtually invisible as far as professional theatre practice is concerned. It points to the importance of the miners' institutes and working-men's clubs in the production of theatre and analyses the history and contemporary practices of the Coliseum Theatre, the Little Theatre and the Cwmaman Institute. Chapter 2 investigates a range of performance practices in the Valleys to reveal their relationships with familiar congregation and the lived experience. Here, the material will include the Muni in Pontypridd, the Parc and Dare, Treorchy, and the Blackwood Miners' Institute. In a departure from the usual material of books on theatre, there will be some consideration of popular performance in pubs and clubs, including discussion of the place of Welsh rock music. Other organizations described include the Arts Factory, Valley and Vale, Rhondda Community Arts and Spectacle theatre company.

The purpose of chapter 3 is to explain how colluding with the Arts Council's ideology actually brought about the Valleys' invisibility in terms of a formal, professional profile. The chapter's focus is on a substantial history and analysis of the Arts Council in Wales from its early days, when the issue of the dichotomy between art for the people and art for an elite first emerged. Contained within this is an account of two Welshmen, William Emrys Williams and Dr Thomas Jones, who embodied this division. The case of Williams is particularly interesting because it shows how his high-profile career effectively sabotaged the democratization of theatre in Wales; and this is linked to, and underpins, an exposition of the debacle of the Drama Strategy of 1999–2000.

In chapter 4, the dominant ideas manoeuvring theatre in Wales are identified and accompanied by an account of the disabling, binary divisions of Welsh performance practice. Additionally, there is a discussion of the role that official opinion-forming plays in disempowering the local, the indigenous, the politically inconvenient and the unorthodox.

The thread which runs through this book is the marginalization of the working classes. The 1991 census showed that the 'working classes' accounted for almost 60 per cent of the population of the Cynon Valley (in comparison, and according to figures in *Regional Trends* (1998), 37 per cent of the population of England, as a whole, can be described as working class). Since the Valleys contain the largest concentration of Welsh population, you might expect that their class complexion would influence differentiated theatre practices. But, in fact, formal theatre production, as supported by the Arts Council, is remarkably similar across the UK. This is because 'invisible' performance traditions tend to be excluded from the territory of public subsidy, even though they have a long and continuing history of support and are directly related to the lived experience. It is partly out of those traditions that the Welsh rock bands have emerged who, paradoxically, have had more international success than Welsh theatre.

This book tells the story of theatre in one small Welsh, English-speaking, working-class town in the Valleys and, out of that, attempts to engage with the bigger issues of the south Wales Valleys: class, poverty, theatre, rock music, small nations, the struggle to find a voice, state subsidy of the arts, and the politics of culture, colonialism and international corporatism.

1

Aberdare – The Construction and Deconstruction of the 'Athens of Wales'

During the nineteenth century, Aberdare was known as the 'Athens of Wales' because of its range of cultural activities; in the twenty-first, however, and as local band the Stereophonics avers, you could argue that there is 'more life in a tramp's vest'. Indeed, if you apply the usual range of performance indicators, there would seem to be no particularly good reason why Aberdare should be renowned. It is a place that appears to be below the radar of significance: famous people come from elsewhere and important events happen somewhere else. It is not even a town you would have to pass through on the way to somewhere more eminent; you need to choose to go there, for a specific purpose. In fact, Aberdare could be defined by what it is not, what it does not possess and who does not live there. In this sense, it is culturally, architecturally, economically and ethnically invisible.

You might wonder, then, what is the use of featuring Aberdare as the starting point for a book about Welsh theatre and performance; yet the point is that its very position outside the loop of cultural significance is what makes it crucial. The fact that Aberdare was once culturally notable, but was not able to capitalize on this status when the advent of the Arts Council might to have made this a possibility, suggests that there is a story to be told about the hidden outcomes of public subsidy and that Aberdare can serve as a symbol of many other places where indigenous theatre and performance practices were displaced by official versions of 'art'. Aberdare's performance activities reveal the gap between the authorized and unauthorized aesthetic worlds. By examining them, we can come to appreciate the real nature of the failure of the post-war grand project to provide public subsidy of the arts and to acknowledge that Aberdare and all those hundreds of towns like it – in Wales, the UK and internationally – are not culturally negligible but, rather, have been constructed to seem so.

My approach is to excavate the hidden history of theatre in Aberdare to show how much theatre there has been in an area which does not feature on the official map of significant theatrical sites in Wales or in the UK. There are sections on the history of the Coliseum, as Aberdare's 'premier' theatre building, and others on the Little Theatre and the Cwmaman Institute as a means of cross-referencing and of drawing comparisons about theatre function. This history is contextualized by accounts of local theatre before and after the Arts Council's inception. The conclusions take the shape of a description of the means of production and an outline of how they form an essential basis for a reconfiguration of theatre in Wales and the UK that might offer the possibility of cultural democracy.

The demographics

Aberdare is a small town at the head of the Cynon Valley in Mid Glamorgan, south Wales. Sandwiched between the Rhondda and Merthyr Tydfil, it is a typical Welsh Valleys town: indeed, its typicality is what makes it particularly suitable source material for this book; the conditions which apply to Aberdare also relate to the Valleys as a whole and the arguments which can be marshalled about theatre practice in Aberdare are equally pertinent to the larger environs.

In terms of language, Aberdare is a predominantly English-speaking area, although a little over 9 per cent of the population of the Cynon Valley speak Welsh. Some would take the view that the language issue is evidence that Aberdarians are 'less' Welsh. What Gwyn Alf Williams describes as 'the long and dismal history of indifference and contempt towards English-speaking Welsh people'[1] has had an impact on how English-language theatre has been viewed by both its local producers and its outside critics. Whilst the success of bands like the Stereophonics and the Manic Street Preachers has meant that the English-speaking Welsh are no longer denied 'membership of Wales',[2] there is still a sense that English-language performance practices are not distinctively Welsh enough. But the question of language is something of a red herring; the important distinguishing characteristic concerns 'class'.

The concept of class as a determinant is much contested. It is central to Marxist theory, where class is understood to be directly related to capitalist modes of production. However, there is disagreement about the extent to which class distinctions can be fixed, the connection between class conscious-ness and class struggle and the significance of the 'means of production' in a post-industrial context. André Gorz, in *Farewell to the Working Class* (1983), asserted that using (old) class definitions is untenable, because work should not be regarded as critical to an individual's identity.

Gorz's thinking is challenged by the work of Gordon Marshall (1997). Marshall's methodology for investigating class structures does not involve a theory of class conflict, neither does he assume that the interests of one class necessarily disadvantage another, and nor does he embrace a concept of class-based collective action. But Marshall provides evidence that class positions continue to be crucial and argues that 'postmodern' critiques of class analysis have tended to be removed from 'empirical reality', a position he shares with Christopher Norris, who contended, appositely, in *Truth and the Ethics of Criticism* (1994), that, given its proximity to the 'real world', there is 'less excuse for being a postmodernist in Cardiff'.

In this book, I have used the ABC1 (or Registrar-General's) system of social grade definitions. These six social classifications have been used for every census since 1911. However, a new system was introduced for the 2001 census with eight categories. Both systems are somewhat crude in that they are based on occupation and therefore can lead to over-simplification. However, there is no universally agreed way of under-standing social relations. In the absence of that, I am using the ABC1 system because it is widely recognized and has been used by market researchers, the census, the Arts Council, Beaufort Research Ltd (whose research has been used by WAC/ACW), and by Valleys Arts Marketing. Although it is subjective and flawed, ABC1 ensures at least some consistency in examining the evidence that is available to us.

The location of theatre practitioners, in class terms, throws up some interesting questions. Whilst some could be considered to be members of the *salariat* (using Gordon Marshall's definitions), in fact, for many, their acknowledged job insecurity, short-term contracts and slender incomes are more suggestive of skilled manual workers. However, under the revised system, actors are in category 2; that is, as one of the Lower Managerial and Professional Occupations, which places them in the middle classes. So we must expect that 'class' relationships between professional actors and their audiences will be complex and variable.

In choosing to point to the significance of class, I am agreeing with Gordon Marshall that, even if class analysis is based on occupation patterns, it is still of value as a way of understanding social relations: in this case, those implicit in theatre practice in Wales. This analysis is not, therefore, about class conflict. It is not intended to posit the notion that theatre practices associated with the 'middle classes' are invariably arid, or that 'working class' performance practices are essentially vigorous. It does, however, acknowledge the importance of class in Wales and is influenced by Marshall's view that the social classes continue to demonstrate 'social cohesion' and 'ideological distinctiveness'. (Further discussion of 'class' is contained in chapter 2.)

The most telling aspect of theatre in Aberdare, as far as this book is concerned, is that it takes place in a particular sociocultural and economic context: by this I mean that the local population is concentrated in social categories C1 and C2, albeit with strong representation in categories B and D. (See Table 1 for sources of the statistics used here and for a detailed breakdown of the class profile of the Cynon Valley. Endnote 3 of chapter 1 provides details of the social grade definitions which are being applied here. See also Table 2 for a comparison between the Cynon Valley and the UK as a whole.) There is, though, an important gender differential, in that the single largest percentage of men can be found in group C2, whereas for women it is in group C1. Hence, the class tendency of women in the Cynon Valley could be described as lower middle class and of men as skilled working class.[3] However, the second largest percentage, for both genders, is that of group D, the working class.

Table 1.
The class profile of the Cynon Valley, as % of those in employment

	Total	F	M
A: Professional	1.8	0.6	2.7
B: Managerial	20.0	20.6	19.6
C1: Skilled non-manual	19.8	33.1	10.0
C2: Skilled manual	27.0	11.1	38.8
D: Partly skilled	21.9	24.6	20.0
E: Unskilled	9.1	9.8	8.6

Source: Office for National Statistics, 1991 Census Extract (Cardiff: Welsh Office Statistical Directorate, 1998).

Table 2.
Social-class breakdown for Cynon Valley (%),
compared with UK population

	Cynon Valley	UK
A	1.8	3
B	20.0	14
C1	19.8	26
C2	27.0	25
D	21.9	19
E	9.1	13

UK figures taken from the 'Definition of social groupings', in Brigitta Horup, *Arts Attendance and Participation in Wales, June 1993–November 1997. A Report based on the ACW/Beaufort Omnibus Surveys* (Aberdare: VAM, 1997), 45.

But Aberdare also has a middle-class element; and, although this might reveal itself in ways different from those displayed by an English middle class, it has often been responsible, as Dai Smith argues, for setting the 'public tone'.[4] The Aberdare middle classes, particularly in relation to education (most noticeably the grammar schools), have been instrumental in the development of theatre practice. This picture is complicated by the contribution of individuals who come from the working classes but, by virtue of an education, often espouse notions of 'high' culture, yet regard themselves as doing so in the interests of enhancing the culture of the working classes.

Although broadly working-class, communities in Aberdare are more varied than outsiders might think. If they were to define themselves in their own terms, locals would attest to the generational and geographical differences between them, as well as to that which unites them. Younger generations tend to be more mobile, less chapel-centred, more responsive to international popular culture and, to some extent at least, less sensible of a very particular, and perhaps narrow, construction of their identity as 'Welsh'. Moreover, this picture is complicated by the fact that very young Aberdarians are more likely to be in receipt of Welsh-language education than were their parents, and it is premature to speculate on how this might express itself in the way in which they choose to lead their lives.

Aberdare's identity is complicated by its composition, as it comprises a series of variously located villages (for example, Cwmbach, Cwmaman, Penywaun, Hirwaun) which, historically, have been proud of their own separate identities even though they are only a few miles apart. Additionally, the Cynon Valley includes the towns of Mountain Ash and Abercynon, which also have a sense of their own identities. Despite differences, communities in Aberdare share a significant historical, geographical, cultural and sociopolitical context.

Aberdare as the 'Athens of Wales'

The thriving status of Aberdare in the nineteenth century was closely allied to the exponential growth in population and its concomitant industrial strength. But the significance of the 'Athens' description relates to the critical thinking about culture at that time; and an understanding of this enables us to explain both the historical background to the Arts Council and the excorporation (that is, the marginalization of Aberdare's theatre practices by the Arts Council) of Aberdare from the contemporary reckoning.

The major success of Aberdare, as Athens of Wales, was the manipulation by the local 'great and good' of popular culture so that indigenous folk forms and local practices were imperceptibly replaced by authenticated 'high' theatre. Standards were set down and accepted; modes of working were endorsed and emulated. But, more than this, agencies of familiar congregation – chapels, miners' institutes, eisteddfodau, schools, public houses and Friendly Societies – were either sidelined (as in the case of the last two) or transformed from sites of popular culture to locations used to establish high quality art-forms.

The account of John (Pendar) Davies[5] includes references to the proliferation of local practices in public houses during the second half of the nineteenth century, comprising performances of the Mari Lwyd tradition in Cardiff Street and Trecynon; ballad singing and the performance of old Welsh folk songs; and the playing of the Welsh harp for step-dancers.[6] Davies also describes the entertainments of the Friendly Societies. But his retrospective view that there had been a 'great development in culture'[7] since the late nineteenth century tells us that the move towards 'high' art was consistent with a diminishing perception that culture could be located outside of authorized buildings. This suggests that the 'performance indicators', or criteria for excellence, of the Athens project were synonymous with definitions of what those who were prominent in developing the arts locally, and later the Arts Council, believed constituted high quality.

The activities of the chapels, and their offshoot the Temperance Movement, along with the miners' institutes, eisteddfodau and the gentry, denote the development of a preferred way of approaching the arts. Whilst not formally collaborative, these 'groups' moved towards a similar (incorporated) view of the function, practice and content of theatre. Methodism tended to discourage theatre practices: 'in 1887 . . . the Methodist Sessions meeting . . . urged the chapels to shun all dramatic performances.'[8] Pendar Davies asserts that, in the 1870s, 'it was considered a very improper thing for church members to visit [theatres]'.[9] But chapel ideology had considerable bearing on the functioning of the miners' institutes, which were crucial to the development of English-language theatre in the Valleys: D. L. Davies comments that 'nonconformist values . . . were a major influence in creating and directing the Institute'.[10] Allied to Methodism was the work of the Temperance Movement, which believed in providing designated spaces within which sobriety would be encouraged through the presentation of (high) culture. Thus the Temperance Society established the Temperance Hall in 1858, which was to become Aberdare's 'most important place of popular entertainment' during the late nineteenth century.[11]

From the 1870s, the eisteddfodau encouraged the developing interest in secular drama by offering prizes. Indeed, the status of Aberdare-as-Athens is substantiated by the fact that the first 'National' Eisteddfod was held there in 1861, with a revisit in 1885. There had been local, 'informal', eisteddfodau, held in public houses at Christmas time. But the fact that Pendar considered that their disappearance by the 1920s was 'an indication that the tone of the district [was] improving'[12] provides some confirmation that the Eisteddfod was an important mechanism through which standards were established and upheld. Dai Smith suggests that the formal eisteddfodau, with their strict competition rules, were encouraged by the middle classes as the acceptable face of working-class culture to the point where the Eisteddfod came to be seen as the 'true representation' of the miner.[13] The discrimination between the informal and the formal eisteddfodau indicates that the thinking about 'standards' which was later to form a major aspect of the Arts Council's strategies was already evident in Aberdare at least as early as the First World War.

The role of the gentry, or at any rate the wealthy, was crucial in developing ideas about quality theatre and in making that synonymous with professional players. As Geoffrey Evans points out:

> It was believed by many eminent Victorians, including Henry Austin Bruce, the most influential of Aberdare's landowners, that the provision of amusement was a means of extending the education of the working classes . . . [to] improve the manners, elevate the tone and expand the intellect of that class . . . [provided it was] harmless and innocent.[14]

We can understand what was meant by 'harmless amusement' from the evidence of the later nineteenth century which shows that travelling English players entertained the gentry with plays from the English classical repertoire: a production of *Macbeth*, for example, in 1881.

The landowners recognized an opportunity to appropriate the culture in their own interests so that they might exercise control over which modes of performance were seen. By authorizing the manifestation of performance practices, the gentry could define what it was to be *cultured*, and in inculturating the proletariat, they rendered them docile and malleable in the interests of social control. Despite evidence of the vigour of popular cultural practices, the working-class people of Aberdare were considered to be *without* culture. In the gentry's terms, evidence of the success of the Aberdare-as-Athens project can be found, as Evans shows, in a concert of Handel's *Saul*, which was attended by a large audience of working men capable, a local periodical records, of 'listening with intelligence', despite the fact that there were few in the audience from the 'higher classes of society'.[15]

Towards the end of the nineteenth century, there was a tension between developing notions of what constituted quality, as recognized by the cultural 'agencies', and popular tastes. We can see from the evidence of theatre companies who were dependent on ticket revenue, and not patronized by the gentry, what kind of performer/audience relationship was successful with the Aberdare constituency. The nature of the plays they performed tends to confirm that locally relevant material attracted a crowd. From the 1850s on, there were many performances from portable or fit-up theatres; and they often presented melodramas, like *The Corsican Brothers*. But the companies also performed plays which had a direct relevance to the area; for instance: *Twm Shon Catti*; *The Maid of Cefn Ydfa*; *Will Pontypridd*; and *The Blind Witness of Aberdare*.[16] The readiness of the town's people to stage a benefit concert for one of the travelling companies confirms the popularity of the fit-ups, perhaps *because* they offered productions of local relevance: the first recorded example of a benefit performance in Aberdare, as documented by Geoffrey Evans, was in aid of Warren's (fit-up) Theatre Company, whose theatre was demolished during a snowstorm in 1881.

Analysis of the Athens 'project' shows that Aberdare contained many of the conditions necessary to become a theatre 'centre', not the least of which was that it had a vibrant theatre-going tradition offering a range of different performance practices. Not all of these were indigenous, in the sense that they were produced from Aberdare. But they were well-attended, and audiences clearly felt connected enough to the theatre companies to offer support in kind. Moreover, that most difficult of contemporary audiences to attract into a theatre, young adults, were 'constant in attendance', according to Pendar.[17]

The Arts Council would not have had to initiate a theatre-going tradition in Aberdare, so it is intriguing that Aberdare's theatre profile declined against a background of public funding of the arts. ACGB's emergence coincided with a number of factors which would have contributed to the weakening of Aberdare's status, including cinema, radio, a move towards a less congregational culture, the effects of the Second World War and changing socio-economic conditions. Nevertheless, the development of the Arts Council ought, in theory, to have offered Aberdare the potential to capitalize on its existing performance traditions.

The miners' institutes

In the twentieth century, theatre in Aberdare, amateur and professional, developed in concert with, and because of, the establishment of the institutes. The main venues for performance in Aberdare now – the Coliseum, the Cwmaman Welfare Hall and the Little Theatre – all materialized as a result of the work of the miners' institutes. There is, therefore, a crucial, determining link between working practices (in this case, the mining industry) and cultural practices.

During the space of almost fifty years, between 1868 and 1914, nine institutes were opened in the Cynon Valley, all in the outlying villages. Originally, the institutes were primarily devoted to the idea of a literary education and offered reading rooms and a library. However, they embraced the notion of cultural provision, extending into performance, at a very early stage in their development. D. L. Davies comments that, in the early part of the twentieth century, 'the local press [was] chequered with reports of . . . drama'.[18]

The institutes reflected the particularity of the villages, repositioned culture away from the orbit of the gentry, and promulgated the idea of a community centre which was, literally, in the middle of communities. But while, in general terms, the 'people' reappropriated their performance practices, those who took the lead on their behalf took the view that a 'professional' model needed to be followed: specifically one which would promote high standards. Aberdare's cultural leaders absorbed the need for standards to establish their credibility, so they could stand their ground against the gentry, while using the gentry's criteria to do so. Whilst the institutes offered a form of cultural democracy, they nevertheless embraced the same objectives as the gentry; the records of the Aberaman Public Hall show that thinking about culture focused on 'high' art: 'music composed by the great masters'.[19] The notion that the arts should be guided by the *great and the good*, which was later to become enshrined in Arts Council policy, was also evident. In setting up its Eisteddfod Committee, for example, the Conveners of the Aberaman Public Hall invited the collaboration of 'the *leading* musicians, literateurs [and] artists' (my emphasis).[20]

The Trecynon Institute: the Coliseum before 1938

The Trecynon Institute (Public Hall and Free Library), out of which the Coliseum theatre later evolved, was opened in 1902, and the progress of its Amateur Dramatic Society (which, in time, spawned the Little Theatre) typifies the functioning of amateur drama in the context of the institutes: 'Trecynon Amateur Dramatic Society . . . brought to the village much fame, and notable productions were staged there before the outbreak of the 1914–1918 war'.[21]

Theatre was used at this time as a means of making visible the lives of otherwise anonymous working people and this gave them a sense of identity. In proving that they were capable of producing validated ('notable') forms, local amateur theatre practitioners also challenged the need for the involvement of the gentry.

Trecynon was then a thriving village capable of sustaining its own discrete leisure practices and the institute's site was, to an extent, a reaction against the gentry's meanness. The research of D. L. Davies, a local historian who has written about the Cwmaman Institute, suggests one significant reason why there is today no theatre or performance site in Aberdare itself as being the parsimony of the bourgeoisie, who would not pay to build a library and institute in the town centre.[22] So, in effect, what we can see in the establishment of the Coliseum, via the institute, is a movement away from the gentry's/bourgeoisie's influence on the arts. Eventually, the Trecynon Institute came under the aegis of the South Wales Miners' Welfare Association, which provided the finance to build the Coliseum (from 1925).

The Little Theatre

The Little Theatre company developed out of the Trecynon Institute (and, therefore, its inception may be attributed to the miners' institute movement). But by 1931, when it ceased to be the Trecynon Amateur Dramatic Society and became the Aberdare Little Theatre Company, with its own designated theatre building (converted from an old engine shed), the group had made a decisive break with the institute.

At that time, Aberdare did not have a purpose-built theatre and, by building one, the Little Theatre's members may have thought they were moving theatre to its 'proper' place. The novelist and playwright, Jack Jones,[23] speaking about the Little Theatre, found it 'heartening' that 'the amateurs of a distressed mining valley [discussed] the need for a bigger stage so that they could produce *bigger and better* plays' (my emphasis).[24] But the physical transformation meant that the company also shifted the context of its aesthetic. Theatre practice in the institutes took place in the context of the totality of cultural practices: 'actors' were juxtaposed with, say, miners playing billiards. Performance did not float free of the reality of the lived experience but was placed within it. However, by building their own theatre (the Little Theatre was the first in the UK to be privately owned by an amateur dramatic society), the company took the aesthetic out of public ownership and privatized it. (The Executive Committee even guaranteed the bank loan out of their own pockets.) In consequence, to become professionalized, they separated the means of production from the modes of consumption. By building a theatre which was unaligned to local working practices, the Little Theatre submitted to free-market forces; and in this, it replicated a commercial, professional mode of practice.

There was a particular class bias to the Little Theatre company which might explain why it wanted to remove itself from the institute. The Executive Committee was composed of the middle classes. In 1931, its committee included a builder, an outfitter and a schoolteacher; and its producer was a minister of religion. But its actors were miners, engine drivers, mechanics and carpenters.[25]

The Little Theatre was able to sustain a professional (and hierarchical) approach in an amateur setting because prizes were discerned as conferring an aesthetic imprimatur, and accounts of the company point to the *quantity* of prizes it won.[26] These provided the working classes (the actors) with tangible proof that the middle classes (the management) were qualified to ensure that proper standards of excellence could be achieved. Furthermore, it suggested that a discrete theatre practice was superior to a mixed cultural practice because the Little Theatre gave the appearance that it was a more successful enterprise, in professional terms, than the Trecynon Hall.

Even though this predates the Arts Council, thinking about quality, standards and professionalism prevailed in the obsession with 'prizes' (a feature shared with eisteddfod culture). Play productions seem not to have had value unless a British Drama League adjudicator said they had. We can see from this that the amateurs allowed the professionals to distinguish for them between a good production and a poor one. This collaboration between the gentry (prize-givers), the middle classes (play producers), theatre professionals (adjudicators) and the working classes (actors) ensured that the Lord Howard de Walden Silver Trophy authenticated the value of *Lady Windermere's Fan*, while Ben Evans's *Conscience* (see below) was consigned to aesthetic oblivion. This process, which actually seemed to serve everyone's interests, taught the amateurs what professional standards were, but also gradually damaged the integrity of their own modes of production.

The Little Theatre was destabilized by the post-ACGB climate, as is evident from its deliberations over whether 'a more modern play with a smaller cast and lower costs [would] halt the decline'.[27] Nevertheless, it continued to deploy a democratic labour process: 'plays are chosen by a reading committee. Nominations are made at the Annual General Meeting . . . the Committee also selects the cast.'[28] However, the decision to work with small casts (in 1998, for instance, it presented Sue Townsend's *Bazaar and Rummage* and *Dead Guilty* by Richard Harris) takes the practice away from the full potential of cultural democracy because so few people are involved in the labour process; and this might partially explain why during the 1990s the company had average attendance figures of 52 per cent.[29]

Some context to amateur theatre

To comprehend the functioning of theatre in Aberdare as a whole, professional and amateur, we have to take into account the Welsh amateur theatre context from 1918 to 1939. Between the two world wars, there were around 500 amateur drama companies throughout Wales who developed a strong tradition, but one which diminished dramatically after the Second World War. In the Cynon Valley, and Aberdare in particular, there was a corresponding proliferation of amateur drama companies providing an indigenous Welsh theatre practice that attracted a substantial constituency, irrespective of its non-professional status.

The nomenclature of the amateur companies suggests that there was a wide range of social participation in theatre practice in Aberdare and that it was not restricted to the occupational middle classes. By the 1930s and 1940s, examples of companies included the Telynog Players of Cwmbach, Aberdare Teachers' Dramatic Society, the Plasdraw Players, St Elvan's Drama Club, Cwmdare Dramatic Society, Cwmaman Institute Theatre Group, Abernant Unemployed Dramatic Section and the drama group from the Settlement.[30] The play-texts which these groups performed suggest differences in the way in which they related to theatre practice. Whilst Aberdare Teachers' Dramatic Society performed a classic, Oscar Wilde's *Lady Windermere's Fan* in 1948, the Abernant Unemployed Dramatic Section presented in 1937 a new play written by a local man, Ben Evans, entitled *Conscience*.[31]

Such companies declined as the Arts Council developed; and a disdain towards amateur theatre became evident: hence, an article entitled 'I Indict Welsh Amateur Acting'.[32] Gradually, amateur theatre was taught to perceive itself (and audiences to recognize amateur theatre) as deficient, inferior and inadequate. In 1967, the ACGB *Report for Wales* argued that 'for too long the dominance of the amateur tradition and standards has deprived Wales of the full benefits of its own talent'; and this prejudice has persisted.[33] This suggests that we should speculate whether there is a correlation between the decline in amateur theatre and the difficulties faced by professional theatre companies in establishing a deeply rooted theatre practice in the south Wales Valleys. As Gilly Adams, Drama Director of WAC between 1976 and 1982, says: 'it is difficult to claim either that the arts have been made accessible to every inhabitant of Wales or that much has been created which demonstrates a distinct Welsh identity in either language'.[34]

The theatre practice of the amateurs in Aberdare changed during the late twentieth century. From the 1940s to the 1980s, Shakespeare constituted a significant source for amateur players. But whereas they once concentrated on presenting the classics, gradually they started to perform recent, popular plays. The Phoenix Theatre, which had specialized in Shakespeare, could be found performing Frank Vickery's *Trivial Pursuits* ('about Valleys' folk, for Valleys' folk'). Many amateurs incorporated what might be described as commercial theatre practice, as is evident in a plethora of musicals – *Godspell*, *Carousel*, *South Pacific*, *Guys and Dolls* and *The King and I*, for example. The notable contemporary absence in the amateur work is the range of plays, written in English by Welsh writers, which were performed, usually for British Drama League competitions, during the 1930s, 1940s and 1950s.

The Coliseum: post-1938 – place and space

The conundrum at the heart of public subsidy for the theatre is why, when the Coliseum might have been a candidate for Arts Council incorporation, it finds itself on the margins, while newer theatres of comparable size, like Clwyd Theatr Cymru (or smaller, like the Sherman), are positioned as ACW mainstream-funded buildings. The Coliseum's resources, local support, location, relationship with a pre-existing theatre practice, and its interconnectedness with other cultural and working practices convey the impression of a theatre which might have been expected to have been incorporated as a flagship theatre by the Arts Council. Its history, understood in the context of the Arts Council project, explains how exclusion works through selectivity. At various points, the Coliseum has evinced a large number of incorporatable characteristics. Its architecture, size and facilities display the hallmarks of mainstream theatre; when it was built in the 1930s, it was a purpose-built theatre, with 725 seats, a state-of-the-art lighting system and electric switchboard, sizeable dressing rooms, and a proscenium arch stage. Indeed, size was crucial to its establishment and respected figures of the time were quick to introduce the idea that amplitude was synonymous with quality in theatre.

Whilst the Coliseum attracted superlatives from all quarters, there was no consensus over what that quality would mean in practice. The detail of the language used indicates that the Coliseum evoked disparate points of view from its inception, and it is worth examining two serious differences of opinion – relating to buildings and programmes – which were not recognized as such at the time, to illustrate why privileging a particular notion of quality can be a mechanism for disenfranchisement.

When it was first built, the Coliseum was viewed as an extraordinary achievement, and it quickly gained referential power as a building. W. Daniel (South Wales Mining Welfare Association Organizer) described it at the opening ceremony as, 'the best building owned by a Welfare Committee that I have encountered'.[35] Daniel's emphasis on the comparative architectural merits of the Coliseum theatre epitomizes an important strand in thinking about quality: the view that excellence in theatre practice is in itself produced by a high standard in theatre buildings. But this is a very different mode of thinking from that which understands quality in relation to content and its proliferation. For instance, the MP, G. H. Hall, contended that 'the success of [the Coliseum] is going to be measured by the amount of work done in it by the people of the district, and by the quality of their work',[36] an opinion which represents an altogether different set of values about theatre practice from W. Daniel's; and this discrepancy prefigured the major tension in the future functioning of the theatre between local imperatives and high standards. Hall's notion of 'quality' included local amateurs, but the development of the Coliseum, as a formal theatre, was coterminous with the growth of CEMA/ACGB, and that institutional development produced a situation in which amateur and professional work became segregated by notions of quality, so that incorporateable quality came to be the preserve of the professional.

The Coliseum was meant to continue the nineteenth-century project of educating and raising the cultural standards of the working classes; and this philosophy engendered a third way of looking at quality in relation to the theatre, which moved towards prescribing the kinds of content that would be acceptable. We can see this perspective in the words of Oliver Harries, the Joint Secretary of the South Wales Miners' Welfare Federation, who, at the stone-laying ceremony of 1937, stated that he 'wanted to see miners aspire to something much higher than [billiards]'.[37] His agenda for the Coliseum was similar to that of Henry Austin Bruce: a project which would serve the interests of 'high' culture.

The Coliseum was, in fact, still known as the Trecynon Welfare Hall when it was opened in 1938 (it was renamed the Coliseum Theatre between 1938 and 1939). Hence, the Coliseum theatre *is* the Trecynon Welfare Hall, and this nomenclature is significant because it is indicative of the shift in thinking about the functioning of theatre practice within the community. A 'hall' is a generic description of place which carries with it no formal conception of 'arts' practice. It is an empty space which may receive any collective community endeavour. In contrast, embedded within the notion of a 'theatre' are more formal constraints which concern themselves with aesthetic programming. Moreover, a hall is a non-delineated space, whereas a theatre suggests some form of separation between performance and audience. Locally, there was some early recognition of the implications of the name of the Coliseum: in a letter to the *Aberdare Leader* in 1939, the Reverend Cynog Williams commented on 'the very aristocratic name you have pinned on the Welfare Hall'.[38]

The Coliseum's committee, however, in choosing a name more commonly associated with a Roman amphitheatre known for spectacle rather than theatre per se, revealed the scale of its aspirations for the building, and the gulf between those hopes and the reality of the theatre's location. The transformation of the Trecynon Hall into the Coliseum Theatre actually brought into play a quite different set of relations between performance and audience.

The original committee of the Coliseum did not acknowledge that a large theatre would inevitably function in a very different way from a community hall; nor did it comprehend that the new hall was not a continuation of a tradition but, rather, a crucial break with it. What this early history of the Coliseum shows is that the Coliseum, unlike Clwyd Theatr Cymru, for instance, was an organic theatre space in a socio-centric location; it was built to exploit an existing theatre practice. Indeed, the decision, taken in the early 1920s, to construct a flagship theatre was made *because* Trecynon's drama activities were already successful.

That social relationship between the Coliseum and its constituency was reflected in the choice of *Cold Coal* by E. Eynon Evans, performed by the local Carmel Dramatic Society from Trecynon, as the first production to be presented at the Coliseum in 1938. Evans was a bus-driver from Caerphilly, although he eventually became a professional playwright;[39] hence he was 'authentic', in that his theatre practice was intrinsically related both to his and to the constituency's lived/working experience.

Cold Coal[40] is a three-act play which depicts events occurring over several weeks in the life of the Llewellyn family. It is set in a fictional Valleys mining village and the action takes place in the family's terraced house. The play shows the consequences of unemployment caused by pit closures. David, the oldest Llewellyn son, is already unemployed; his father, John, loses his job during the play; Arthur, his sister Mair's fiancé, is also unemployed. Only Wensley, the youngest son, has prospects underground and is expected to be promoted in the near future. Unfolding events place the family under further pressure. Mair becomes pregnant out of wedlock; so Arthur and, later, David, work as blacklegs in a nearby pit, which is engaged in a strike. Wensley is thus positioned as the main family breadwinner. However, in the climax of the play, Wensley is killed in a pit accident during an enforced overtime shift.

What is striking about *Cold Coal* is Evans's use of symbolism. His stage direction that the coal fire 'burns brightly throughout the play' is visually powerful as well as emblematic. All of the characters are working-class and poor; yet none is caricatured or stereotyped. Evans includes a number of small, telling details. Older characters integrate Welsh expressions into their English speech, whilst the younger characters do not use Welsh. The playwright emphasizes that the house is spotless and that the Llewellyns have 'well-chosen' pictures on their walls. The family's poverty is indicated through the detail of David's clothes: his trousers are 'recently pressed', even though they are 'the worse for wear'.

At the play's heart is a debate about the value of religious belief in an apparently God-forsaken landscape – the Llewellyns, a God-fearing couple who have worked hard, been law-abiding, raised three able and decent children and given much to the community, are rewarded with the loss of their livelihood, the death of one child, the social disgrace of a second and the political censure of the third. But Evans juxtaposes the question about the purpose of religious faith with political and social issues, like the emotional and cultural consequences of Valleys' people having to migrate to find work. He also raises issues about unmarried mothers, the purpose of trade unions and gender roles:

ANN: It's not a man's job, cutting bread and butter.
JOHN: It's difficult to know what a man's job is nowadays.[41]

Evans uses the play to ask questions about Welsh politics: 'The trouble with
Wales today is that we have pinned our faith to a lot of empty, high-sounding
slogans', says Arthur. 'The trouble with Wales today', replies David, 'is that
we still have men who will sell their rights for a mess of pottage.'[42] Above all,
Evans provides a real insight into the texture of unemployment:

DAVID: I'm fed up . . . with being told that there is a job, or there was a
           job, or there's going to be a job, or there might be a job. I've
           looked for, hoped for, prayed for a job so much that now – now I
           don't want a blasted job . . . if this wave of prosperity eventually
           arrives, let them come and look for me and they'll find me . . .
           damn well rotted.[43]

Although the play tackles serious issues and is, ultimately, a tragedy, it is also
humorous and uses local patois well: Wensley announces that he is 'dwli
mad' on kippers, for instance.

When this play was originally performed at the Coliseum, it would have
been a cutting-edge piece of new writing about local concerns. Amateurs,
like Evans, once made a critical contribution to the development of indigenous theatre, and it was this kind of practice which was lost in the later drive
towards professionalization and quality. The climate in which the local
amateur could be recognized as having the potential to produce quality
theatre disappeared and this also meant that professionalization damaged
indigenous Welsh theatre. During the Second World War, Jack Jones
claimed that '[the Coliseum was] one of the few real "people's theatres" in
Britain',[44] because it enabled local people to find self-expression through
theatre practice – as was evident in a performance of Jones's own play,
Rhondda Roundabout, of which he said: 'a band of Rhondda amateur players,
in a play about the Rhondda valley and its people, gave a performance which
bettered . . . the play as originally conceived by me.'[45]

Just four years later, and shortly after the inception of the Arts Council of
Great Britain, the formal connection between cultural and working practices
was gradually superseded by an explicit and, in the sense that it became
divorced from the mining industry, decontextualized theatre practice. By
1948, the Coliseum's committee still had a direct relationship with the
mining industry: 32 per cent of its members were representatives of the
mining industry. But while this was the largest single group represented, its
relative proportions indicated that the mining industry's direct involvement
in cultural management was diminishing.[46]

The Coliseum: its management in the age of CEMA/ACGB

The committee structure, while giving the appearance of a community-based initiative, was actually a means of concentrating decision-making in the hands of a select few, who also defined standards. This sense that they were curators with a directive role was later confirmed by the attitude of the Coliseum's Secretary of the late 1950s, Ivor Rees, who argued that a vigorous theatre practice was something which the management committee needed to '*instil* into the community' (my emphasis).[47]

But the understanding of what kind of theatre it was that needed to be instilled varied, because the concept of quality meant distinct things at different times; and, also, it was used for contrasting purposes to support divergent agendas. From the outset, the (amateur) management committee took the view that, in order to achieve quality, the Coliseum should pursue forms of theatre which were validated by the Arts Council.

Both ENSA and CEMA (the forerunner to the Arts Council) made an early claim for involvement in the Coliseum, which might be viewed as a pre-emptive move towards incorporation. D. R. Davies documents that in 1940 both organizations announced that they intended to make *use* of the Coliseum as 'an oasis in the provinces'.[48] This suggests that, as far as CEMA was concerned, the south Wales Valleys were an extension of the Home Counties, rather than an area with its own differentiated theatre practice. CEMA's desire to spread its quality product represented a form of missionary work.[49] Thus, during the Second World War, Aberdare received the word of CEMA during a visit from Dame Sybil Thorndike and the Old Vic. Of course, the capacity audience which saw *Macbeth* at the Coliseum in 1941 were not, directly, forced into attending, but the culture of asserting that this kind of production defines excellence is constitutive of a form of persuasion.

In its last Annual Report, CEMA had noted the importance of the 'collaboration of local audiences with their own existing theatre managements';[50] yet the evidence of D. R. Davies's handwritten minutes (from 1948 to 1955) suggests that the Coliseum committee had a directive relationship with the audience. Indeed, the committee behaved, at times, in an autocratic manner. For example, in 1948, it refused permission for a local grocer to sell icecream during the interval. Also in 1948, it forbade the Salvation Army, or anyone else, from making a collection inside or outside the Coliseum. Most telling are the minutes of 22 March 1948, which record the Chair's dismay at learning that members of the management committee had been making public disclosures of committee business to non-committee members. From this, we gain an impression of a group of custodians rather than curators, because ownership of the space was assumed by the committee. The paradox of this situation is that, whilst operating a 'closed' management, the theatre was also attempting to encourage an 'open' performance practice, having advertised in the local paper a general meeting 'to bring into being a Dramatic Society, an Operatic Society and a Choral Society'.[51]

What made the committee consider opening itself out to members of the general public was not a belief in cultural democracy but rather a realization that it needed to develop its financial resources (most particularly because in 1951 the local council refused to provide financial support and the Coliseum was threatened with closure). Before 1948, the Coliseum's status as a 'mining leisure organization' enabled it to apply for grants from the Miners' Welfare Fund. But the Nationalization of the Coal Mines Act changed the terms of the Miners' Welfare Scheme and, therefore, less money and fewer opportunities for grants from the Welfare Fund were available. At the same time, the committee was ineligible – because it was a 'closed shop' – to apply for grants from the Glamorgan education authorities, which became possible after the passing of the 1944 Education Act. D. R. Davies's minutes record the committee's intense deliberations. It was a momentous decision to cast off from the mining industry, as it marked the formal end of a long cultural relationship with the working-men's institutes. But, although the structure of the committee appeared to become more democratic, the change was not fundamental because new members, who were not from the mining industry, did not have executive power.

However, that there was resistance to the undemocratic committee struc-ture suggests there was an awareness of the inadequacy of the Coliseum's social relations and that the amateur performers had a sense of themselves as workers with labour power which was undervalued by management. For example, in 1948, a large majority of the male section of the chorus of a production called *Balalaika* walked out, leading to the resignation of the musical director and the suspension of the production. This was because the singers demanded first choice of tickets for the Saturday night performance. However, the Coliseum Committee wanted to retain control over ticket sales. The choir members took the view that because '[they] were doing the show . . they should have the priority in the choice of tickets'.[52] The opera group realized that the Coliseum committee regarded the product of its (the opera group's) creative labour as its own property. Given that Saturday night tickets were at a premium, the chorus would have expended its efforts only to find that friends and family (the most important conduit for the validation of the chorus's endeavours) were a low priority. Whilst this may appear to be a minor disagreement, it shows that (even) amateur chorus members have a sense of themselves as stakeholders in the production process.

The difficulty with the Coliseum (and, indeed, with many theatres after the creation of the Arts Council) was that, when the theatre's position became complicated by public subsidy, its ownership was unclear, and it was not obvious to whom 'value' should accrue. In amateur practice, the 'audience' was, in effect, both producer and consumer of the product. But, against a more professionalized background, the audience's power to determine what kinds of theatre were produced and presented, and under what circumstances, was compromised. When an audience attends professional theatre, it does so as a consumer; and, as such, it is tangential to the enterprise because its main purpose is to bear witness and to buy a ticket. Individuals either attend or do not attend, and this is the extent of the audience's involvement with the production process. In contrast, when an audience is part of the local production process, it has a different relationship with the theatre venue, because that theatre becomes symbolic of the audience's power to impact on production processes; and this creates a very different set of social relations. In attempting to dictate the terms of the sale of tickets, the Coliseum's committee not only appropriated the amateur theatre product, but also established conditions of engagement with all theatre practice within that venue: namely that the role of the audience is limited to that of passive consumer, even where it might also be making an active contribution to the production process. We can see from the evidence of audience attendance that the more local amateurs were included in the production process, the more local audiences were active in supporting the Coliseum's programme. But the approach epitomized by the Arts Council did not seem to prioritize the kinds of theatre that Coliseum audiences necessarily wanted to participate in or watch.

After its inception in 1946, ACGB's strategies for incorporation included demonstrating through its authorized productions what standards were; and, conveniently, ACGB product became the means by which the Coliseum committee could instil standards. But whilst the committee had its own understanding of an appropriate repertoire (the Coliseum had a successful strategy of presenting residual performance practices displaying a marked difference from ACGB thinking: in 1946, its first Noson Lawen, for example, attracted a 'substantial' audience, according to D. R. Davies), it did not have the self-confidence to assert its views and allowed the Arts Council to determine what a quality product for the theatre would be. For instance, in 1948, Huw Wheldon[53] wrote to the committee in April and July requesting that it present the Covent Garden Opera chorus and an ACGB tour of two plays, including J. B. Priestley's *When We Are Married*. Both these requests were acceded to, despite the fact that the committee recorded in its minutes that it did not think that the Priestley play would 'take very well'. This suggests that the Coliseum committee acknowledged ACGB's influence, and was prepared to accept the Arts Council's thinking as superior to its own, even where the committee's knowledge of local interest might have led it to consider alternative programming.

The chief interest in the documentation of the Coliseum at this time is the picture of a theatre practice functioning, for the most part, outside of the Arts Council; and this information is useful because it enables us to engage with an unincorporated notion of quality and, therefore, to posit what an indigenous Aberdare theatre practice might be. What we can presume is that, before ACGB established quality as exclusively the preserve of professionals, amateurs in Aberdare were regarded as having an equal potential to produce high standards. The Coliseum committee had confidence in the quality of amateur practice even to the point where it would prioritize amateur over professional productions; for instance, an amateur variety show from Port Talbot was accepted, whereas a professional company from London with an 'all-star' show was rejected; and in 1948, the committee took the initiative of securing a performance from the amateur Landore Dramatic Society because it thought that the production had 'quality'.[54] But, through the 1950s, the Coliseum committee increasingly accepted Arts Council touring professional productions, as was the case in 1949, 1950, 1953, 1954 and 1958.

The Welsh media endorsed ACGB's status as standard-makers: Haydn Davies comments in the *Western Mail* that, '[tours continue] the Arts Council's policy of bringing worth-while productions to the theatreless towns of north and south Wales'.[55] But Aberdare was by no means 'theatreless' without ACGB, nor was it a stranger to 'worthwhile productions', in local terms. What Davies meant by this was that an Arts Council notion of the 'worthwhile' was being developed which embraced a professional concept of quality theatre and that touring was a mechanism for this strategic formation.

If we consider the 'worthwhile' plays which were presented at the Coliseum by ACGB at this time – *Pygmalion*; *The Rivals*; *Romeo and Juliet*; and *The Duenna*, for example – we can observe that they were almost exclusively from the classical 'canon'.[56] Moreover, it is noticeable how those involved with theatre practice learned to use the language of incorporation, which endorsed the canon, to demonstrate the worth of what they were doing: D. R. Davies boasted that 'no Welfare Hall in Wales has had more Shakespeare, professional and amateur, than the Coliseum'.[57]

The Coliseum and incorporation

By the 1950s, the Coliseum achieved the aim of presenting 'high' culture. But more than that, it possessed the conditions to become an incorporated venue. A key factor in its 'incorporateability' was the relationship between the Coliseum and opera, which is particularly indicative of the Coliseum committee's thinking about quality in the context of ACGB's objectives.[58] The minutes from 1948 to 1955 show how the Coliseum committee prioritized the development of opera, in concert with ACGB's development of the Welsh National Opera. What is significant about this to a comprehension that there is a hegemony of quality is the way in which ACGB set about achieving its project. The next example illustrates the working of its methodology.

In April 1948, the Coliseum committee received an invitation from ACGB's director to attend a 'first class' concert of classical music, including operatic arias, in Cardiff, from which it could select 'suitable' acts for booking at the Coliseum.[59] This implies a strategy by ACGB (Wales) to establish a connection between its authenticated product and inherent quality. Secondly, it promotes the idea that opera was of particular value; and, thirdly, the implication is that by presenting validated material, venues would *ipso facto* become authorized theatre practices.

A later incident shows how ACGB was able to construct a model of exemplary practice while creating a list of candidates for incorporation, some of whom, including the Coliseum, could be discarded once they had served their purpose. In 1951, the Coliseum might have closed as a theatre because it did not have a safety curtain, and Aberdare Urban District Council was unwilling to endow sufficient grant aid. The committee approached ACGB, which provided the necessary funds. In her speech given at the unveiling of the new safety curtain, Myra Owen, director of the Wales Office of ACGB, outlined the nature of the Coliseum's relationship with the Arts Council in terms of what each could do for the other:

> One of our great needs, as an Arts Council, is to find people with an enlightened policy in respect of the arts, and people willing to co-operate with us. The Coliseum has done everything possible to help us. After the deputation had visited me in Cardiff in 1950, I was determined that, whatever else happened, the doors of the Coliseum had to be kept open.[60]

We should note that Owen's speech was given during a performance by the Welsh National Opera, its first in Aberdare; so that, in a sense, the Coliseum was literally kept open to promote the WNO. The Coliseum had the size of stage and auditorium suitable for opera and, in holding the theatre open, Owen protected an outlet for the WNO. Therefore, opera served the interests of both ACGB and the Coliseum's committee, providing a link between the notion of quality, as it was perceived in the 1950s, and the identification of, and support for, those who might provide the conditions necessary to produce it.

For some twenty years – from the late 1930s to the late 1950s – the Coliseum was successful in attracting audiences and we can draw certain conclusions from this. Audiences at the Coliseum were substantial when there was a direct relationship between the means of production and the modes of consumption and, generally, this happened when the performance developed out of familiar congregation. This might take the form of local provenance; for example, the old Trecynon Public Hall 'was packed for the opening of the Trecynon drama competition'.[61] Or it can relate to a shared experience: during the Second World War audiences at the Coliseum were often large and the theatre played an important role in raising morale; councillor Tom Phillips, chairman of the Little Theatre, wondered how the people of Aberdare would have coped without the Coliseum during the war.[62] We can also note the response of audiences to indigenous performance traditions: D. R. Davies states that, during the Mountain Ash National Eisteddfod of 1946, the Coliseum was not only full every night, but 'was besieged' for a specially commissioned play performed by a local cast and directed by two local people.[63] Consequently, we can contend that programming which integrated production and consumption *caused* audiences to attend.

In contrast, in the post-ACGB, incorporative climate, where amateur work was held under suspicion, the local constituency was alienated from the means of production; and this impacted upon its willingness to consume theatre. While a British Drama League adjudicator could still maintain in 1959 that 'the Coliseum, Aberdare, is the Mecca of drama in Wales',[64] audiences in Aberdare seemed unmoved by this assessment. At an annual meeting of the Little Theatre in the late 1950s, the chairman, Alan Morgan, asked whether 'Aberdare audiences [had had] a surfeit of drama'.[65] Then in 1962, the *Aberdare Leader* opined that 'apathy by the Aberdare public is threatening the future of the Coliseum'.[66] Those closely involved with the management of the Coliseum held audiences responsible for the decline of enthusiasm for theatre practice: 'the blame must lie entirely on the people of Aberdare'.[67] The discussion about the 'vanishing' audience continued to exercise the *Aberdare Leader* from the early 1960s until the 1980s: 'where's the audience? . . . Whatever happened to the theatre-goers of the Cynon Valley?'[68] This suggests that something dramatic happened to audiences post-ACGB and after the Second World War. Some might say it was a combination of TV, increased pub-going, the growth of rock music, attitudes towards community. But these factors, although important, do not provide a full explanation.

In the 1960s, many of the old welfare theatres and halls became derelict, or were converted into licensed clubs, cinemas and bingo halls. While there was some recognition of a 'wind of change abroad in S. Wales as far as people's tastes for entertainment are concerned', it did not produce the kind of debate which was necessary to the Coliseum; instead, while there was a will to 'enable the Coliseum to go on catering for cultural activities', this was to be done while retaining 'the purpose for which it [was] intended'.[69] We can assume from this that the original idea was to provide a formal, flagship theatre capable of presenting 'Culture', as distinct from the wider,

popular cultural practices espoused by the institutes; and this is substantiated by an editorial in the *Aberdare Leader* (1966) which asserted that
'without the Coliseum the cultural life of the town, and indeed much of the
valley, would be very bleak'.[70]

The Coliseum was caught between a developing popular culture, on the
one hand, and an Arts Council thrust towards the establishment of new
theatres, on the other. At the same time that the Coliseum was acknowledged within Aberdare to be the major cultural institution, the Arts
Council considered that venues like it were symptomatic of unsatisfactory
theatre provision in Wales. The 1966 ACGB (Wales) Report, for example,
refers to the 'serious deficiency of suitable buildings';[71] the 1967 Report
describes the lack of 'appropriate' theatres;[72] and the 1970 Report points
to the prioritization of new theatre-building with the appointment of an
assistant director for Drama and Housing the Arts.[73] The Coliseum was not
a local authority venue. But it was neither a commercial enterprise nor an
amateur theatre company with referential power, like the Questors Theatre,
Ealing.[74] Most importantly, it did not comply with WAC's objectives for
flagship buildings.

The problem for venues like the Coliseum was that, while they had been
useful to ACGB in the 1950s, they were much less so in the 1960s, when the
WNO, for instance, was able to extend its relationship with the New Theatre
in Cardiff and an increasing car-owning constituency in the Valleys was
prepared to travel to see the WNO. Then in the 1970s, ACGB (WAC) prioritized the building of new theatres, which, as Graham Taylor pointed out,
were mainly located next to universities,[75] in areas that were not central to
community life, in contrast with older theatres like the Coliseum, which
were in the middle of the lived experience.

In comparison with new concrete showcases like Clwyd Theatr Cymru,
the Coliseum looked shabby and evoked an older, inconvenient working-
class history out of step with the image which the Arts Council was trying to
project (even though the Coliseum, at 617 seats, is about the same size as
CTC's main auditorium). The Coliseum did not resemble what WAC
thought of as a quality theatre experience and, worse, local people absorbed
the idea that their theatre was unworthy; as this 1982 report in the *Aberdare
Leader* states: 'at times, there are reasons to believe that the up-to-date
Coliseum is not appreciated as much as was the old Trecynon Hall'.[76] So
when the Coliseum was transformed into a professional touring venue in the
early 1990s, its potential within the Arts Council's quality matrix was
already compromised because the local constituency had already been
educated into recognizing that a quality theatre practice was rather different
from that which was offered at the Coliseum.

The Coliseum in the 1990s

The purchase of the Coliseum by CVBC from the Coal Industry Social Welfare Organization (CISWO) in 1989 marked an end to a formal relationship between theatre and the totality of the lived experience.[77] Pat Murphy, former deputy director of leisure for RCT County Borough Council, suggests that the refurbishment project of the early 1990s was steered by members of the council:

> If we, as officers, had . . . said that it was our recommendation that [the Coliseum] should not be taken on board by the authority . . . [that would not] have been acceptable to the members . . . the decision was taken that it was going to be a flagship site for the arts in the Valleys.[78]

Murphy's view that it was elected councillors who were most committed to the (new) Coliseum project is corroborated by Martyn Green, the former general manager of the Coliseum: 'the members were, if anything, more supportive and much more encouraging [than the officers]'. It is significant that it was local councillors and not 'professionals' who made the decision to refurbish because they were the 'local voice' in this case, who carried with them a sense of the tradition of the Coliseum, of its history as the new successor to the old Trecynon Institute, and of its potential to attract attention to the area. They saw in it a concrete symbol of what the people of Aberdare might aspire to be: a cultured society. The local authority could at least imagine the Coliseum as a flagship theatre. Eric Hitchings, the local authority's then director of leisure services, describes the Coliseum as '[a contribution] to the quality of life in the Cynon Valley [which provides] a broad based programme of top quality entertainment and arts based activities'.[79]

The difficulty is, though, that Eric Hitchings's view on what the Coliseum is or how its effective functioning may be achieved is by no means universally accepted. The crux of the matter was the complexity of establishing a coherent reading out of a disparate set of groups (comprising, in this case, elected members of the local council; appointed officers of the leisure services department; management of the theatre; ACW; local amateurs; visiting professionals; participants in local community arts advocacy; and constituent audiences), who had no shared history or formal mechanisms of talking to each other.

It is unsurprising, then, that when Martyn Green started his job 'no arts strategy had been put together'. But, in appointing a general manager, as opposed to an artistic director, the local authority determined an arts strategy by default because, as Green asserts, 'there was no talk of the Coliseum being a producing venue'.[80] While a resident theatre company was ruled out, the local authority nevertheless had an accidental agenda for a professionalized theatre practice which limited the possibilities in Aberdare of a successful professional outcome. A theatre led by an artistic director might have enabled the Coliseum to become the 'flagship' which the council members wanted it to be, because such a director could have integrated the processes of production and consumption in a locally relevant way; but a manager is primarily a programmer who places the theatre in the position of a recipient, separating at source the relationship between production and consumption.

The outcomes of this ill-conceived professionalization in the 1990s can be assessed from audience responses.[81] Between April 1993 and March 1994, for example, only a quarter of seats for professional plays/drama were sold and between April 1994 and March 1995 this figure dropped to less than a fifth. In contrast, between two-thirds and three-quarters of seats were filled for amateur events. These statistics need to be understood in the context of the lack of verification for amateur events, because amateur companies sell their own tickets. Nevertheless, during 1994–5 the percentage of seats sold declined in all areas except for amateur and children's events

Table 3.
The Coliseum's programme in 1949-50 and 1992-5
(proportions shown as %)

	1992-5	1949-50
Total theatre events	32	46
Professional	64	12.5
Amateur	36	87.5
Concerts or variety events	59	52.4
Professional	60	3.8
Amateur	40	48.5
Total dance events	9	0.9
Professional	78	100
Amateur	22	0

Table 3 provides a comparative analysis between the 1992–5 programmes[82] and the 1949–50 programme[83] and demonstrates the difficulties of professionalizing theatre at the Coliseum. In comparison with 1949–50, the professionalized Coliseum increased its total output of live events by 50 per cent; but the amateur-managed Coliseum offered 14 per cent more live theatre in 1950 than in the 1990s. In 1950, however, productions were mainly amateur, whereas in the mid-1990s two-thirds were professional. Martyn Green adhered to an agreed ratio of 60 per cent professional product, and 40 per cent amateur product; but the extent of the differentiation between amateur and professional performances provides evidence of the impact of Arts Council thinking on programming.

For the most part, productions were traditional theatre in form and content, with a reliance on Frank Vickery's plays. Examples included: Vickery's *Breaking the String* (a 'study of the destructive power of mother love'), *Sleeping with Mickey Mouse* ('Two Welsh talents in a moving and compassionate tale'), and *Love Forty* ('Rhondda playwright . . . two characters . . . miraculously married to each other for forty years'); Theatre West Glamorgan's *Desperate Measures* ('when desperate people try to sort things out for themselves'); Wales Actors Company in *Germinal* ('When the mine owners cut the already pitiful wages the town is ripe for revolt'); and John Godber's *Teechers* ('If you like Frank Vickery you'll love John Godber').

The few developmental productions were isolated, as though they were in the programme to justify ACW's South East Wales Office's (SEWO) Programme Support funding. For example, Y Cwmni's production of Ed Thomas's *East from the Gantry* ('Into this morass of emotional turmoil comes not only the complication of a pizza delivery phone call, but the arrival of a lone drifter from the television series *The Virginian*') did not appear to connect well with the rest of the programming. *East from the Gantry* was funded by ACW, but the production did not attract a large audience at the Coliseum (Green estimated that there were approximately thirty to forty people in the audience), which illustrates the difficulty of presenting a piece of theatre that has no clearly defined, direct relationship with the venue's constituency, even though Ed Thomas originates from an area near Aberdare.

The position at the end of the twentieth century was that ACW did not directly support the Coliseum from its main drama funding categories, although SEWO funded the Coliseum through its Programme Support Grant; and, as a receiving venue, the theatre was indirectly subsidized by receiving ACW-funded productions (WNO, Sherman Theatre Company, Y Cwmni, Theatre West Glamorgan, Volcano).

By the autumn season 1998, the Coliseum was receiving far less by way of Arts Council theatre product than it had been earlier in the 1990s. Subsidized material represented just 18 per cent of the Coliseum's live performance programme,[84] as compared with 81 per cent at Clwyd Theatr Cymru. A single performance by Volcano of Alan Ayckbourn's *Time of My Life* actually represented a third of the Coliseum's professional portfolio that autumn, yet audience attendance for that production was only 11 per cent of capacity.[85]

To contextualize this, in 1997/98, average attendance at each live performance was around 40 per cent.[86] However, only 8 per cent of the capacity was filled for professional plays. Even the Coliseum's own promoted pantomime obtained just 39 per cent capacity,[87] which suggests that not only did professionalizing the Coliseum not develop audiences for professional theatre but it also had repercussions for amateur theatre.

Moreover, audiences were atypical of the Cynon Valley. While the Coliseum's audience tendencies reflect the social class breakdown of its immediate catchment area – in Aberdare West, the ward which includes the Coliseum, 53 per cent of the population falls in groups ABC1 – the audience is non-representative of the locality as a whole. So the Coliseum had an increasingly tangential relationship with the community, not least because its audiences were, in local terms, verging on the 'rarefied', as the figures in Table 4 demonstrate.

Table 4.
Comparative demographics

	Coliseum audiences	The Cynon Valley
Largest constituency	Middle-class	Working-class
	Mainly C1	Mainly C2
2nd largest	AB	DE[c]
Gender	Female[a]	More even[d]
Age	25–54[b]	16–59[e]

a) 67.3% female; 32.7% male. VAM, *The Coliseum, Aberdare: Three Year Plan* (Aberdare: VAM, 1995), 22.

b) Central Statistical Office, *Digest of Welsh Statistics 38* (Cardiff: Welsh Office, 1992), 21–3. VAM found 67.3% of Coliseum audience are female, 46% from C1, 36.3% from AB and 15% from C2; 28.7% aged 35–44, 19.2% aged 25–34 and 18.6% aged 45–54; 50.9% of audience are employed, 23.5% unemployed (47.5% retired or unemployed and 19% retired).

c) Source: ONS. Data concentrate on economically active members of population.

d) Total population of the Cynon Valley at 1991 census: 65,800, males 32,100, females 33,700. That is, male 48.7%, female 51.2%.

e) Age statistics are difficult to assess because different sources use different methodologies. According to *Digest of Welsh Statistics 38*, 38,700 in the Cynon Valley are in the 16–59 age range, that is, 58.8%.

The fact that these figures are consistent with those for audiences in Wales, as a whole – except with regard to age: the audience at the Coliseum is a little younger than the average Welsh audience – demonstrates the homogenizing effects of the Arts Council on theatre audiences.[88]

The Coliseum's marginalization and the development of Arts Council thinking

From the end of the Second World War onwards, the Coliseum's ethos was informed by Arts Council policies, even though the benefits of public subsidy to the Coliseum were so limited as to suggest that it might have made more sense for it to have developed itself as an independent commercial enterprise. The reason for this is that the Arts Council came to be seen as the expert institution in the field of theatre, and the perception of this led those who ran theatres, like the Coliseum's management committee, to discipline themselves into attempting to replicate the conditions for theatre which the Arts Council seemed to endorse, irrespective of whether this was appropriate or useful.

This gave the Arts Council an authority which was disproportionate to its income. In Wales, its prioritization of professionalization and normative standards produced a powerful 'gaze', the effect of which was to homogenize the theatre practices of a heterogeneous, Welsh culture. Consequently, a 'reality' of theatre was created which has tended to exclude those who do not conform to the established 'norms' of the Arts Council.

In Aberdare, the Coliseum theatre has been disenfranchised from Arts Council structures largely because it is situated in a 'difficult' location where the audience is thought to be unreceptive to 'serious' theatre.[89] The reality of this marginalization can be detected from relative programming proportions.[90] In 1999–2000, for example, plays/theatre (including musicals) represented only 15 per cent of the Coliseum's programme, which means that the Coliseum delivered 17 per cent less theatre in 2000 than it did in the early 1990s; and 31 per cent less than in the late 1940s. The fact that over three-quarters of its programme was devoted to film suggests that the Coliseum has, in effect, become a cinema: hardly a successful outcome to the Arts Council's original aim of bringing theatre to the 'theatreless' towns of the Valleys.

The more the Coliseum adopted Arts Council thinking, the more distanced it became from the lived experience and, when that happened, the Coliseum started to lose its audience. This then impacted on its ability to function as a theatre and, constrained by market forces, it has mutated largely into a cinema to attract audiences. The Cwmaman Institute, however, has had a different history because its location outside the Arts Council nexus has enabled it to produce performances which derive from the lived experience, and this has been an effective means of attracting audiences.

The Cwmaman Institute

The key to the Cwmaman Institute's theatre practice lies in its range of social and leisure activities. The problem of the Coliseum is that it tries to function as a discrete flagship theatre open for the presentation of theatre product to a generic theatre-going audience, which means that it does not benefit from a core lived constituency. Although it has a social use, in that it offers evening meals and a bar, the Coliseum positions itself as 'somewhere for that Special Occasion'.[91]

In contrast, the Cwmaman Institute serves as a cultural centre for the immediate community. A further important difference between the Coliseum and the Cwmaman Welfare Hall/Institute is that, in Cwmaman, theatre is performed in a *public hall* and not a theatre; and this use of terminology refers not just to the notion of space and its ownership, but also to a shared history of performance traditions.

The Cwmaman Institute has a long history of presenting drama. By 1929, according to D. L. Davies, four dramatic societies were based there. Indeed, some of Aberdare's most distinguished professionals were involved in performance activities at the institute. Amongst these was the poet Alun Lewis's father,[92] who became Aberdare's Director of Education. Alun Lewis's mother was also involved in local theatre and wrote a prize-winning one-act play, first performed in 1933, which is set in Cwmaman. *Pleasant Place*[93] is notable because its central character is a woman, thus giving voice to one of 'King Coal's lowliest subjects'.[94] The play introduces Mari Jones, a poor collier's wife, and portrays her struggle to survive in the Valleys during the Depression.

The Cwmaman Institute's Theatre Group has always been able to draw large audiences for its productions because, as D. L. Davies observes, the company has 'its roots in the local community'.[95] Unlike the Coliseum and the Little Theatre, which are both discrete theatres, Cwmaman is still a working-people's institute and theatre takes place alongside a wealth of other activities – bars and catering, cinema, silver band, operatic society, Brownies, sports teams and so on. Many Cwmaman people use the institute as a matter of course and, therefore, theatre does not float free of other activities. What the theatre group presents is, to a considerable degree, irrelevant (*Blithe Spirit*, *A Night on the Tiles*, *My Giddy Aunt*, pantomimes at Christmas, Frank Vickery's plays and comedies by Norman Robbins and Derek Benfield). The point is that it shares ownership of the space and the economic means of production, and creates its own value from the labour process: its members own their own labour power.

Theatre practice at the Cwmaman Institute exists in the context of a history which is known to, and shared by, those who produce the performances. When, say, the women in Cwmaman's productions enter the performance space, they may carry with them the histories of their own mothers, grandmothers and great-grandmothers *in that space*, and a community sensibility is thus inscribed in the performance text to transform the general into the particular. There is no distance between the lived experience of the audience and that of the performers and this translates into attendance figures. But when the Cwmaman Institute Theatre Group accounts for its preference for comedies, for instance, by stating that, '[comedy] is [its] best audience seller',[96] it does not mean that simply in economic terms; what is also indicated here is the totality of the social experience of theatre-going, which includes the critical aspect of comedy, namely that it produces an observable, collective, public response.

The old Cwmaman Institute's lack of 'distinction' helped to make it popular. It was unintimidating, accessible and it served a useful purpose as an amenity (it has been estimated that during the mid-1990s around a third of the local population used the facilities every week[97]); and this functionality seems to affect responses to its presentation of formal theatre because the Cwmaman Institute's attendances have been proportionately better than the Coliseum's. In 1994, for example, 84 per cent of seats for amateur theatre events were sold and over three-quarters of the seating capacity was filled for a professional pantomime.[98] According to the late Brenda Culliford, the former secretary of the Cwmaman Institute Theatre Group, the average attendance for amateur plays in 1998 was 58 per cent of capacity.[99]

We should, however, be mindful of the global totals here: while the percentages show the Coliseum lagging behind Cwmaman, 40 per cent of its capacity actually represents a total of 250 people, whereas 58 per cent at Cwmaman denotes only 200 people. But the significance of the relative proportions increases when we take into account audience sizes in relation to ease of access. Cwmaman is in a geographical cul-de-sac approached by narrow, winding roads on an incline; whereas the Coliseum is just off the main Aberdare to Hirwaun road.

The significance of Cwmaman's non-professional performance work (as contrasted with the Coliseum's work) lies in its resemblance to orature. The evidence of engagement with the theatre practices of the Coliseum, the Little Theatre and the Cwmaman Institute implies a relationship between local modes of production and audience support, to the extent that the more a theatre practice resembles orature the more marginal to the Arts Council it is likely to be. For instance, in funding terms the Cwmaman Institute, which manifests a high degree of orature, is (merely) Lottery and not revenue funded.

There is, though, a connection between receipt of Arts Council subsidy and self-identification with its external standards of professionalism, as evidenced by this response to its Lottery award: 'when [the theatre] reopens, it will be a state-of-the-art theatre . . . [and we hope] to attract more professional companies into our area.'[100]

The Cwmaman Institute experienced considerable change during the late 1990s and early part of the 2000s. It secured around £3.5 million, including a large Lottery award, which enabled it to complete a major redevelopment of the building along with a refurbishment of the theatre. The institute appointed a manager in 2001 and, in 2002, an Arts Development Officer, with three-year funding from ACW. But these developments, whilst providing much-improved facilities, also increased the likelihood of tensions, because the institute now has to juggle the potentially competing demands made by its Board of Trustees, a Board of Directors, various user-groups, the local authority and ACW. Since annual running costs are met through trading and, equally, given that it will be important to exploit the theatre's capacity, there is the possibility of ideological differences between those two organizational arms. Cwmaman's cinema and theatre have a turnover of around £50K. However, in comparison with the bars, which involve a turnover of some £1 million, and catering, which is in the region of £70K, performance activities could find themselves compromised if hard choices need to be made. Certainly, a number of Lottery-funded venues have found themselves weakened by refurbishment, discovering that agreeable facilities come at a price increased official intervention, unrealistic expect-ations and proprietorial attitudes towards the building. A subtle remove from the local constituency is symbolized by the fact that the institute chose to welcome Prince Charles to reopen the refurbished building. The contrast between the institute's beginnings, when local colliers donated a halfpenny a week from their meagre wages, and the material wealth of the Royal Family was stark.

Whilst it is admirable that the institute is able to meet its own running costs, it is brave of it to claim that it does not 'require' continual revenue funding. That said, its arts events already attract some 15,000 attendances per year (and this in a village with a population of only 10,000); so revenue funding with its concomitant professionalization might actually diminish audiences. But if, as was claimed in the *Cynon Valley Leader*,[101] the institute wants to become 'the premier cultural centre in Wales' it would need to acquire revenue funding from ACW, as manager Ian Roberts has acknow-ledged. However, the discrepancy between the institute's perception of itself and ACW's understanding of it is already apparent in the contrast between that vision of a national cultural centre and ACW Chairman Sybil Crouch's comment that the institute is of 'central importance to the *local* community' (my emphasis). For ACW, the Institute is a useful venue for presenting and increasing the value of ACW product; but perhaps no more than that. Indeed, some support for this idea can be found in the institute's struggle to obtain funding for the Arts Development Worker post, which Ian Roberts ascribes to the fact that Cwmaman Institute is neither a local authority nor an ACW-funded building and does not, therefore, fit in with either organization's strategic thinking.

Since its reopening, Cwmaman Institute has won the Carling Best Club in Britain award of 2001, out of 35,000 entrants. It has joined VAM, which will enable it to receive properly audited statistics about its programming, and it has started to build a performance programme. The events it has run confirm that locally produced projects attract the biggest audiences. The institute's own pantomime played to about three-quarters capacity in comparison with around 30 per cent for the professional Christmas show. But, at present, cinema is, in Ian Roberts's words, 'Cwmaman's bread and butter' and one problem with this is that the institute is then in competition with the Coliseum for the earliest date to show a film.

When it did not have much money, the institute put on plays it thought that local people would want to see. The by-product of having significant capital funding is that the institute will be required to bring in (professional) theatre from outside the area, even though it may not attract local audiences. Thus, Arts Council funding could have the effect of decreasing audiences, particularly when you consider that in Aberaman South, the ward which includes Cwmaman, only 31 per cent of the constituency falls in ABC1, the typical constituency for traditional theatre product.[102]

Until the twenty-first century, Cwmaman was an effective unincorporated venue, despite the fact that its own theatre work did not conform with Arts Council definitions of quality. It was capable of attracting substantial audiences for its theatre performances largely by 'word of mouth',[103] even though it was not a professional touring venue – it did not host performances from ACW's Night Out touring scheme, for example. So two things are puzzling. First, why Cwmaman Institute would want to accept the terms of incorporation (it has already entered into discussions with ACW about hosting Night Out product) and, secondly, why a theatre practice which was inclusive, supported and effective within its own terms was not, in any case, incorporateable by the Arts Council.

The means of production

The key factor in the effectiveness of the Cwmaman Institute has been the relationship between its performance practices and the lived experience of its audiences. In particular, it is determined by the 'means of production'. This term originates in Marxist terminology and it refers to the exercise of labour power, the uses of technology, the labour process, ownership of space, the education of the proletariat, economic ownership of the means of production and the relationship between the bourgeoisie and the proletariat.[104] Whilst complex, these concepts enable us to understand the nature of the transactions which take place during theatre practice in Aberdare. But we need to be cautious about two aspects of the modes of production, labour power and the labour process, because these are more properly associated with professional work for a wage, and industrial work, at that.

In brief, labour power refers to the *capacity* to exercise a skill, or to the possession of a talent; but the 'employee' needs to be 'empowered' to put that capacity into practice by being given a space, or resources, or the opportunity to work or make a product. The labour process describes the work itself: the object on which the work is carried out, and the tools which make the work possible. Strictly speaking, it is these last two which are the *means* of production, where the point of the exercise is to create qualitative value which can be sold at a profit.

Theatre is an intricate working practice to analyse because those who give practitioners the resources to produce theatre are not perceived as being 'capitalist' in the Marxist sense; nor is the 'product' understood to have economic value, as such – subsidized venues would not generally benefit from significant surplus value because the cost margins are too small. Moreover, when theatre companies 'sell' a production, they are not alienated from the object of their creative powers, as they perform it or are credited with having created it. Nevertheless, what is crucial is the nature of social relations in theatre practice: and concepts of ownership, even if they relate to quite small sums of money, have at least some part to play in cultural transactions. Moreover, there must be some (dis)connection between the (theoretical) capacity to make theatre and the exercise of that, or not, in the context of a system of practice which empowers certain groups instead of others. Additionally, there is an unequal distribution of resources and the potential to create value (and we can associate this with 'quality', rather than price) is determined by selection. Consequently, there is a power struggle in relation to theatre practice and this has disenfranchised theatre in Aberdare to a particular degree because it falls outside even the impoverished circumstances of much professional theatre. Whilst theatre practice in Aberdare connects work with leisure to reflect the totality of the lived experience, it both places itself and is placed outside of referential power because of its non-conformance to Arts Council funding (and aesthetic) criteria.

The importance of theatre in Aberdare to an understanding of how theatre works in general across the UK lies in the residual presence there of forms of theatre which prefigure those privileged by the Arts Council, coexisting with theatre practices which are obviously influenced by Arts Council thinking. Hence, it is a place which enables us to evaluate the whole role of the Arts Council because we can still find there the traces of indigenous, local impulses to produce theatre and, as such, this is important evidence of what Raymond Williams advocates: 'communities [defining] themselves in their own terms'.[105] The first-hand, practical experience of the internationally acclaimed German director, Peter Zadek, provides further corroboration for a strategy which relates to the lived experience. Zadek ran a theatre in Pontypridd in the 1950s but failed to attract an audience because 'the miners weren't interested in what [he] was doing, and there was no reason why they should [have been]'. He now considers that what ought to be done in Wales is '[bring] into the theatre the audience who *should* be in it. [He would present] a popular revue-type show . . . [to give him] the courage to do Shakespeare in a very open and popular way.'[106] There is a problem in what Zadek says, in that he seems to see the popular as merely a means by which the classical canon of theatre can – must, even – eventually be established. But at least he acknowledges the importance of starting where the audience is at and of not imposing externally created stories. (We might note here Edward Said's contention that the power to obstruct local narratives is a defining aspect of imperialist discourses.) Zadek's discovery is endorsed by Owen Kelly who argues in *Community, Art and the State* that: 'It is an act of oppression . . . to attempt to "work with" a community as part of a directive, professionalised role, since this will impose an externally manufactured shape and direction.'[107]

The casual reader could be forgiven for thinking that this chapter is 'merely' a description of theatre in a small town in the south Wales Valleys; in which case, their very understandable response might be: 'well, so what?' But the reality is that, in microcosm, this is the story of twentieth-century British theatre from the perspective of those who normally feature only as a footnote. In fact, Aberdare exemplifies what has happened to theatre in countless places all over the UK, if not in many other countries. The introduction of public subsidy was supposed to benefit the relationship between theatre and its audiences by enhancing the possibilities for connecting the two. Of course, if you test this out on, say, the National Theatre or the West Yorkshire Playhouse, you would probably draw the conclusion that the Arts Council has been, on the whole, a Good Thing. What critiques do not generally do, though, is assess the Arts Council against the 'undistinguished'. Criticism of the Arts Council is invariably premised on its failure to reward adequately that which is deemed to be of quality. But consider this: what happens if we view subsidy from a different angle and, instead of valuing the theatre product itself, we look first towards the needs and wants of an area and fund theatre which is fit for that community's purpose?

Aberdare is an important case study in this context because, at their best, its performance practices provide the direct link between production and consumption that Owen Kelly argues for: 'What is needed is a new kind of market, in which there is no strictly hierarchical division between those who produce and those who consume, but rather a series of interchangeable and interchanging roles.'[108] The reason why we do not have this and why Aberdare is marginalized is because many theatre companies, arts managers and arts funders have a vested interest in ensuring that subsidy is never provided on this basis, not least because they are squeamish about the possibility that, left to their own devices, the working classes would choose to present the kinds of plays that Aberdare's amateurs have, indeed, often chosen to do. And this is the reason why Aberdare is important – because it forces us to engage with the real issues of public subsidy, the ones we do not really want to talk about. It is relatively easy to make a case for professional theatres and companies who do 'proper' theatre; it is much more difficult to argue for those who wilfully put on productions that local people actually want to see.

There is an analogy to be drawn here with Cwmaman's Stereophonics. Their way of performing live – their social relations – has strong similarities with the attitudes of those who run the Cwmaman Institute's theatre group. Irrespective of their international success, their involvement in the capital of the music industry and their wealth, what they do in live performance is, in essence, informed by the lived experience of Cwmaman: for instance, much of the material for their songs, both literal and figurative, originates in Cwmaman; the way in which they use language, their attitudes towards people and the texture of the sound they produce are examples of the way in which what the Stereophonics do can be understood in relation to the means of production. The Stereophonics, as Tragic Love Company, used to rehearse and have performed at Cwmaman Institute. (Indeed, drummer Stuart Cable is now a trustee.) Hence, the band demonstrates that performance practices emanating from Cwmaman can be effective and powerful in a larger context.

What is true about the Stereophonics can also be true of Cwmaman's theatre, and if this is understood, the notion that Cwmaman or Aberdare are unlikely places for significant theatre can be seen as a failure of the imagination. The importance of the Stereophonics lies in the imaginative possibilities they have created for people in their local area as much as in the music. Their success encourages writers, performers and directors in Aberdare to reclaim the style, form and content of performance practices on their own terms because the legitimization provided by the Stereophonics enables them to have some belief in themselves; and it is this self-confidence which has been eroded by the Arts Council's methods. What Aberdare can be is not a new 'Athens of Wales' but something more fundamental than that. It could be what Raymond Williams described as '[a] distinctively Welsh, English-speaking working-class culture'.[109]

In the next chapter, I am going to broaden the picture to examine how the culture of performance in the south Wales Valleys, as a whole, features distinctive and compelling characteristics sufficient to indicate the primary importance of performance practices which connect with the lived experience and with familiar congregation.

2

Valley Lines

The Valleys resemble a saucer, which reaches from Llanelli in the west to Torfaen in the east, and from its northern edges at the top of Merthyr to Taff-Ely in the south. They incorporate the former coalfields of south Wales. It is not a homogeneous place, but, rather, a series of communities with a common focus on industrial production and the socio-economic relations implied. Originally, it was sparse and rural, but it is now dense and urban, particularly at the centre of the saucer, where the deepest coal seams were to be found. The largest concentration of the Welsh population lives in this area, for the combined population of Mid Glamorgan (Cynon Valley, Merthyr Tydfil, Ogwr, Rhondda, Rhymney Valley, Taff-Ely), Blaenau Gwent and Islwyn constitutes almost a quarter of the people of Wales.[1]

In 1947, there were 214 collieries in south Wales. By 1994, there were none and many of the current economic problems of the south Wales Valleys have been caused by the speed with which the coalmines closed during the 1980s.[2] Bennett et al. (2000) argue that alternative forms of occupation to coalmining were deliberately blocked to ensure that there was a sufficiently large workforce to make the mines productive. Consequently, when the pits closed, there was an impact on social, cultural and leisure activities and, because they did not have much in the way of resources, the Valleys were ill-equipped to compensate by competing in a market-led economy. Bennett shows that it has been difficult for the Valleys to attract new investment and that, to encourage public-sector funding, they have had to emphasize the poverty and deprivation of the area, thus producing a negative image which further discourages inward investment. A low-wage economy has been created, therefore, with a workforce which is increasingly female and in part-time or insecure jobs. Bennett contends that the predicament of the Valleys is that they are 'uncertain whether they are caught in a period of transformation, or just trapped on the long road of decline'.[3]

Outsiders are presented with difficulties when forming an understanding of the Valleys. The media, for instance, seem to find it difficult to capture an unique selling point for the Valleys. The prelapsarian iconography of singing miners and mams-in-shawls has been rightly criticized; yet it served a purpose in that it at least provided a symbolic landscape which could function as an entry point to discussion of Wales, and any *Cymro* with initiative and wit was able to manipulate the mythology to his/her own advantage.

There was a time when, to the outside observer, the Valleys stood for Wales. But, during the last twenty years, the particularity of the Valleys has been subsumed under a mass of Welsh identity generalities; which is a pity, because this, the most densely populated area of Wales, has an image problem that is not only culturally impoverishing but potentially economically damaging too. That 'image problem' has developed commensurate with the collapse of the mining industry. When the Valleys are written about, it tends to be as a badlands, an area whose chief interest lies in its social problems. Hence, the Valleys have come to be synonymous with negative imagery.

Whilst the distinguished Welsh academic Raymond Williams could describe the Valleys as having 'some of the most remarkably solid and mutually loyal communities of which we have record',[4] more recent observations focus on deleterious aspects of the area, as this British broadsheet newspaper headline shows: 'Heroin epidemic grips the valleys';[5] which is remarkably similar to a headline from six years earlier, 'Epidemic of hard drugs amid jobless valleys'.[6] Likewise, six years separate the headline, 'growing up on grim estates like the Gurnos in south Wales is hard'[7] from one on the 'despair' of (the Gurnos estate) Merthyr Tydfil, where '55 per cent of households are economically inactive'.[8] Indeed, Merthyr was subsequently described by the *Observer* as 'the sickest town in Britain'.[9] But reports in Welsh newspapers, like the *Western Mail*, are no more positive: 'Poverty and sickness blight pit communities'.[10]

The outcome of this is the creation of a two-tier Valleys, with the subtle development of an approved Valleys alongside a Valleys culture which 'dare not speak its name'. Thus, the Welsh Assembly Member for Merthyr, Huw Lewis, stated in 2001 that the inhabitants of the Gurnos live in a 'parallel society with their own economy and their own points of reference that *bear no relation to how the rest of us live*' (my emphasis).[11] The logic of this statement seems to be that Valleys people who are 'lower' working class, who refuse, or cannot afford, to play at being bourgeois and who have often borne the brunt of monetarist policies, can be written out of the culture if they make the consequences of brutalist economic tactics all too apparent, because they can be consigned to a special, separate place from 'us': the 'tidy' Welsh.

The Valleys are not, then, generally a magnet for the rich and successful. When they are featured in the media, it tends to be because of their insalubrity – see, for instance, the way in which HTV's soap opera *Nuts and Bolts* was advertised as '[bringing] the rough and tumble of modern day life in the Valleys to our screens'.[12] Reduced to its essence, perceptions of the

Valleys largely revolve around the idea that the population consists of 'white trash' – drunken, bigoted, ignorant, threadbare junkies – and in which women are slappers, men are pumped up on steroids and both are itching for a good fight. The *Observer's* rugby correspondent Will Buckley suggests as much in 'Doing the full Ponty', an article ostensibly about a Pontypridd versus Saracens match in December 1999, in which he recounts a night out with three locals. His account endorses the usual depiction described above, but misses the point that Valleys people may actually be capable of being playful with their external image. When one of Buckley's companions invites Buckley and his wife to return to Pontypridd, saying: 'my brother can shag your missus and we can go out drinking', Buckley does not twig that he is probably being teased.

Buckley's article indicates a subtext which seems to operate when referring to Valleys people. On the one hand, they are the deserving poor for whom 'something must be done'. But, on the other, that imperative is subtly undermined by pointing to the ways in which Valleys people are undeserving poor

they will only go and spend money on heroin, or alcohol, or say politically incorrect things, or be racist, or get involved in punch-ups.

You have to wonder whose interests are served by the media's depiction of the Valleys, which has an inevitable impact on attitudes towards its cultural practices: specifically, that it is worthwhile supporting the arts when they conform to an ideal, but not when they are associated with modes of behaviour which might well be distasteful to the theatre-going middle classes. Although one of the most deprived parts of Britain, the Valleys pose problems for potential benefactors because their inhabitants lack charisma as victims, being too white, too 'British' and too 'bolshie' to be worthy.

The Valleys and their lived experience

The Valleys have a long history of being depicted as 'working class', the second part of which term is defined by Diana Coole thus: 'Class refers primarily to material differences between groups of persons: [these include] measurable indices [which] sometimes correspond with cultural differences: values, perspectives, practices, self-identity. But the major phenomenon . . . is that of structured economic inequality.'[13] Gordon Marshall, who has conducted extensive research into class, concludes that in Britain there is 'a remarkable persistence of class-linked inequalities and of class-differentiated patterns of social action'.[14] Given that the population of the Valleys contains a large number of those who could be described as 'working' class, using the conventional indices for measuring class-orientation, the relationship between performance practices and class is, at the least, an important factor. Of course, such an investigation might also be applicable to certain parts of England and my discussion could be transferable to non-Welsh contexts.

Some commentators, however, counsel against taking a narrow view of class in Wales. David Adamson and Stuart Jones of the University of Glamorgan, for instance, argue that 'the south Wales Valleys are easy to present as archetypal working class communities . . . [and that] images associated with this perspective need re-examination'.[15] Nevertheless, we should be suspicious of the relativist argument that 'we are all middle-class now', which would be a singularly inadequate description of a place like Penrhiwceiber, where only 23 per cent of the population are in socio-economic groups ABC1.[16] Adamson and Jones are right to differentiate between the working classes, and they identify three such groups in the Valleys: the traditional working classes, the new working classes and the marginalized working class.[17] But this does not invalidate the assertion that class is a particularly significant factor in the analysis of theatre in Wales – in the south Wales Valleys, in particular, where the evidence of class orientation by income and social position is considerable. For example, in the south Wales Valleys, life expectancy is lower than that for the rest of Wales: people are 30 per cent more likely to die before the age of 75; and over two-thirds of the population of RCT earn less than £10K per year.[18] Class is important because it has very significant bearings on whether people go to the theatre. One report on Ireland, for instance, suggests that people with very low incomes would not attend the theatre even if it was free because they feel so alienated from it.[19]

Adamson and Jones's research has a further area of relevance to discussion of Welsh theatre because it supports the argument that the Valleys are collectively orientated and culturally specific. While people in the Valleys believe that their communities are diminishing, they also 'report high levels of community association in their daily lives'. More than 70 per cent considered that a 'sense of community' defines the Valleys. Adamson and Jones show that there is 'a strong sense of identity located spatially and socially in both the immediate locality of the Valleys and a more general Welsh identity'. Significantly, 85 per cent of their respondents defined themselves as Welsh, whereas only 9 per cent described themselves as British, 70 per cent declaring that being Welsh is important in shaping who they are.[20]

Cultural practices

Adamson and Jones help explain the nature of cultural practices because their analysis includes age and gender descriptions. They find that the older, female generation still involves itself in chapel/church culture and that older middle-aged men frequent working-men's clubs. The two largest constituencies, however, are for leisure centres and the public house.[21] This is important because working-men's clubs, public houses, night clubs and leisure centres often offer forms of performance. Rhydycar Leisure Centre in Merthyr serves as a performance venue for theatre and music. Public houses and rugby clubs present rock bands and club acts. There is also a crossover between chapel and performance: the former Soar chapel in Penygraig is now the Soar Ffrwdamos Centre. This knowledge enables us to assert that the notion of the performance space in the Valleys is flexible and open to the idea that theatre can take place in buildings other than those called theatres. Performance, in the broadest sense, is understood in the context of other congregational activities: sport, team games, dancing and so on.

Cultural and performance practices are organic developments which have emerged out of the lived experience of the people in the Valleys. Of course, discrete theatres exist too. But, even here, theatres have often developed out of a specific relationship with other cultural practices, like the miners' institutes.

Whilst the south Wales Valleys have changed considerably, the culture continues to be congregational and an *effective* theatre practice would start from this point. But if we examine what that common culture is offered in the form of subsidized theatre, there seems to be a gap between what Valleys' people take informal pleasure from and what they are asked to experience as a formal audience. We need to tease out further what the implications are of the local, organic performance practices and how those relate to conventionally perceived notions of subsidized theatre.

If Adamson and Jones's table of organized leisure activities is used as a reference point – which includes working-men's clubs, choirs, sports teams, public houses, chapels/churches, leisure centres, night clubs and wine bars – it becomes possible to provide a description of available performance practices in the Valleys. It is perhaps worth stating the obvious, that participation figures show that people in the Valleys are keen to engage in public social activities. Although simple, it is an important point, because one of the problems of theatre is that of encouraging people to come out of the home and into a public arena. Television, video, domestic sound systems and computer technology are all generally perceived as having diminished the potential audience for theatre. But, in the Valleys, there is still an appetite for congregation. Further, we can detect certain common threads running through the apparently dissimilar cultural practices outlined earlier. It is significant that all offer the opportunity for participation in the organization. For example, working-men's clubs and rugby clubs have committees. But it is also possible to have a participatory investment in public houses through, for instance, a darts team. Moreover, when public houses present rock bands, they do so having regard for what they know to be the tastes of their clientele. They are able to do this because, and this is the case with all of these practices, they have a regular constituency. Individuals and groups use these outlets in order to know, and be known by, other individuals and groups. Hence, these leisure 'agencies' function through the use of what I shall call 'familiar congregation'.

Familiar congregation

Familiar congregation refers to the relationship between 'audience' and 'performer' during an event. It encompasses how near to the performance venue people live and how closely the audience's lifestyle resembles that of the performers; whether individuals are known to others through relatives and friends, and the extent to which an individual's poverty or personal disadvantage is accommodated; the knowledge of previous events in the venue; the sense of a non-hierarchical relationship with other members of the audience and with the performers; the feeling of being empowered by the circumstances of the event; the extent to which audience members feel a sense of ownership towards the venue; the way in which the content of the event is plugged in to the local culture; the ability to come and go without discomfort; and the opportunity for social interaction after and on leaving the event.

One way of describing the effect of familiar congregation is by using the analogy of wine production. In France, the term *terroir* describes the region, soil, climate, history, human agency and traditions which affect the taste, texture, aroma, colour and value of the wine. The *terroir* is what makes different wines individually distinctive. In the Valleys, the performance *terroir* has developed out of those events and activities which are available and which might become theatricalized, or which might influence theatre structures.

The following are examples of what takes place on a daily basis in the Valleys and, therefore, what might constitute the raw ingredients of theatre.

- storytelling
- anecdotes
- joke-telling
- debate/discussion
- gossip
- song
- music and instrumentation
- drinking games
- team darts/snooker

- choral singing
- rhetoric
- sermonizing
- character sketches and impersonation
- dance
- gesture
- the expression of sports partisanship
- business negotiation

What provides the hallmark (or *terroir*) of Valleys culture is the melding together of different elements. Cross-fertilization occurs naturally, as this extract from the *Cynon Valley Leader* in 2000 shows. Under the heading of 'Community News', notices about healthy eating are juxtaposed with a description (itself a form of storytelling) of an anniversary service, a note about a silver band, and assorted jokes. This one follows on immediately after serious advice on how to use a computer: 'a man turns up to a club wrapped in a pair of jump leads. The bouncer says to him, "You can come in, as long as you don't start anything."'

The effect of this is to produce quite startling leaps from humour, to tragedy, to the provision of information, yet such transitions are not only accepted with ease but seem to define how the culture works, in a cumulative and episodic way with connections constantly being made by the audience.

But content and form are not the only factors. The mode of expression is also an important contributory factor to the locally produced performative, because vocal elements are particularized by ways of speaking. Consider, for instance, John Edwards's translation of *Little Red Riding Hood* into Wenglish, his term for Valleys patois:

> Red Riding Hood was flabbergasted – it shook 'er rigid – but she was kokum. She shiggled 'er way out of that cloak an' was out of there in a winky. She went off, full pelt, along the road to where 'er father was 'ard at it. Talkin' twenty to the dozen she told 'im all that 'ad 'appened. 'E took 'is chopper, ran all the way back to mamgu's and gave that wolf a real belter.[22]

The use of local vocabulary, coupled with various permutations of the wide variety of forms identified earlier, creates a rich and complex layering effect and it is that, I would argue, which typifies performance structures produced in the Valleys.

When combined, informal elements can develop into more formal performance practices. The Noson Lawen (light entertainment evening), for instance, uses an integrated structure of storytelling, song, character impressions, music and dance. Originally, these 'merry evenings' were informal entertainments which took place in a domestic setting. In common with the ceilidh, they might often combine work with socializing. The Noson Lawen is now understood as a formal concert and it features as a series of programmes on S4C. But while that television series is produced in the Welsh language, the format of the Noson Lawen is recognizable in popular English-language cultural practices in the Valleys.

Indeed, the integrated structure, such as that found in the Noson Lawen, is evident to the point where we might say that it is the dominant popular performance practice. But the dominant *theatre* practice is very different from the Noson Lawen for two reasons. First, it does not draw on the methodology of familiar congregation and, secondly, it derives from the (English) tradition of the formal, single-authored play-text. Now, not all forms of theatre in Wales resemble what we might commonly understand to be 'the play'. There is a significant presence of what the WAC used to call 'developmental' theatre, and Brith Gof, for example, championed the use of a range of popular oral traditions. However, the developmental theatre companies have not, in the main, adopted the methodology of familiar congregation. Most companies are not Valleys-based and their functioning is comparable to that of mainstream touring companies. That is, they visit their audiences to perform but do not generally work out of, or with, a particular local sensibility.

Issues of participation and fellowship in the Valleys have been fore-grounded because I want to argue that the *methodology* of congregation is the crux of the matter and that the content of what 'audiences' see is of lesser importance, even immaterial in certain circumstances; and this is a very different approach from that of the Arts Council, where the quality and integrity of the *product* are paramount. Of course, this is not to say that familiar congregations are uninterested in content; when dissatisfied with club acts, for example, their response tends to be immediate. But, equally, accommodations are made for entertainments which are viewed as relating to the lived experience. For instance, Rhondda playwright Frank Vickery's standing is, at least in part, due to the fact that he lives in and is a part of the locale.

Orature

An important reference point for this discussion is African orature because, in a number of respects, orature resembles the performance practices in Wales I have described. Orature involves a quite different set of relation-ships from those inherent in the British tradition of subsidized theatre; and, by contrasting the strategies of orature with British practices, we can recognize that the British tradition is neither universal nor inevitable. Orature, as described by Kwesi Owusu, is an integrated arts practice which utilizes social cooperation; combines different art-forms (dance, storytelling, music, song, design, physical action); takes place in a circle in the centre of the living space, which would also be used for a wide variety of other social activities; transforms the local environment and its resources; incorporates the 'amateur' with the 'professional' in a non-hierarchical structure; and acknowledges the interdependence of members of communities. It does not separate creative expression from the local, lived experience.[23] As in orature, collective association is fundamental to the Valleys lived experience where there is an incorporation of the 'real life processes and . . . experiences of people involved in production'.[24] Orature does not, though, imply exclusion; neither the play-text nor the formal production event need necessarily be ruled out of orature practices.

In contrast, the classical European tradition, which dominates the kind of theatre available through subsidy to Valleys audiences, foregrounds the central importance of the play-text, and privileges the contribution of the professional theatre practitioner. There is also a separation between the audience and the performance space, quite literally through the way in which the stage area is defined and the discrete theatre venue located. Although, in broad terms, theatre practitioners live in the same political climate, the creative world is segregated from that of the audience because performance practice tends to derive from the aesthetic autonomy of the (professional) theatre company and not from a collaboration with local communities.

One of the central techniques of orature is *call and response*,[25] which can be understood both as a specific technique and as a metaphor. Within perform ance, it is used to describe how a storyteller, for example, will articulate a familiar phrase which can be completed, echoed or even contradicted by the audience. But this is also an analogy for the performance experience as a whole: 'the call springs from a subjective reality, and the response from a collective or communal one'.[26] This suggests a quite different order of social relations as made manifest through performance traditions, not least because the audience has a direct and democratic relationship with the performance.

In European theatre, *calling* is conventionally the province of the player, while *response* is confined to the non-participatory position of the audience. Theatre companies are traditionally apprehended as the catalysts for the event and as agents of both the action of the play and the occasion itself. Performances take place because theatre companies determine what the subject matter, form, style and structure will be and make these available to the audience through the play-product. Given the way in which theatre is organized, it is unusual for an audience to make any contribution to the aesthetics of the event. Moreover, audiences do not, as a rule, choose the circumstances – the place, the time – because they are arranged by official intermediaries: theatre administrators or managers. Audiences are literally positioned, even captured, by theatre companies. The business of issuing tickets for specific seats, the atmosphere of polite silence during a performance, the opprobrium which is meted out to latecomers, owners of digital watches and mobile telephones and those with a persistent cough, those who shift in their seats and those who laugh in the 'wrong' places: all of this suggests a regimented notion of courtesy surrounding theatre. Orthodox theatre finds it difficult to cope with unorthodox responses, and recalcitrant audiences have sometimes been disciplined.[27] In African performance, and also in black British theatre, direct *response* from the audience to the *call* of the performers, through dialogue, characterization and dramatic incident, is welcomed.

Call and response is also a feature of audiences in the south Wales Valleys. At the Muni in Pontypridd, for example, during a production of Frank Vickery's *A Kiss on the Bottom* by the amateur Parc and Dare Theatre Company, the audience had a traditional end-on physical relationship with the performance, with the audience on one side of the proscenium arch and the performance on the other. Even so, the audience *chose* to involve itself in the performance by talking back to it. When the central character, Marlene, learns that her daughter has paid £47.50 for her wedding bouquet, she exclaims that she 'could have had a second-hand fridge for that'. Many members of the audience, women in particular, responded audibly by agreeing with the sentiment. But in the bourgeois English theatre, this would be considered rude or, at best, quaint, unless it took place during a pantomime. Whilst it might be argued that there are sound reasons for a code of theatre behaviour – sensitivity towards the needs of others, for instance – the real beneficiary of this is the orthodox status quo of English, middle-class theatre which, in ensuring that appropriate standards are established and maintained, consolidates its status as the instrument of best practice. Orature encourages and acknowledges a different way of establishing relationships between audience and performers, one that has marked similarities with the familiar congregation inherent to the Valleys.

A wide range of examples of orature can be found in Wales, in addition to the aforementioned Noson Lawen, where work and cultural practices have been interconnected – *gwylmabsant* (patron saint's festival), *cymanfa ganu* (great gathering or singing festival) and the Mari Lwyd (a Christmas event of pre-Christian origin, involving the procession of a horse's head accompanied by mummers). There are also, of course, the festival activities of the eisteddfodau, and the example cited by Gwyn Alf Williams of quarrymen turning their lunchtime sessions 'into an eisteddfod-cum-trade union of improvised verse, song, quizzes and debates'.[28]

But orature in Wales is not the relic of the past that these older forms might suggest and new theatre practices have emerged out of the traditions of folklore. When professional Welsh theatre companies Moving Being presented *The Mabinogi* and Brith Gof *The Gododdin* in the 1980s, they were continuing in the tradition of professional storytellers performing heroic epics, yet finding new forms to present old material.

Despite these examples, orature is generally to be found at the margins of theatre and it is atypical of standardized, incorporated theatre practice. Valley and Vale Community Arts, for instance, has been based in the village of Betws since 1981 and it works out of venues like the Blaengarw Workmen's Hall. Its first community play, in 1986, took as its theme the notion of community in the context of the closure of the pits. The production inspired a video and discussions and offered the community the opportunity to communicate and work with each other: 'much of the work is informed by a very strong commitment to and use of local oral history'.[29] In 1992, the play, *How Jacko Davies Became the God of Racing Pigeons*, was coordinated by playwright Tim Rhys, who is from the area. Much of the material came from a team of local contributors who interviewed people from the locality, and the production included a wide range of community involvement through dance, writing, research, performance and music.

Valley and Vale runs workshops in music, dance and drama and also develops large-scale community arts events. In addition, it has established an archive of local oral history and photographs. Its main focus is on working with people who are disenfranchised from mainstream arts provision; but it also provides training and consultancy services and produces books relevant to the Valleys.

Valley and Vale has been able to incorporate conditions of production which are reflective of local imperatives: the transformation of an old working men's hall is an important means by which a culture's past may resonate in the present. Forms used to animate its productions are those which are to be found within the totality of local cultural practices, an approach which resembles Raymond Williams's definition of drama as a 'special' use of 'common modes for new and specific ends'.[30] Narrative content and characterization are shaped by the community's structure of feeling and particular experience, and this constitutes direct action, which enables the whole community to share in the means of production.

But note how Valley and Vale is financially positioned by the Arts Council and what that says about how theatre which resembles orature is regarded. In 1993–4, Valley and Vale received a total of £16.6K – spread across dance, theatre writing, film, and literature.[31] But this represented only 3.4 per cent of Theatr Clwyd's grant in that year. Some six years later, the picture had improved somewhat. In 1999–2000, Valley and Vale received around £101K and (the by-now-renamed) Clwyd Theatr Cymru (CTC) was given close to £1.1 million. This meant that Valley and Vale had, in fact, achieved something like a 500 per cent increase in its own income from ACW. In absolute terms, Valley and Vale was less marginal than it had been. Nevertheless, in relative terms, Valley and Vale's income represented less than 1 per cent of ACW's total expenditure, whereas CTC's income amounted to 8 per cent of the ACW total.[32] Curiously, by 2001, Valley and Vale's funding represented an even smaller percentage of ACW's total expenditure on revenue grants, because it received only 0.35 per cent of that funding. Although ACW could argue that Valley and Vale received a 3 per cent increase, in line with other organizations, in proportionate terms it was actually receiving less, and this is particularly significant when we take into account that CTC's share of the total had risen to 9.4 per cent. The financial proportions described here suggest that those practices which most resemble orature have been the least likely to be significantly rewarded by the ACW. In this, ACW resembles ACE and the former English Regional Arts Boards. If we take just the year 1996–7, as an example (all figures taken from the respective annual reports) we can observe that the ACE grant to the Royal Shakespeare Company was £8.4 million (31 per cent of ACE's drama budget), whereas the amount ACE gave to Welfare State International was £140,000 (0.51 per cent of ACE's total drama budget in that year). In the same year, West Midlands Arts (WMA) gave the Birmingham Rep £870,000 (16 per cent of WMA's drama budget) and Pentabus Theatre Company £91,000 (1.6 per cent of WMA's drama budget in that year). As a comparison, ACW gave CTC £700,000 in 1996–7 (20 per cent of ACW's drama budget) and Spectacle Theatre received £87,000 (2.5 per cent of ACW's drama budget). The discrepancy is telling. In each case, theatre companies/venues that are considered to be flagship organizations tend to be given at least 15 per cent of a drama budget, whereas theatre practices which resemble orature receive less than 3 per cent. (In fact, in this respect, ACW is comparatively generous.)

Orature does not, however, emanate only from the margins and there are examples of its use in the mainstream. *Everything Must Go* was presented by the Sherman Theatre in Cardiff in March 1999.[33] Patrick Jones's play was performed in the main theatre and, on the face of it, this might seem to be a typically orthodox mainstream theatre venture. It was performed in a mainhouse theatre, using professional actors, directed by the Sherman's artistic director himself (Phil Clark) in a conventional end-on fashion, with an author-originated play-text which proceeded through a linear narrative; and the presentation achieved standardized high production values. All of which seems to confirm its consistency with an English, middle-class paradigm for theatre.

But, in fact, the totality of the experience was far from such an orthodox model and aspects of the play actually make it more like orature. The setting of the play was localized in the Valleys (Blackwood) and its author writes from his own lived experience. Both the characters and the world of the play are Welsh, English-speaking and working-class. The production combined professionals and amateurs, albeit that the latter were students from the

Welsh College of Music and Drama in Cardiff. There was a large cast, which helped to make the play an authentic social and collective landscape. Its politics, too, reflect local concerns in that they critique the New Labour project and reappropriate the critical thinking of Aneurin Bevan. The play's language both draws on and reconfigures the poeticism of Dylan Thomas, the lyricism of the Bible and the rhythmic poetry of the Welsh national anthem: 'Oh land of my fathers so dear to me . . . thy rocks and thy crags o'er thy valleys keep guard . . . thy mountains still shelter the haunts of the bard . . thy harpstrings unbroken by traitor's fell hand . . . still sing to me songs of my land'.[34] Yet this is not a nostalgic exercise, as the play includes many contemporary references – most particularly the music and lyrics of Catatonia and the Manic Street Preachers – and uses stereotypical images (girls in 'traditional' Welsh costume) in order to place them under suspicion.

The production was noteworthy in that it attracted a different audience into mainstream theatre: younger, from the Valleys, with a limited experience of conventional theatre. It was also very well-attended with capacity audiences. Some would argue that this was because the playwright is the brother of Nicky Wire, bass player with the Manic Street Preachers. But that would not fully explain the level of genuine interest in the production from a very mixed constituency.

Rock music

Patrick Jones's theatre work connects with an area of Welsh performance efficacy which has hitherto remained outside the parameters of formal theatre and performance – that of rock music. Rock music is important because it is a form of orature and the Manics are especially emblematic of that connection between rock and the Valleys. Their achievement has been to find a credible way of being English-speaking, working-class and Welsh, and being all of those things while also earning international success. One of the most crucial symbolic moments for contemporary Welsh culture occurred when the Manic Street Preachers placed the Red Dragon (the Welsh flag) prominently on their amplification equipment, because this made their position explicit and enabled audiences to understand their provenance as specifically Welsh rock musicians. Moreover, this becomes particularly apparent during their live performances, when the Red Dragon visually underscores all their songs; and this is not a nationalistic process, as the image can be understood in a complex way. What they – and, indeed, Welsh rock musicians generally – have accomplished has more implications for theatre than has perhaps been recognized.

In general, theatre practitioners in Wales have not acknowledged the significance of Welsh rock bands as live performers; they seem to take the view that rock music occupies a different territory. They ignore the fact that, through what they do live, the bands have actually developed an effective performance practice which has a direct relationship with the lived experience, particularly in the Valleys, in keeping with the spirit of orature and familiar congregation described earlier. Moreover, rock bands can formally position themselves within the broader cultural context, as this quote from Nicky Wire demonstrates:

> We, as a band from Wales, support any cultural enterprise that gives people
> the chance to . . . attack established forms of behaviour . . . We all must
> have a chance to bear witness to our reality . . . [including] to act it . . . We
> fully support the Sherman [Theatre] and all it stands for.[35]

The Manics have established a formal relationship with the Sherman Theatre. However, there are many other rock bands who are of critical importance to understanding performance practices in the Valleys, even if theirs is a more indeterminate relationship with professional theatre; and, by examining how they function, we can develop the evidence for asserting that orature is the authentic mode of performance in the Valleys.

Rock music combines a large number of the elements of orature. It draws audiences together in a shared experience, and incorporates different skills, like poetry, political comment and technology, along with music. Gigs create symbiotic performer/audience relationships and take place in community venues that are not often the province of traditional theatre, which has the effect of transforming the venue and encouraging an audience to look at the 'meaning' of the space in a different way. Musicians do not have the same kinds of boundaries between the amateur and the professional that formal theatre has. For instance, guitarists do not need conventional qualifications in order to progress: in rock music, the conservatoire has never been of much relevance; but, while actors have not necessarily attended drama schools, they usually have had some kind of formal training.

The contrasting definitions of the language used to describe the rock band as opposed to the theatre company are instructive. A 'band' is an entity which connects, binds and unites, an organized group having a common object, which bands together for mutual advantage. A company, however, is more obviously business-like, referring to a number of people who are assembled, a commercial business, partners or associates in a firm. Rock bands often form out of personal friendships derived from living in proximity, whereas theatre companies rarely emerge out of local fellowship. Moreover, Valleys' musicians do not tend to live in arts 'ghettos'; but actors seem to cluster around arts communities, and, in consequence, they might appear to be less connected to the local lived experience.

Rock music has an ability to cultivate organic 'call and response' through the emergence of 'anthems', which are informally designated as such by audiences, like 'They Shoot Horses, Don't They' by Racing Cars. Air-guitar is a good example of an organic response; and the demotic tradition of using a pointed index finger aimed at the lead guitarist to underscore guitar solos is also a form of orature. Theatre, on the other hand, has a tendency to discourage anything other than orchestrated responses, outside of panto-mime. Rock music is also adept at producing short narratives about local life, a process akin to the griot, or storyteller, of orature: see, for instance, 'Local Boy in the Photograph' by the Stereophonics.

If we take a broad perspective of rock bands, comparisons can be drawn between them and the totality of historical Welsh cultural practices (the festivals, great occasions, processional events and so on) because they work in the same way. That is, they provide a sense of occasion in the context of everyday life; the gathering, the event itself and the dispersal from it, all create a scene which is transformative. Moreover, Valleys rock music sometimes provides an echo of the chapel sermon and an inclusion of the people's history (consider, for instance, the Manics' 'If You Tolerate This, Your Children Will Be Next').

The detail of the English-language rock bands from the Valleys demon-strates how they have been able to connect with the lived experience (I have included for discussion some bands who are from the Cardiff or Swansea areas but who are relevant because they have been successful performers in the Valleys.) Invariably working-class and usually grammar school-educated, most band members became rock musicians because they wanted to live outside mainstream conventions, to be dissenting and subversive, and saw rock music as a way of achieving that. Martin Ace of Man avers that the musical lineage of the Welsh rock musicians emerging during the 1960s–1970s owed much to poor, black people in the southern states of America; and because of that, even if it was at a subconscious level, they related to their audiences in ways similar to those of the early black blues musicians.[36] They produced music out of the lived experience, in terms of the content of the material and the way in which they comported themselves as performers; and that lived experience was, largely, Welsh, working-class and English-speaking. Paul Rosser of the Watermelons, for instance, 'really wanted' to write and sing songs about his local community, even though he thinks that Valleys communities do not wish to encounter such subject matter in a naked format, which is why he 'disguises' the localism and (makes the songs) 'pretty abstract'.[37]

The early Welsh rock musicians emerged directly out of the industrial workforce and they seem to have transferred characteristics of the labour process to performance. Burke Shelley of Budgie, for example, was a trainee surveyor and carries industrial terminology through to his music. He sees a rock band as essentially 'the workmen . . . we're [there] to build rock walls'.

Former factory worker Chris Thomas of Racing Cars also employs the work-metaphor. For him, 'the bass guitar is the equivalent of a trowel'.

It is unsurprising that the early rock musicians took a workmanlike approach to performing because they were, in fact, workmen. In the early 1960s, musicians were undifferentiated from those who did a 'proper' job because they often had full-time jobs while working in bands during the evenings. The increase in performance venues in Wales during the 1960s meant that, in time, musicians became comparatively well-remunerated – it was just about possible to earn as much playing in a band as in a factory – and could then turn professional. By the late 1960s, Budgie were earning £15–£25 a night, working about five gigs a week. In 1970, Man, who by that time were well-known in the UK, were earning £70–£100 a gig. In the 1970s, Chris Thomas's first paid gig earned him £35, which was £3 more than he had been receiving for a week's shift-work in the Rhondda. So, locally, Valleys rock musicians were able to earn a living slightly above that of a skilled labourer and this ensured that, like the griot, they had a certain status; but it was very much one which relied on their ability to connect with the audiences whose support ensured their livelihood.

Perhaps because of this, musicians often believe that the human connections made during live performance are more important than technical skill. Morty, the singer in Racing Cars, points out that, 'intimacy [with the audience] is an integral part of any band . . . [and] it's a reciprocal relationship'. Chris Thomas goes further in defining the purpose of the relationship between bands and their audiences: '[bands] are there [for the audience]; [the audience is] not there for [the bands]'.

The symbiotic relationship between bands and audiences probably developed because, during the 1960s, there were no music venues in Wales, as such – there was no commercial market in Wales then – and bands had to cultivate a circuit for live performance. At a time when theatres in the Valleys were noticing a decline in their audiences, rock music quickly became an important performance practice. Morty recalls that, 'you could go anywhere in the Valleys . . . and see a live band every night of the week'. Danny Chang (guitarist in Dozy, composer and record producer) even suggests that, 'you could play in the Rhondda every night'. Amongst the liveliest venues were Merthyr's Sands; Aberdare Memorial Hall; Judges Hall and the Naval Club in Tonypandy; Tylorstown Rugby Club; the Ace of Spades and the Cymmer Club, Porth; Penrhys Community Centre; the Boathouse, Cwmparc; Blaenrhondda Rugby Club; Rhymney Renco; Dinas Powis youth club; Pontypridd's Muni; Trefforest Polytechnic; Newbridge 'Memo'; and Maerdy Junior School on Friday nights.

Gigs moved into those venues which were already part of the community's cultural network, like schools, and working-men's and rugby clubs. From the musicians' point of view, that practice had its limitations. Martin Ace points to the problems of juxtaposing bingo with rock, as does Thomas, who suggests that clubs wanted 'a Saturday-night-special band, that plays [covers]'. In the 1980s, the Watermelons tried to avoid working-men's clubs because, in Rosser's opinion, the culture of the clubs led to a certain closedness in the audience: 'If they are in a familiar environment, then [the audience wants] familiar music.' It was difficult to perform original, new work in clubs, which is why pubs started putting on bands. Despite this, it was problematic for bands writing their own material to find venues in which to play. The Watermelons, for instance, had been successful in Wales and England; but, on home ground in the Valleys, they had to drop songs without a 'hook' and play covers.

The practice of orature has its downside, as can be seen from the above description of the pressures on bands to construct an audience-preferred repertoire. Cultural democracy does not mean that there will always be an easy relationship between performers and audiences, but, rather, that the performance process involves ongoing difficult negotiations which demand responsibilities on both sides. Audiences in working-men's clubs have not always allowed bands to determine their own material. That said, an important reason why there were so many bands in Wales from the 1960s is that audiences were often well-informed about popular music; hence, there was a knowledgeable constituency to become musicians and/or audience. Rosser remembers that four or five people in any one street might play the guitar. In the Valleys, small record shops, like 'Gracie's' in Aberdare, played an important role in disseminating information (and, indeed, in forming musical tastes) about rock music. Orature works best when, as in the case of rock music, it is the result of a collaboration between committed performers and a discerning audience.

What also helped develop rock music, and which is distinctive of orature, in addition to knowledge about it, was the congregational aspect caused, in part, by the fact that it was difficult for audiences to obtain public transport home and there were few taxis to be had – none, as Mike Monk (manager and sound engineer for many bands) recalls, in the Rhondda. So bands created a community effect, with large numbers of people walking through the streets after gigs, having had an experience in common.

Those audiences not only knew about rock music's roots in the blues, but also had a sense of what the blues meant; and the blues provided an apposite expression for the local culture's history. Whilst the blues may have developed in America, when Valleys musicians played them they were not, as some mistakenly argue, imitating an alien form but, on the contrary, making it their own by giving it local resonance. Valleys musicians adopted the blues not because the music was American, but because it was part of an international language relating to working people and to the struggle against poverty. Graham Hedley Williams, Racing Cars' guitarist, asserts that, being

Welsh 'suits playing blues'. He believes that Valleys musicians can produce a 'depth of feeling' because of their knowledge of the hardships caused by poverty and the circumstances of mining. The relationship between the blues, rock and the Valleys is summarized by Chris Thomas thus: '[the Valleys are] a deprived area [and] deprived areas and rock bands seem to go hand in hand'.

But there were other aspects to south Wales rock. Paul Rosser points to the connection between folk music, rock and the Valleys: 'Rock and roll is the folk music of the Rhondda . . . Folk is hand-me-down music, mixing the traditional with the contemporary; and rock is also, in the Valleys.' Folk music, like the blues, is the international lingua franca of struggle, so that singing about 'a man of constant sorrow' or the Gresford Mining Disaster, for instance, became a means by which the 1965 Cambrian Pit disaster in Clydach Vale could be referred to at one remove, but in such a way that local allusions could be drawn.

The familiar congregation which was created out of this use of form and content produced a powerful physical dynamic. Burke Shelley loved Valleys venues for their 'electric atmosphere' and actively sought them out. He 'couldn't get up there to play quick enough' and ascribes the ambience to the fact that Valleys audiences know each other, in contrast to those in Cardiff, where there is 'no cameraderie'. Even when Budgie became successful recording artists, he would still try to obtain gigs up in the Valleys.

Indeed, the issue of the Americanization of Welsh culture is raised into sharp relief by Budgie. Burke Shelley's song 'Breadfan' was recorded by Metallica as a homage to Budgie. During the 1990s, Metallica was one of the biggest bands in the world capable of filling enormous stadia. So, when it plays 'Breadfan' live, a song that was honed in the south Wales Valleys, is that the Americanization of Welsh culture, or the 'Welshization' of American culture? Whichever is the case, Metallica's adoption of 'Breadfan' points to the existence of a Welsh culture that has been able to infiltrate the international scene in ways that are often overlooked, which suggests that south Walian cultural practices, irrespective of whether they are parochial, are capable of communicating to a wider audience. Material produced out of familiar congregation is able to transcend its origins.

It has been argued that rock bands emerging from the Valleys were, comparatively, less interested in conventional notions of success in the music industry than, perhaps, many comparable English bands. Certainly, Graham Hedley Williams and Paul Rosser, for example, were reluctant to move to London, wanting to be able to work out of south Wales. Danny Chang, himself English, believes that there was a shift of emphasis between English and Welsh bands in that 'bands in England would want to play the whole game [which involved a divide between audience and artist]; whereas in Wales it [was not] about the game, [it was] about [musicians as] folk heroes'.

The relationship that many Welsh bands developed with their audiences demonstrated familiar congregation in that it drew on shared cultural and geographical experiences. In that sense, the front-man, for instance, was, as Morty says, a 'face of the people'.

Of course, those bands which emerged out of the Valleys during the 1960s and 1970s were part of a very different rock music world when it was possible to have personal access at gigs, even to very famous bands, because security was less evident and audiences were, in any case, perhaps less intrusive. It is more difficult to make the case for the Manics and the Stereophonics as being exemplars of orature because their fame has affected their ability to function in that context. These days, bands are generally less accessible. Moreover, as *performers*, the Manics did not operate as 'oraturists' in the sense that I have been discussing because they performed very few gigs in the Valleys. One such, at the Star pub in Trealaw, attracted only a handful of people; so, at that stage, the Manics were not gathering much of a familiar congregation. That said, and as suggested earlier, the content of the Manics' material is suggestive of orature.

The Stereophonics, though, more than any other of the raft of successful contemporary Welsh bands, are a good example of orature, even though their fame means that they function very differently now. But, during their formative years, their attitude defined orature, because they incorporated their background into their songs, performed in local venues, worked locally and built an audience out of people with whom they were familiar. Their success emphasizes the point that orature – the most local of performance practices – can speak internationally.

Performance practices

The following section aims to provide the reader with a description of what performance is like in the south Wales Valleys. It takes the form of a series of case studies which can be used to test the limits of the concepts involved in orature and of familar congregation. It is, however, necessarily selective and there are, of course, exceptions to the rule.

The *Beaufort Welsh Omnibus Survey*, research conducted on behalf of ACW, gives us an idea of the kinds of performances people in the Valleys appreciate. Here is the 2000 list of Valleys-preferred arts activities in order of attendance percentages.

1. Cinema (41.3%)
2. Live music, like rock (26.1%)
3. Galleries (17.4%)
4. Musicals (14%)

5. Plays (13.6%)
6. Classical music (10.9%)
7. Jazz (8.6%)
8. Literary events (3.8%)
9. Opera (2.9%)
10. Ballet (2.1%)
11. Contemporary dance (2%)

If the figures for plays are added to those of musicals, theatre occupies second place, just ahead of rock and folk music, although still a long way behind film. (VAM has noted, however, that in 2000–1 cinema attendance decreased nationally in the UK by 12 per cent and that this trend is also reflected in the Valleys.) Nevertheless, these figures suggest that more than a quarter of people in the Valleys are watching theatre, of some kind, which is significant given that there is not a single revenue-funded, producing house in the whole of the south Wales Valleys.

The Night Out scheme

An important means by which ACW services the Valleys is through its community touring 'Night Out' scheme. The purpose of it is to provide professional performances in local venues (not necessarily theatres) at 'affordable prices' and ACW describes the organizations hosting this scheme as being 'grass-roots'. In 1999–2000, ACW boasted that the scheme attracted an average attendance rate of 70 per cent. The most interesting area of the Night Out scheme concerns the kinds of productions that are available to Valleys audiences. What makes them intriguing is the comparison between the *terroir* of the piece of theatre and Valleys audiences.

To demonstrate some of the ideological complexities of touring theatre, and the possible gap between theatre product and its potential audience, I shall use as an example one production that was on offer to venues in relation to the Night Out scheme in the 2001–2 season. My discussion of this production is purely theoretical and I have chosen it merely as a case study. At that time, Valleys venues might have chosen to present *WonderVision TM*, a touring production by Proteus Theatre Company in association with Blow Up Theatre. The publicity described it as featuring a TV repairman who starts to shrink. Its style was influenced by American B-movies of the 1950s and was intended to be a piece of visual theatre with a triphop soundtrack. On the face of it, this would seem to be a suitable choice. The central character is working-class, Valleys audiences are keen film-goers, so they could pick up the cinematic allusions, and they might also respond to the music.[38]

Let us look at this more closely, though. Proteus is a company which was established to tour work to Hampshire and the southern region of England, an area which is, largely, Tory-voting, with a middle-class constituency that has a higher than average income.[39] Even so, its audiences are wide-ranging and include arts centres, village halls, prisons and schools. The company itself works in a way which ought to be relevant to the Valleys – its approach towards non-theatre venues and 'community' audiences is especially appropriate. The problem, however, lies in the delicate interplay between the specific provenance of the piece of theatre and its particular applications. By this I mean that a product designed for a southern English audience (even if that audience is liberal, politically aware and egalitarian) will have been produced as a result of the theatre company having absorbed a multiplicity of sensibilities and imperatives that are quite different from those in the Valleys. The problem of touring theatre is that it makes the false assumption that what is appropriate in Portsmouth is as appropriate in Porth.

This issue of universality is widely misunderstood; and it is rather a complex subject. However, it is one which needs addressing, because the whole question of what happens when you take a piece of theatre made in place X to venue Y is central to any critique of theatre practices in the Valleys, and, indeed, everywhere. Briefly, my contention is that many pieces of touring theatre function in a manner comparable with imperialism. That is, they have the effect of promoting ideologies, belief-systems and models of behaviour which, in a subtle way, demean local values. Now, theatre ought to be in the business of interrogating ideology. Nevertheless, pieces of theatre which do so might achieve that aim more successfully if they developed out of theatre companies with a local basis, not least because they would be likely to have detailed knowledge at their disposal with which to make a more convincing argument.

But some contend that local theatre companies are too parochial, meaning narrow. However, parochialism need not necessarily imply small-minded-ness, as it can simply refer to the fact that the immediate starting point for a piece of theatre is the local environment. It is perfectly feasible that a piece of theatre made in a very small, local way could engage audiences inter-nationally, even when audiences do not speak the language in which the piece is presented (and we have seen that this can be so in rock music).

The key element of touring is that of class and of the lived experience. Where touring theatre companies emanate from a very different socio-economic reality, the practice of touring theatre starts to become problematic in terms of the ideological exchange that is taking place. In such instances, the theatre company can take on a colonialist or missionary role, even where this is unintentional (which, in most cases, it is).

So, to return to Proteus, what matters is the lived reality of the members of the company, collectively and severally, and what, in fact, they would be bringing to the Valleys in the form of hidden meanings. This is awkward territory because actors are not well-paid and may be living close to poverty themselves. But what matters is the class relationships which are being exchanged, and here lies the difficulty. Actors may carry with them sets of values which are 'hegemonic' of those in the community within which they find themselves playing.

In using this term, I am drawing on the definition of hegemony provided by Gwyn Alf Williams:

> An order in which a certain way of life and thought is dominant, in which one concept of reality is diffused throughout society in all its institutional and private manifestations [where] an element of direction and control, not necessarily conscious, is implied.[40]

When applied to theatre, hegemony, as Raymond Williams explains it, takes the form of a selective tradition passing itself off as the only or most important tradition.[41] Thus, professional touring theatre companies might be saying, in effect: 'We are the professionals, so what we say and the way in which we say it is authoritative.'

Consequently, ACW's Night Out scheme carries with it more than just a good night out and, in this respect, theatre is comparable to ethical shoping. If you buy certain brands of trainers, for example, you may be helping to sustain child slavery in the developing world. Similarly, when you watch a piece of theatre, you are being exposed to more than just a performance – the play is not the whole thing. Therefore, to draw on another example of what could be available through the Night Out scheme, the Watermill Theatre's production of *Witch*, ostensibly a 'searing psychological thriller', might, in reality, be about delivering to the Valleys the values of southern England. Theatre is always about that which is not theatre.

That said, audiences are not ciphers and are perfectly capable of choosing which bits of a production are significant to them. Nevertheless, it is uncertain to what extent programmers really consider the sociocultural by-products of the theatre companies they present. The Night Out scheme exemplifies the complications of 'community' theatre programming in that, while it appears to make theatre more inclusive and more accessible, it also conveys ideological baggage which can provide audiences with rather more than they had bargained for.

Venues

The role of the major venues in the south Wales Valleys is decisive in developing the relationship between audiences and theatre companies and in choosing which ideologies are presented to the community through theatre. The Valleys venues were not, in the main, purpose-built as theatres, however. The oldest venue is the Cwmaman Institute (1868 – from 1892 at its present site). But the oldest of what ACW refers to as *the* Valleys venues is the Blaengarw Workmen's Hall (1894). Valleys venues represent just under a fifth of the total number of venues in Wales. The first of these to adopt the discrete title of 'theatre' was the Parc and Dare in 1913. Of the eight venues (see Table 5) five were started because local people wanted to have such a facility and they were financed with money direct from miners' wages or from the coal industry. The majority of the Valleys venues had a symbiotic relationship with the local workforce and located theatre within the totality of local cultural and social activities so that performance informed and was informed by the lived experience.

Table 5.
Valleys Venues

Blaengarw Workmen's Hall	1894
Parc and Dare Theatre	1913
Blackwood Miners' Institute	1925
Ystradgynlais Miners' Welfare and Community Hall	1934
Coliseum Theatre	1938
The Muni Arts Centre (formerly a church) developed during the 1960s	
Beaufort Theatre and Ballroom	1960s
Rhydycar Leisure Centre	1975

For the most part, the venues are old buildings, big and acoustically awkward, with performance spaces which hark back to an age before the advent of television when considerable audiences could be amassed for plays and shows, which were themselves grand in scope and with sizeable casts. The once-imposing architecture of the buildings can seem reproachful now and, during the 1980s, many of these buildings were decaying badly. A certain amount of refurbishment was made possible by the Welsh Office's Valleys Initiative Scheme of the early 1990s. Lottery funding has also enabled some of the venues to improve their look and facilities; but their modest revenue funding means that they struggle to offer imaginative programmes because they lack the money to take risks, or to become producing houses.

The biggest difficulty, though, is that Valleys venues display a deep confusion over what they ought to be doing. On one hand, they have to be cost-effective and draw in audiences yet, on the other, they need to demonstrate that they can provide stimulating programmes, if they are to stand any chance of earning the kind of artistic credibility that would make them eligible for increased revenue funding.

A general introduction to the Valleys venues can be provided by drawing on tendencies demonstrated by two of the venues, the largest, Blackwood, and the smallest, Beaufort.[42] Before doing that, however, a word about the use of data and statistics. Figures about theatre are often inconclusive, contradictory or limited, either because they are incomplete, or because they are available but restricted. Many statistics about theatre are unavailable to the general public. (Some of the figures used in this book are not in the public domain.) Whilst Arts Council annual reports can provide useful information, the telling details are often 'owned' by the body that paid for the research. Few organizations have the resources to conduct the kind of research that would enable the public to make really informed decisions about theatre practice. Of those in existence, doubt has been cast on the accuracy of the figures – for instance, some consider that the Beaufort data is inflated by around a third which, if true, could lead to the size of potential audiences being overestimated. Equally, others have disputed the validity of the VAM data because of the size of the sampling. Nevertheless, it is helpful to refer to the available data, albeit with some caution.

Ticket sales at both the Blackwood and Beaufort theatres are reminders of the difficulties of the local economy: only just over half are sold at full price. This obviously has an impact on attendances and, in overall terms, both these venues play to less than half their capacity.[43] In 2000–1, there was, however, a big difference in the average number· of attenders, forty-four at Blackwood and 128 at Beaufort, which is, in part, accounted for by the fact that over two-thirds of the audience visit the venue only once a year. According to Valleys Arts Marketing, this is usually because they have attended the cinema on one occasion or have attended a big, annual event, like a pantomime. But this pattern of consumption might also be indicative of the extent to which the Valleys venues function as places where the consumer goes to buy theatre-as-product, rather than as cultural centres where theatre is one of a range of services. And this is why, I would argue, professional plays are often poorly attended: Blackwood and Beaufort filled less than 20 per cent of their available seating capacity for 'straight' plays. Indeed, VAM notes that plays are a product type that is 'becoming virtually impossible to support at the majority of [VAM venues]'.[44]

There is, though, a significant difference between professional and amateur drama. Blackwood was able to achieve 33 per cent of its capacity for amateur plays; at Beaufort, nearly 50 per cent of the available seats were filled for amateur drama; and this professional/amateur divide is evident in other performance modes. Whilst Blackwood was able to occupy only 14 per cent of its capacity for professional rock music events, amateur rock events filled almost half the available seats. The obvious conclusion to draw from this is that it is not plays, or other particular performance forms, which disengage audiences but the context in which they take place; and the differential between audiences for professional and amateur performances is telling in this respect. (The total average number of attendances for amateur events at the Coliseum, for instance, is nearly double that for professional events.[45]) It is noticeable, though, that it is possible to attract Valleys audiences to specialized events, even when it might be assumed that there would not be a constituency for such product, which is further evidence that it is connective relationships that create audiences, not the product in itself. For instance, Blackwood was able to fill over three-quarters of its seats for opera and Beaufort has developed a significant audience for folk music.

The autumn programmes for 2001 give some idea of how the Valleys venues function. For the purposes of this discussion, I am going to develop the material about the Coliseum, Aberdare (617 seats), which featured in chapter 1, and compare it with the Muni, Pontypridd (313 seats), the Beaufort, Ebbw Vale (302 seats), Blackwood Miners' Institute (651 seats) and the Parc and Dare, Treorchy (641 seats).

What is most noticeable is that the Muni and the Coliseum have virtually become cinemas. Film takes up 75 per cent of the Muni's programme (and this is a venue which describes itself as an 'arts centre') and 67 per cent of the Coliseum's. Only a quarter or less of their output is devoted to live performance. Live music is the most strongly represented live form at the Muni, with 16 per cent of its events in that category. But just 6.6 per cent of its events are live drama or musicals. In contrast, at the Coliseum, drama/musicals represent 22 per cent of the programme. It is perhaps telling that the venue which still identifies itself as a 'miners' institute', Blackwood, offers the most drama/musicals – 58 per cent of its programme, more than twice what the Coliseum offers and eight times the Muni's output. The Beaufort, which defines itself as a 'theatre and ballroom', presents nearly 53 per cent of its programme in the form of drama/musicals; and, at 38 per cent, its programme contains the second highest incidence of live music. The Parc and Dare has the greatest percentage of live music: almost 41 per cent of its programme falls in this category. However, its major output (at nearly 59 per cent) is drama/musicals.

Of course, these percentages indicate proportions rather than absolute totals. The Muni has by far the greatest number of events on its programme (135) and the Parc and Dare has the lowest (49). However, whilst we might expect the Coliseum to follow the Muni, given that it, too, has a substantial film programme, in fact it is Blackwood that has the second highest number of events (91) and this excludes any film programme. If you subtract their film programmes, the Muni and the Coliseum have the lowest live perform-ance output of any of the Valleys venues studied. Hence, Blackwood Miners'

Institute has the most active live performance programme in the Valleys. Moreover, it has the largest capacity of seats to fill, so this makes its policy particularly brave.

It is important to take into account the rather complex and opaque funding arrangements for these Valleys venues. They are all owned by local authorities: the Coliseum, the Muni and the Parc and Dare by RCT County Borough Council, Blackwood Miners' Institute by Caerphilly County Borough Council, and the Beaufort by Blaenau Gwent Borough Council. This makes it difficult to ascertain by how much each venue is subsidized as local authority accounts are not easily accessed; and this is a pity because it then becomes difficult to make the case for these theatres by comparing their funding positions with those of Arts Council-funded venues. It does seem anomalous that there is not a single Valleys venue that is revenue-funded by the Arts Council to be a producing venue. The sums that have been given to the Valleys venues directly from the Arts Council are relatively small, amounting to around £50,000 in 1999–2000, although the total was only £18,000 the year before that. Of course, these venues have received Lottery funding for capital projects. Nevertheless, what we are looking at in general is relatively low-status Arts Council funding.

The content of the 2001 autumn programmes of the Valleys venues provides a real challenge to anyone interested in thinking about contemporary theatre practice. There was such a plethora of tribute shows – ABBA, Elvis Presley, Elton John, Tina Turner – that it came as a surprise to see the real Lonnie Donegan. The interchangeability of the programmes was obvious – Max Boyce, an evening of clairvoyance, Peter Karrie and Owen Money's pantomime could be seen in most places. What we might call 'straight' plays were in the minority and, again, often replicated, like Hijinx's production of Charles Way's *Ill Met By Moonlight*. (Blackwood and the Beaufort both featured this production and yet you can drive from Ebbw Vale to Blackwood in about thirty minutes.) A children's show, *Mr Men and Little Miss*, was on at three of the venues; the Sherman Theatre Company's production for children was performed at two.

The preponderance of tribute shows is a curious phenomenon of the early twenty-first century. Such performances often attract big audiences, who choose to pay £9.50 to see a replica of Elvis, when the original is available on CDs. Given that Elvis is dead, a simulacrum makes some sense; but many artists are still alive. Tribute shows are testament to something in the *Zeitgeist*, however. The replicas seem to carry with them some kind of reassurance for the audience of what the evening will entail, whereas performances of, say, new plays are an unknown quantity. Performers in tribute shows 'quote' the original, rather than copy them, and are often very accomplished performers in their own right; and these shows can have high production values. Audiences can laugh at, or perhaps with, the artiste, which they could not if s/he was actually there. This form of impersonation is the equivalent of designer copies in supermarkets. It is a means by which Valleys audiences can see people whom they might not be able to afford to see, or are too young to have seen, and, in that respect, the tribute show is an egalitarian exercise.

Tribute bands are generally professional shows, however, and the Valleys venues are reliant on amateur events to bulk out their programmes. Some two-thirds of the Coliseum's live performances are amateur, although only around one-seventh of Blackwood's events are amateur in origin. Generally, about half of the programmes in these venues comprises amateur events. In the autumn of 2001, they included the Colstars in *Oliver*, Pontypridd Theatre Company's *A Celebration of Rodgers and Hammerstein*, Blaenau Gwent Young Stars in *Alice – The Musical*, Ystrad Mynach College Performing Arts Students in *Breaking the String* (by Frank Vickery), Blackwood Operatic Society's *Annie* and Tredegar Operatic Society in *The Sound of Music*.

This catalogue shows how the amateurs have taken over the role of providing large-scale performances in the Valleys and the significance of that lies in two details. First, the size of the venues and, secondly, patterns of arts attendance. Now, we know that the Valleys venues have large capacities to fill – over 600 in the case of three of them. Equally, large-cast amateur shows are capable of attracting sizeable audiences, because each cast member can generate a number of audience members from family and friends. So the musical is an ideal means by which the local community can enjoy familiar congregation in large theatres. However, the musical, as such, is a declining force outside London's West End. The *Beaufort Welsh Omnibus Survey* (2000) observes that 'frequent attendance at a musical dropped quite significantly' in 2000. Furthermore, that same survey shows that in every region in Wales, bar one, attendance at musicals was lower than for plays. That region is mid-south Wales, that is, the Valleys. We might surmise that the reason why the musical remains an attraction in the Valleys is because of the activity of local amateurs.

We could go further and suggest that the amateur musicals are the main channel of orature in the Valleys and also that, despite the fact that these shows are mainly American, they are actually reflective of indigenous south Walian theatre practice, for these reasons: they create and are inspired by local congregation; musicals integrate different performative elements; their process involves taking ownership of the material; those on the stage are known to and by those in the audience and there is no hierarchical separation between them; the effect of familiar congregation leads to a feeling of ownership of the venue; and creative expression draws on the local lived experience. Thus, *Annie*, for example, becomes a metaphor for Blackwood, without that transition being laboured or self-conscious.

This is not, though, a view that would probably be shared by either the Arts Council of Wales or the major voices of theatre in Wales. There is an unstated, yet understood, attitude towards some of the entertainments described above which is, at best, sniffy. Both local musicals and imported tribute shows tend to be well-attended. However, neither is valued by those with referential power; and here is the nub of the problem of theatre in the Valleys. There is a massive taste discrepancy between the Arts Council of Wales and its cohorts on the one hand and Valleys audiences on the other; and it is that gap which has caused the hole in the Valleys where state funding of the arts ought to be.

Organizations

It is curious how that taste discrepancy has evolved. One explanation may lie in the fact that it was 'proper' theatre venues which came to be dominant in cultural production (even before the advent of the Arts Council in the 1940s), rather than the other available cultural organizations in the Valleys. Of these, the most interesting were the settlements, because they had a very different concept of cultural production from theatres.

Through the 1920s and 1930s, the settlements made an important contribution to cultural practices in the Valleys. Maes-yr-haf at Trealaw, near Tonypandy, was the first to be developed in the south Wales coalfield and, from 1927 onwards, it established a blueprint for the creation of settlements elsewhere.[46] The purpose of the settlements was to provide educational and cultural succour to the long-term unemployed during the Depression. They were places to which the unemployed could go to make contacts and receive legal and financial advice. But they also provided a range of other services: they owned their own buildings, including a holiday camp by the sea, ran allotments, and had permanent lecturers, PT instructors, handicraftsmen, musicians and social workers. The Pilgrim Trust's report suggests that some settlements were, at times, turned into the 'dramatic centre for the neighbourhood' and performance activities, which included the production of plays and operas, developed out of the totality of the settlements' endeavours. They were, therefore, contextualized and informed by the whole lived experience of the environment and, in this, the settlements had much in common with the practice of orature. There was a real emphasis on the organization's being conducted by local people on their own behalf – building work was mainly carried out by settlement members – and each settlement was run by a democratically elected committee. Wardens were expected to be responsive, rather than prescriptive, and to 'feel [their] way into the life of the society' in which they were living.[47] The settlements were a very good cultural model for the Valleys and it is a shame that their influence on the organization of performance was limited and short-term.

There are, however, several contemporary arts agencies in the Valleys which exhibit some of the features of the settlements and these hybridized organizations are of significance because they occupy the space between Arts Council territory, on the one hand, and the amateur world, on the other.

Whilst not a discrete performance-based organization, Arts Factory has adopted a method of working which provides a model of how theatre practice might move forward in the Valleys.[48] Arts Factory is an independent Development Trust, founded in 1990 and created by local people in Ferndale; it developed in response to high unemployment and was started by local people who thought that they were being perceived as part of the social problems, when they felt that they could be part of the solution. It is based on several sites, one of which is in Tre-Rhondda, a former chapel which Arts Factory now owns.

Arts Factory functions in two ways. The first is through enterprise: it earns its money by developing viable businesses in graphic design, environmental art, woodcraft and a garden centre with a landscaping service; and it also hires out office space. The second is by providing the community with facilities, classes (including drama and dance), training courses, arts activities and a cinema. In order to access these services, local people take out annual membership for one pound, which is all that they pay in the whole year to use any of the facilities. (The organization has over 1,000 members.) To become a member, it is necessary to 'share [Arts Factory's] values'. Those beliefs include profit-sharing within the context of a non-profit-making organization, a philosophy which is consistent with the early co-operative societies.

Arts Factory has made an important contribution to the local economy because it employs forty people. It also helps the economy in more subtle ways, having around one hundred volunteers who might otherwise have been disengaged from the community and, even, in some instances, involved in crime. Its training courses help individuals to improve their employability. Moreover, the reconstruction of the chapel was undertaken by local builders using local labour and materials, which also helps to keep money within the local economy.

This is a good example of 'grounded arts', where a symbiotic relationship occurs between business and the arts and each supports the other: Arts Factory aims to earn money from arts activities which can then be ploughed back into the community. It has a mixed-income base and obtains money from four sources: trading activities, service-level agreements and contracts, European funding, and grants, including the Lottery and charitable trusts. Grants represent the smallest amount of Arts Factory income and more than half its money comes from the first two sources, which means that Arts Factory is not dependent on ACW funding and is not, therefore, subject to the limits and pressures that are associated with being in receipt of Arts Council subvention.

Valleys Kids is another example of a 'grounded' Rhondda community organization; based in Penygraig near Tonypandy, it was established in 1978. It specializes in working with children and its arts activities are, in the broadest sense, therapeutic in that they have a social function, which is to help support children whose backgrounds are affected by unemployment and disadvantage. Like Arts Factory, its strength is that it uses a hybrid model of organization and includes volunteers working alongside professionals. In common with the early settlements, performance coexists with other activities, like homework clubs, computer training and a community gym. Theatre productions, which come under the auspices of ArtWorks (funded by an ACW Lottery grant), may emanate locally from the Penygraig Youth Theatre – in a localized reworking of the story of the Snow Queen, for instance – or from visiting professional companies, like Hijinx and the Sherman Theatre Company. But Valleys Kids does not just present Welsh material or work in the Rhondda: it provides children who could not afford to travel abroad with access to international theatre projects, for example by hosting a Bosnian Youth Theatre and participating in a theatre conference in Jordan.

One of the organizations that works with Valleys Kids is Rhondda Cynon Taff Community Arts (RCTCA), which runs residency and dance projects at Penygraig. RCTCA was established in 1983 as, and this is a significant term in the context of this book, an 'Unincorporated Association'; part of its current funding comes from a service level agreement with RCT County Borough Council. However, from 2002 it will receive increased revenue funding from ACW. Its purpose, according to its mission statement, is to 'ensure that community art plays a central role in the social, cultural, educational and artistic life of the Valleys'. Projects are aimed at people of all ages, abilities and backgrounds but, to some extent, RCTCA works with the marginalized-within-the-marginalized as it has a particular focus on the disabled and on dance. Amongst RCTCA's innovations is a physical theatre group for boys at Treorchy Comprehensive School, whose first production was presented at the Parc and Dare Theatre. Although RCTCA is prepared to involve itself in conventional mainstream projects (it worked in partnership with Spectacle Theatre company to create one of the 'Our Town' pieces for the Millennium Dome, for example), it also provides the wherewithal for the community to reshape performance practice: by offering the kind of technical training which enables 'any performance space' to be turned into a theatre; or by employing local professional musicians, like Paul Rosser, to facilitate amateur musical development. Rosser runs a percussion group for

RCTCA which uses 'found' instruments and empowers local people to make music, even if they have few musical skills at the outset.

The Canolfan Rhys Arts Centre, opened in 1996, is a rather different kind of Rhondda organization: its origins are linked to church activities. Situated on the Penrhys housing estate, where unemployment has reached very high levels, the Penrhys Partnership runs a series of projects, including the arts centre converted from a derelict housing block. The Partnership is a registered charity, which is steered by a mixture of the public and private sectors, including the local authority, and local residents. The arts at Penrhys are linked explicitly to the Community Development Strategy and are perceived as a methodology, rather than an end-product But, as with the other organizations discussed here, performance practices exist alongside other cultural and social activities, like a doctor's surgery, a grocery store, a nearly new shop, the social services and education projects. Among Canolfan Rhys's activities are sessions on rock music, drumming and youth dance. Elan, a professional theatre company from Cardiff, produced a performance project using local, especially young, people at Penrhys in 1999. In 2002, Canolfan Rhys developed a theatre piece from material written by members of its creative writing group, which was a hybrid amateur/professional project run in collaboration with Spectacle Theatre company.

Although the hybrid is a sensible model, it can be difficult for arts professionals to work effectively with local projects, because they do not necessarily have the skills and techniques that are required, a problem that Tim Dwelly alludes to in *Creative Regeneration* (2001), a research report specifically about community arts projects in south Wales. Dwelly cautions against employing 'workers who cannot easily empathize with people in the communities' and advises that artists need to be both physically and 'emotionally [based] in the community'. *Creative Regeneration* underlines the fact that locals and professionals can have differing perceptions about the functioning of performances in the Valleys. Where professionals are not part of the lived experience, they may experience real difficulties in developing or presenting a piece of theatre. Moreover, those problems are often then compounded by the critical reception given to 'community' performance projects by critics and Arts Council officers, who are themselves also not part of the community. Their critiques, which may suspend the usual criteria employed to discuss 'proper' professional theatre – something that, in itself, can be seen as patronizing by local people – are inclined to impose limits on the performance by restricting its value to the worthwhileness of the endeavour, which ultimately serves the interests of the professionals. In effect, the subtext can be that the professionals are doing these poor people a favour for which they should be grateful. When professionals come from outside, their motives for working with Valleys communities can be complex: funders, and theatre practitioners, 'often want to promote themselves through [community projects]'.[49]

The work of the companies discussed here suggests that Valleys arts organizations are at their most effective where the ethos of the early settlements has been retained, a view that is corroborated by Tim Dwelly in *Creative Regeneration* who reinforces the point that visiting professionals need to 'ask [local] people what kind of events they want to be involved in'.

Theatre companies

There is a big difference between visiting professionals working temporarily for a community arts organization and professionals working permanently for a discrete theatre company. The organizations I have discussed use a wide range of performance activities in the course of their work. But I am going to look now at how a specific theatre company functions in the Valleys. Spectacle, which was founded in 1979, is the only producing theatre company situated in the south Wales Valleys and it is based at Pontypridd College, Llwynypia, in the Rhondda Fawr. In its website, the company claims to have 'an international reputation for excellence, innovation and collaboration . . . and [leads] the way in showing just how effective live theatre can be'. Spectacle describes itself as a 'community theatre company' and it tends to make three productions a year.

In 2001, its productions included *Hide and Seek*, by Martin James, a humorous story, aimed at key stages 1 and 2, about how people relate to others and learn through mutual cooperation and understanding. Another of its productions was *The Lazy Ant*, about self-perception, which was aimed at ages 3 to 5. A third production was Dic Edwards's *Into the East*, produced for a schools' tour, which dealt with the story of two children in the Czech Jewish ghetto of Terezin during the Second World War.

The connection between Dic Edwards and Spectacle is particularly interesting and serves as a counterpoint to the analysis of Proteus provided earlier. Furthermore, Edwards's association with the locale has something in common with the way in which the wardens of the settlements operated. Edwards has had a relationship with Spectacle going back over a number of years. In the 1990s, the company commisioned him to write several plays for a project on literacy and oracy, and the fact that this was a five-year project indicates that Edwards's involvement took the form of a lengthy developing relationship between himself, the theatre company and its constituency. He was not, then, being parachuted into a community with which he had only a tenuous link.

Edwards is a south Walian and considers the Valleys to be his 'cultural home';[50] he also espouses views which are consistent with the Valleys, as in his acknowledgement that a lack of confidence is endemic to the area. He understands that places like the Valleys have a sense of being disenfranchised from the Welsh-speaking heartlands of Wales. Edwards's comprehension of the lived experience impacts on his approach to theatre, as in his antipathy to 'proper' theatres and in his willingness to have his work toured to non-theatre venues. He believes in a democratic, collaborative theatre process: his purpose is to 'distance' the audience from 'any bourgeois representation' and to make the audience a 'part of action and argument'.[51] Edwards locates himself as working-class and, in observing that middle-class directors tend not to want to work with working-class playwrights, he makes the case that class is of central importance to the dynamics of theatre practice and, more-over, that middle-class directors are instrumental in producing bourgeois theatre for working-class audiences.

In observing that many children in the Valleys could not afford to see any theatre, he demonstrates a realistic view of the implications of poverty. Hence, his work with Spectacle is an end in itself, whereas for some theatre practitioners Theatre-in-Education (TiE) is a phase in their career develop-ment.

Dic Edwards's plays for Spectacle indicate how Edwards goes about constructing a believable Valleys-orientated theatre practice.[52] In *David* (1996), an exploration of the issue of bullying through a reworking of the story of *David and Goliath*, Edwards's use of local references helps to reassure the audience (key stage 2) that the piece of theatre can communicate with them in their own language. The play contains well-observed local details to reveal the texture of poverty – David's father eats crisp sandwiches, for example – without using them to sneer at the poor. A reference to Cardiff City fans, stalwart even though their team has, at times, had mixed fortunes, is pertinent (and guaranteed to raise a knowing smile). Edwards's inclusion of commonly used aggressive vocabulary ('you calling me a liar'; 'don't get funny with me') enhances the credibility of his writing. The political subtext of *David*, how young people in the Valleys attempt to cope with dignity under challenging domestic circumstances, offers a more constructive view of living in poverty than is sometimes provided elsewhere. Through commissioning a writer like Edwards, Spectacle is able to construct a form of theatre which speaks directly of and to its immediate constituency, yet one which is also able to travel to other areas.

In Arts Council parlance, this is typical of 'community theatre'. However, the use of that term to describe what Spectacle does, and also the organ-izations discussed earlier when the term is extended to include the arts in general, is problematic. Indeed, it could be argued that the notion of community performance is responsible for creating a category of theatre in the Valleys that is subliminally understood to be second-class. Bennett et al. in *Coalfields Regeneration* have some very striking things to say about the complicated concept of community, which are of direct relevance here. They make the point that the term is sometimes used as a substitute for political action, in the hope that communities can be created simply by repeating the word.[53] They also suggest that the task of community workers is to mediate between 'official discourses of community and the lived experiences of people', which then makes them a 'constitutive part of a very messy process'. Although we understand 'community' to be an inclusive term, Bennett et al. assert that it often hides difficult relations of power and inequality; official versions of community empowerment prevent serious questions being asked about who, exactly, is being empowered and whose interests are being served. When agencies like the Welsh Assembly and the Arts Council of Wales use the term 'community' to refer to policies for theatre and performance, we ought to be alert to the possibility of a hidden agenda.

Learning from the present

Whilst there are examples of positive developments which suggest that the lived experience is being acknowledged by arts professionals, there is still a real problem, in that performance practices in the Valleys are often disassociated from local life. There seem to be two parallel cultures: one which is plugged in to the lived experience; and the other which is transported from elsewhere, bringing with it someone else's lifestyle. Formal theatre practice would be more effective if, like the early settlements, it could learn from the present Valleys reality; instead of problematizing certain social behaviours, a more realistic appraisal of how the local culture works would be helpful. The kind of behaviour that is routinely depicted in plays as proof of the tragic consequences of the loss of coalmining is not necessarily that in local parlance.

Look, for instance, at the evidence provided by what people say. The *Knowhere Guide to the Rhondda* on the internet enables local people to comment on their environs, and their remarks are telling.[54] The majority single out pubs, clubs, cinemas and the Arts Centre in Penrhys as their favourite buildings. Their choice of structures that they want to see demolished (Pentre Legion, the Banc nightclub in Pentre, the cricket pitch in Ton-Pentre – selected because the site is no longer available for public, community events, like the annual fair) suggests a sense of cultural engagement at odds with the view that the populace is culturally apathetic.

Whilst the way in which the website's correspondents express themselves would probably occasion an attack of the vapours in the politically correct, they are, in fact, providing very good detail about the lived experience, albeit limited to those who have access to the internet. In identifying the best aspects about the Rhondda, they single out, 'Cheap skag! Cheap cider! Cheap women!'; or 'all the good looking men'; or they extol the virtues of 'listening to (rare) Complex Animals bootlegs recorded in the Prince of Wales, Treorchy'. They are comfortable about volunteering that they enjoy 'getting pissed and crawling home' and that the inhabitants of Treherbert's Ranch estate have a tendency to burn 'any building . . . that is unoccupied for more than 1 day'. Whilst local people recognize the difficulties of their social circumstances, they are more sardonic as commentators than the well-meaning professional observer: 'Leisure time – we are so successful here that NOBODY has to work! Yes, it's true, no work means we have loads of time for drinking ourselves to death and taking heroin in Pentre flats. Fucking great, mine's a pint.' These correspondents are not, though, nostalgic for the time when employment opportunities were better, specifically the coalmining past, 'that we get force-fed as if it means anything to anyone under 50'.

The significance of the findings from internet correspondents is that they shed light on what Raymond Williams called 'the structure of feeling' and they are especially useful because they emanate from a social stratum that would not necessarily be thought of as prime theatre-goers. Consequently, they are an important way of learning about the mindset of at least some of the inhabitants of the Rhondda; and what we learn points to a perception-gap between the people and how they are often characterized in theatre.

For instance, drugs have been used as a means of symbolizing post-1984 deprivation in the Valleys. However, drugs have been widely available in the Valleys for at least thirty-five years and, moreover, a fair number of 'tidy' Valleys people (lawyers, teachers, office workers, theatre practitioners) have been, at least occasional, users. Hence, the emblematic use of drugs, in and of themselves, as indicators of deprivation is inaccurate, particularly so given that local attitudes towards drug use are, as the internet correspondents show, ambivalent and complex.

Another example might be the way in which theatre companies use language to suggest that a character is a 'low-life'. They tend to do this through the use of what the BBC quaintly describes as 'strong language'. However, in the Valleys, such language is simply not viewed in that way by a lot of people. When talking to each other, Valleys people from quite a wide variety of backgrounds will use phrases which might discomfort the anxious arts practitioner. Some theatre companies would consider this a real problem, many local people would not; hence part of the gulf between theatre and local reality.

But perhaps of more importance is the question of form; for it is here that the gap between arts reality and the lived experience is at its most obvious. As demonstrated earlier, Valleys people are familiar with certain kinds of entertainment and, if the objective is to develop theatre practice in the Valleys, it would be sensible to draw on those forms. When the late John McGrath was running 7:84 (Scotland), one of the reasons why the company was successful was because he capitalized on the ceilidh form for productions

which were aimed at Highlanders and on popular music idioms for performances directed at urban Glaswegians. In the Valleys, pubs, clubs and cinemas
ought to be important sources of influence because they have shaped local
perceptions of what a good night out' entails. Furthermore, it is the comparison between what theatre offers and what these other forms of entertainment
give that renders theatre less attractive; and it is not just pubbing and
clubbing that are of relevance here. The means by which local people follow
sport are also of interest.

In all of these examples, it is not the cost of tickets that matters – because
it can often be more expensive to 'consume' these forms of entertainment.
What counts is the fact that, a lot of the time, the pleasure principle is more
obviously at work than it is in many theatres; and this is because these forms
are sensuous, by which I mean that they are tactile and, often, moving. For
instance, cinema, which we know is the most successful entertainment form
in south Wales in terms of attendance, offers compensations, even when the
film is dreary, in the form of the size of the screen, the volume of the music,
and the consequent impact of the images. Moreover, the fact that you can
drink and eat at the same time as watch the film (something which is
forbidden in most theatres) is an attraction to many; and, curiously, cinema
audiences continue to be collectively vocal in response to fear or excitement
when most theatre audiences are more controlled. A lot of theatre productions do not 'move' and have lost sight of how to excite an audience because
theatre companies do not have the kinds of connections with their audiences
which would allow them to understand what moves them.

But it is not just the present from which theatre companies need to learn.
They also need to recognize the past because, as Dai Smith points out,
without an acknowledgement of the past Wales will operate in a cultural
vacuum: theatre companies cannot invent 'any old Wales . . . whenever and
wherever [they wish]'.[55]

The use of local history as a source of professional theatre is quite under-
developed, and the example of para-theatre suggests one way forward. At
Llancaiach Fawr, a group of amateur local historians has developed a way of
telling the history of the house by using theatrical techniques. But you do not
see much of this in the Valleys, although there are many buildings which
could be used in this way. (Brith Gof used to inhabit spaces and reconfigure
their history, as in a piece called *Haearn* (1992), which transformed the old
British Coal Tredegar Works into a theatre venue for that project.) The
Rhondda Heritage Centre (formerly the Lewis-Merthyr pit) is a case in point,
as it has been underexploited in a performance context. That said, it is the
unremembered buildings and forgotten places around the Valleys that would
make for the more interesting work. But to know where they are and why they
might matter, you would need to have a deep knowledge of the area and it is
this that many theatre practitioners coming into the Valleys do not have.

At the Museum of Welsh Life, St Fagans, the former Oakdale Institute, a working-men's club near Blackwood, has been carefully reconstructed using the original materials. It includes a small theatre, which is now used for events, like storytelling for children, and which can be hired. It is quite a sad space, though, because it is a form of heritage-in-aspic. The Oakdale Institute once offered a space in which local people could say something about their history through the medium of performance. Now it is, itself, history. We should not be maudlin about this – old buildings are expensive to maintain – but we should not be blind to the fact that the kinds of cultural relationships which working-men's institutes had with their communities have been eroded. They, along with the settlements, had a regard for history and enabled local people to engage with their own past by providing them with books and classes about it. Because the institutes and settlements also served as venues for drama classes and theatre events, this provided an opportunity for some cross-fertilization between the study of local history and a form for articulating it. What we have lost is this connection and, in the process, an impulse to use theatre practice to investigate our history.

Thus distanced from the past, theatre has become solipsistic and somewhat divorced from the shared experience. When Dai Smith decries the recent tendency of writers to create characters who '[feed] on their own dreams not ours, and so [illuminate] only the backdrop of the writer's mind',[56] his critique of literature is equally apposite to theatre. The idea that you can create an imaginary Wales for the purposes of theatre practice is a nonsense which has developed, in part, to disguise the fact that some of those who are involved in nurturing theatre in the Valleys (in the wider sense, these include ACW officers, theatre company members, arts consultants, educationists, academics) know little about what it is like to live in the Valleys and have no history of the area either. In short, they would rather die than spend an evening in the Pandy Inn; and people in the Valleys know this.

Equally, Valleys people do not much care for arts missionaries who perceive them either as victims who need to be educated out of the unsatisfactory behaviour caused by their disadvantages, or as an opportunity to develop the missionary's career by demonstrating her/his willingness to produce theatre for marginalized communities. Arts careerists do not know what it 'feels' like to live in the Valleys, which is why they so often misjudge or intellectualize theatre practice to the point where all the guts are removed from it. Small wonder, then, that audiences would rather watch a tribute band or an amateur musical: to enjoy something that theatre professionals, who do not really want to know you, would sneer at constitutes a small act of rebellion.

Performance practices in the Valleys illustrate the negative impact of product culture on theatre, a culture which revolves around the idea that the performance is an artefact – a tangible 'thing', rather than a process. Hence, the play as product, and the venue as its surrounding packaging, is a discrete object which can be manipulated to serve the formal needs of official thinking. This suits the interests of theatre practitioners themselves because, although they are constrained by policies, they are still able to function, or at any rate to imagine that they function, as 'free' artists with control over their own aesthetic.

The standard European model, however, is not the only concept of good quality theatre available. There are other ideas about ways of producing '*effective* performance practice',[57] a notion which draws on a combination of ideas expressed by, first, Baz Kershaw (1992) and, secondly, Kwesi Owusu (1986). In *The Politics of Performance*, Kershaw introduces the expression 'performance efficacy' to describe the way in which best theatre practice connects the performers' and the audience's ideologies and to provide an alternative way of identifying 'quality'. He suggests that, in order to be effectual, it is necessary for theatre practitioners to demonstrate an understanding of the particularities of their audiences' modes of social production: of the way in which audiences come together; through the use of theatrical conventions in the context of an audience's expectations of performance and levels of theatre literacy; and in the devices which are used to establish the credibility of the performance content.[58] The link I am making between Kershaw's analysis of (British) theatre practice and African performance traditions is through the notion of *call and response*, as described by Owusu. Both Kershaw and Owusu assert the importance of practitioners and audiences being equal bondholders in the procedures of theatre practice. They recognize that theatre practitioners need to establish their credentials to practise theatre by participating in the lived experiences which condition the responses of their audiences to theatre. Kwesi Owusu confirms the centrality of the relationship between theatre and the culture when he contends that: 'the overall character of [the] creative universe [in African orature] is ultimately determined by the dominant mode of social production'.[59]

Owusu's explanation of African performance practices points to the reasons why British theatre is structured so differently. A capitalist, market-led economy impacts upon the imaginative world to produce a product-orientated theatre practice. Instead of the modes of social production determining the pattern of local theatre, the demands of the (centralized) market construct the shape of the nation's theatre, albeit modified by the Arts Council's emphasis on quality rather than profitable product.

The import of this for theatre practice in Wales is that the Arts Council's system of theatre procedures across the UK does not allow sufficiently for differentiation between modes of social production. This is also true of certain parts of England, of course, particularly in the context of poverty and class orientation, and it is equally applicable to Scotland. However, the difference between Wales and Scotland, on one hand, and England, on the other, is that issues of national and cultural identity, along with complex questions concerning power relations, are added into the mix. Whereas orature is an outcome of 'the masses living out their life dramas and expressing them', the dominant British procedures of theatre tend to work on the basis that the masses can be adequately represented by designated professionals articulating the 'life dramas' on their behalf.[60] But prevailing cultural tendencies in Wales are not necessarily correlative with those found in the *dominant* cultures within England. In Wales, for example, there is a history of slippage between professional and amateur activity. While that may be true of certain activities in England, like folk music traditions, it is not so to the same extent. Bardic conventions associated with the national Eisteddfod elevate the status of the amateur in ways that are not generally evident in England. The relative importance of the poet-farmer, for example, does not appear to have an English equivalent. There are also other differences in patterns of the lived experience – education provision, geographical configurations of social 'exclusion', relative proportions of poverty distribution, and so on – which suggest that subsidized theatre provision does not respond appropriately to modes of social production in Wales. Although we are talking about shifts of emphasis here, rather than absolutes, the *prevailing* lived experience is noticeably different in Wales from that in England, and the statistics and data referred to earlier in this book support that idea. Yet theatre provision is not substantively differentiated to accommodate national, and perhaps even regional, characteristics; and it is this discrepancy which should alert us to the idea that theatre practice is manipulated, albeit not consciously, to produce a homogenizing effect in Wales and across the UK.

The problem is that so many professional theatre companies control audiences and permit their 'participation' on their (the theatre companies') terms. Consequently, the audience is used, in the worst sense, to fulfil the horizons of expectation of the companies, and to complete their predetermined creation of meaning. The audience is confined to the role of consumer: audience participation only exists at the point of consumption. In contrast, the work of Valley and Vale and Canolfan Rhys, for example, represents a version of cultural democracy, because the lived experience of the cultural practice connects directly with that of its south Wales Valleys constituency.

In 1992, the former South East Wales Arts Association organized a month-long celebration called Valleys Live. It boasted 500 events involving over 20,000 people. Its primary purpose was to mark the refurbishment of a number of the major Valleys venues; but, according to its programme, it was intended that the festival would 'have positive results in future years'. In fact, although the event as a whole is still remarked on by local people, many of the projects initiated then did not continue in the way in which they were envisaged and the real task of audience development was much less successful than anticipated. This, I would argue, is because Valleys Live masked a collision between different kinds of critical thinking about perform-ance. On one hand, there was a focus on theatre venues; but, on the other, there was an attempt to incorporate the types of performativity that had been the province of the early settlements. What appeared to be a winning combination of approaches was actually a clash of ideologies; and this tension is endemic to the difficulties the Valleys face in developing perform-ance practices that are indigenous. It is a man-made friction constructed by the very policies that were intended to support theatre in the Valleys. Which brings me to the matter of the Arts Council.

1. The Stereophonics in front of Cwmaman Institute, 1997, just before they released their first album (Source: *The Western Mail*, Cardiff)

2. The Coliseum Theatre, Trecynon, Aberdare, 2002 (Source: R. Shade)

3. The front of the Cwmaman Institute, 2002, Cwmaman, Cynon Valley (Source: R. Shade)

4. The Little Theatre, Gadlys, Aberdare, 2002 (Source: R. Shade)

5. The Phoenix Players in *The Merchant of Venice* on the stage of the Coliseum, Aberdare, *circa* 1970/71 (Source: R. Shade) (The author is among the cast)

6. The Parc and Dare Theatre, Treorchy, Rhondda, 2002 (Source: R. Shade)

7. Ferndale Band Club, Rhondda, 2002 (Source: R. Shade)

8. Llwynypia Workingmen's Club, Rhondda, 2002 (Source: R. Shade)

9. Canolfan Rhys Arts Centre, Penrhys, Rhondda, 2002 (Source: R. Shade)

10. Soar Ffrwdamos Centre (a former chapel), Penygraig, Rhondda, 2002
(Source: R. Shade)

11. Judges Hall, Trealaw, Rhondda, 2002 (Source: R. Shade)
(*Black Sabbath* and *Man* played here)

12. Spectacle Theatre company in Dic Edwards's *Over Milkwood*, 1999
(Photographer: Terry Morgan)

13. The Muni Arts Centre, Pontypridd, 2002 (Source: R. Shade)
(*Cream* and *Status Quo* played here in the 1960s)

14. Rhondda Cynon Taff Community Arts
(Source: Joy Rosser/RCT Community Arts)

15. The Pontypridd Community Play, 1992, *Valley of the Kings*
(Source: Keith Morris)

3

Art for the People: The Arts Council – Power, Discipline and Theatre

This chapter will investigate Arts Council procedures and attempt to dismantle some of the 'natural' assumptions on which Arts Council policies are based in order to demonstrate how use of certain orthodoxies has standardized theatre practice. My purpose is to explain the background to validation and disqualification, which is crucial to a comprehension of the ways in which theatre in general in Wales has been marginalized, and popular, indigenous performance practices, in particular.

The amount of money which the arts receive is small in comparison with overall government expenditure. In the 1990s, that sum was around 0.4 per cent of government spending, which included the total grant given to the Department for Culture, Media and Sport, as well as local authority spending on the arts.[1] Despite this relatively insignificant figure, the level of influence which the Arts Council exerts is, and has been, enormous. The problem is that what little money there is acts as a very powerful determinant. The role of the Arts Council is, then, central to an understanding of the way in which theatre practices have been hegemonized.

This is of particular significance to Wales because the experience of the Arts Council in Wales is that of an ideological transaction between a larger and a smaller country, covering significant differences in terms of class, language, cultural traditions and political complexion. As such, the Arts Council exemplifies the working through of power in practice; it is, for instance, central to the curatorship of Welsh theatre and, as a consequence of that, is critical to the exercise of power in relation to inclusion and incorporation. As Owen Kelly argues: 'the state has assumed the role of patron of the arts, and custodian of a specific national culture, and the establishment of the Arts Council of Great Britain in 1945 is but one example of the ways in which the state enacts that role'.[2]

Discipline and the Panopticon

My contention is that the Arts Council functions as a panoptic, or disciplinary, body and that it is this panopticism which provides the conditions for hegemony. The idea of the Panopticon was originally produced by Jeremy Bentham in the late eighteenth century as a response to the problem of keeping hospital and prison inmates under surveillance for their well-being and protection. It was conceived as an architectural device which took the form of an observation tower, with windows on all sides, which faced on to a circle of cells, each of which had a window facing on to the tower and another facing the outside. A single guard could keep the occupants of the cells under surveillance at all times: 'daylight and the overseer's gaze capture the inmate more effectively than darkness'.[3]

The defining characteristics of the Panopticon are the extent of its 'gaze'; its efficiency in conducting 'surveillance'; the 'universal visibility' of its subjects; and the internalization by the inmate of these functions so that eventually s/he becomes self-surveying and self-disciplining. As Michel Foucault notes, 'it's a machine in which everyone is caught, those who exercise power just as much as those over whom it is exercised'. He accounts for this development by suggesting that the bourgeoisie recognized that legislation alone would not ensure control over the individual and that it would be necessary for a mechanism, such as the Panopticon, to be devised to produce a 'social hegemony which it has never relinquished'.[4]

Foucault does not perceive the power of the Panopticon to be centred on the guard, because s/he is also being watched by peers, superiors and, of course, the subjected inmates. As a result, 'you have an apparatus of total and circulating mistrust'. There is no 'point' of power in the Panopticon, which is its strength. The power of the Panopticon lies in its disciplinary power, consisting of 'structures', 'hierarchies', 'inspections, exercises and methods of training and conditioning'.[5]

Originally a utopian endeavour, the Panopticon was a device designed to reform prisons and hospitals and to improve conditions in a civilized manner by helping inmates to be protected from themselves. Foucault did not see the system as being exclusively repressive, since he accepted the possibility of 'revolts against the gaze'.[6]

Panopticism

The Arts Council can be viewed as a panoptic structure because its modus operandi is primarily disciplinary. Its disciplinary procedures 'reinforce' the Arts Council's 'internal mechanisms of power',[7] the chief purpose of which is to '[regulate] movements . . . [and dissipate] compact groupings of individuals wandering about the country in unpredictable ways'.[8] The source of the Arts Council's power lies in the reach of its 'gaze', which encourages self-discipline and through which an overtly repressive external discipline is avoided.

Like the Panopticon, the Arts Council was established for ostensibly utopian purposes. It was founded after the Second World War but its framework was essentially that of the Council for the Encouragement of Music and the Arts (CEMA).[9] Its aims may be seen as laudable and altruistic, for until this point the theatre was unregulated, in the sense that it was not subsidized by government money.[10] Given the lack of a formal, centralized system of organizing the distribution of theatre, and despite the fact that some actors had achieved social status, performers could still be regarded as little more than the 'rogues and vagabonds' that they had been in the fourteenth century and, as such, could be perceived as 'wandering about the country in unpredictable ways'. CEMA was, then, a radical move towards organization and regularization, arguably the most major historical shift towards a national cultural policy Britain has seen. What it did was to recognize the arts as *disciplines*. But this laid the foundation for those incorporative procedures which also exclude. As Foucault noted: 'the disciplines characterize, classify, and specialize, they distribute along a scale, around a norm, hierarchize individuals in relation to one another and, if necessary, disqualify and invalidate.'[11]

The shift towards a systematized approach to the funding of the arts, while producing a situation where the arts could, for the first time, be formally recognized through government sponsorship, made the arts more vulnerable to 'discipline' in the form of normalization and categorization. From the outset, it was acknowledged that there would always be too many demands on the limited supply of money and, consequently, there was always the need to exclude. The important questions in relation to panopticism and the arts relate to the means by which disqualification and invalidation have been exercised for 'at the heart of all disciplinary systems functions a small penal mechanism'.[12] It is important, then, to acknowledge that the Arts Council developed policies which disqualify certain theatre practices, bearing in mind that, by withholding subsidy, the Arts Council is, in effect, imposing a penalty.

The history of the Arts Council is the history of cultural policy in the context of government subsidy and, as such, evokes the 'uninterrupted play of calculated gazes'.[13] In order to make decisions about who receives public subsidy, the Arts Council has developed a system of surveillance, in effect a 'gaze', which ensures that arts organizations are 'always to be seen'; and it is this state of visibility that 'maintains the disciplined individual in his subjection'.[14] The concept of 'visibility' works in the interests of the Arts Council; and evidence suggests that one of the ways in which the Arts Council exercises disciplinary power is through its control of what it is appropriate for the public to know and, by implication, through its encouragement of self-censorship. For example, as this extract from a document relating to the former Welsh Committee shows, what happens in Arts

Council committees is private, that is, secret: 'Members should treat as strictly confidential all matters discussed . . . No statements should be made to the press [by Council, committee or panel members] without prior approval of the appropriate chairman.'[15] Confidentiality ensures that, while the activities of the occupants of the Panopticon's cells (or, for the purposes of this investigation, theatre companies) are exposed, the deliberations of the Arts Council, or watchtower, remain invisible when it suits the Arts Council for them to be so.

Performing arts organizations are ideal subjects of panopticism because the content of what they do is, by definition, visible. The problem is the extent to which they have colluded with the demands of the Arts Council to become self-disciplining, trained bodies. Like the inmates of the Panopticon, the performer 'does not know whether the supervisor is there . . . so he behaves as though he were under constant surveillance from the gaze'.[16] In this way, the performer/performance is not produced exclusively by the creative process, but rather by the effects of power through 'discipline': 'power produces; it produces reality; it produces domains of objects and rituals of truth'.[17]

We can demonstrate *how* the reality of theatre practice is produced through panoptic strategies by describing the fundamental characteristic of the Arts Council, which is that it categorizes the elements of theatre constitutive of best practice. Hence, it defines theatre literacy in its establishment of a polarity between high and low quality theatre, so that what seems to be an imaginative attempt to offer theatre financial support is a means by which the Arts Council can introduce a set of imperatives to close, manipulate and limit theatre practice: the Arts Council determines what it is appropriate to fund and, in so doing, disciplines what can be seen, by whom and under which circumstances.

The development of panopticism in theatre practice

CEMA, which emerged in January 1940, was introduced as part of the war effort to demonstrate 'that the Government cares about the cultural life of the country'.[18] But it is clear that CEMA understood its function as being to distribute 'high' culture to the working classes. Lord (John Maynard) Keynes, the first chairman of the Arts Council, identified CEMA's purpose thus: 'to carry [theatre] to places which otherwise would be cut off from all contact with the masterpieces of happier days . . . to air-raid shelters, to wartime hostels, to factories, [and] to mining villages'.[19]

The Second World War enabled government to recognize the power-potential of cultural practices and, therefore, the opportunities which would accrue in *centralizing* the organization of the arts; and the government took sole charge of funding CEMA in 1942. By 1945, a panoptic structure for theatre had been established before the Arts Council was fully in place. The 'gaze' of the Council was evident; theatre companies were trained and disciplined, observed, examined and supervised; theatre forms were hierarchized and differentiated; and London, which was perceived as being at the centre of the activity, was, in effect, the 'watchtower' of theatre practice. The last *CEMA Report* (1944–5), illustrates the way in which, even by this early stage, the Council used the language of panopticism. Appendix D, entitled 'Theatre Companies: *Conditions* [my emphasis] of Association with CEMA', exemplifes the 'penal mechanism' at work: theatre companies were expected to subscribe to the Council's ideals before they could be eligible for sponsorship and, therefore, incorporation. But these principles introduced a value system ('the highest possible standards in the arts'; and 'all that is best in the theatre'[20]) without defining what it was that actually constituted the apex of achievement.

In return for achieving these standards, theatre companies would be subjected to a system of surveillance and would find that 'an assessor appointed by the [Arts] Council had the right to be present at all meetings'. Theatre companies were also to be supervised: 'the Council [is] entitled to nominate an accountant to investigate the accounts and financial position of any company'. Moreover, a relationship with the Arts Council included the threat of a penalty for non-compliance: 'the [Arts] Council shall retain the right to withhold support from any production of which it shall signify its disapproval'.[21]

The Arts Council

A crucial stage in the development of the Arts Council's panoptic power structure might be said to correlate with Keynes's decision that CEMA advisory panels should 'lose their executive function'.[22] The construction of the power nexus brought with it the distinction between those who could vote, and therefore had direct power, and those who could advise, a much more ambiguous form of power. This procedure was inextricably related to the fact that executive power came to rest in the hands of the appointed, rather than the elected, and the complexion of the appointed was that of the upper classes, who were critical to the mechanism which has engendered social hegemony.

The Arts Council emerged as a philanthropic venture on the part of the 'great and the good', as can be seen from the list of members incorporated and appointed by the Charter – *Sir* Ernest Pooley (who replaced Keynes), *Sir* Lewis Casson, *Sir* Kenneth Clark. Whilst the purpose of the Arts Council, at this point in time, was to act as custodians of the *public* purse, 'the real power of decision lay with council members and their executive officers'.[23]

The first *ACGB Report* (1945–6) demonstrates the continuation of CEMA's panoptic policies, and provides further illustration of the means by which universal visibility was developed. The conditions for theatre companies included the caveat that 'no affiliated organisation shall accept any engagement abroad . . . without first . . . obtaining the Council's permission to do so'.[24] The Arts Council was, then, in a position to control not only what was seen inside the UK but also what theatre companies could present outside it.

Against a background of economic stringency and post-war reconstruction, the Arts Council shaped cultural policy and, in common with other social reforms, its cultural project was intended as a means by which well-being might be induced. However, the strategies employed by the Arts Council, whilst appearing as elements of utopian endeavour, are also open to interpretation as aspects of panopticism. Of particular interest is the way in which, in order to produce civilizing reforms, the Arts Council developed a system of discrimination. This was an economically pragmatic strategy, because it was a means by which a set of imperatives could be established for the distribution of a modest sum of money through an impractically large arts constituency. However, the outcomes of this are at variance with the original aim, because the practice of distinguishing 'good' from 'bad' and the 'worthy of subsidy' from the 'unworthy' involved the Council in codifying a set of rules from which it has been difficult to depart. Consequently, its concept of excellence induced the Council to encourage a range of discriminatory and penal mechanisms. For example, the regional repertory system, conceived of as functioning through centres of excellence, had the effect of displacing small, local, non-theatre venues; by emphasizing the need for training actors to be 'appropriately' well-qualified, the value of amateur actors was diminished; and by focusing on the 'need' for a London-based National Theatre, capable of producing work of the highest, exemplary, and most *visible* quality, the Council endorsed the notion that theatre could be perceived in a single, unifying, British context.

In the interests of reform, the Arts Council pursued a policy of 'raising standards' but, in so doing, it bestowed a legacy of expensive regional repertory buildings which, because it would be politically difficult to close them, remain. The Arts Council project created a cultural hegemony by ensuring that the capital expenditure upon which it embarked would need to be upheld indefinitely. Most of the immediate post-war subsidy was spent on the English repertory system. However, although Wales did not benefit from the Arts Council's building improvements programme for a further twenty years, nevertheless it, too, eventually found itself with buildings whose upkeep limits other possibilities.

The conundrum at the heart of the Arts Council is the way in which utopian strategies produced a disciplinary and discriminatory organization. The problem of the Arts Council in Wales is that, because of the panoptic process, it absorbed forms of critical thinking which persist in conditioning how it analyses theatre and performance practices in Wales. Thus, although ACW has been an independent organization since 1994 and even though aspects of the government of Wales have been devolved since 1999, the way in which forms of performance are discussed in Wales is heavily influenced by the established thinking of ACGB and decades of central government. Wales is having more difficulty in 'unlearning the dominant mode' than it likes to admit. It is telling that, despite a considerable amount of attention and a number of important reports, the performance culture in Wales is struggling to divest itself of old ACGB precepts.

These axioms appear in five manifestations. They are: the arm's length principle, ideas about quality, the drive towards professionalization, the establishment of flagship buildings or companies, and the development of a national theatre. In all but the last, Wales continues to hold with ACGB principles, albeit with some modifications.

The arm's length principle

The 'arm's length' principle is the term used to describe the relationship between central government, the Arts Council and theatre practice. The value of the term is that it suggests, correctly in a simple sense, that theatre practitioners are free from direct state interference. But relationships are more intricate than the arm's length principle admits and we can look to the example of the Panopticon as a means of explaining why this is so.

In the Panopticon, there is no *point* of power: everyone is caught up in the mechanism. The atmosphere of circulating mistrust is caused by the impossibility of identifying the source of power and the consequent difficulty of apportioning blame. Everyone within the Panopticon is blameless, because it is unclear who has the absolute power to make decisions. This is also the case with the central government/Arts Council/subsidized theatre sector network. Central government cannot be held accountable, because it (merely) makes funding available; the Arts Council is not culpable, because it can only work within its budget; and theatre companies are not responsible, because they function within the joint constraints of the government's economic policy and the Arts Council's imperatives.

The idea that theatre practice occupies a coercion-free realm is a convenient but entirely bogus notion. Yet theatre practitioners have been told so often that government is at arm's length from British theatre that they have absorbed the idea. Lord Redcliffe-Maud, for instance, insisted in his 1976 report that the relationship between the government and the Arts Council is at 'arm's length'.[25]

Keynes described the Arts Council as 'independent in constitution [even though it was] financed by the Treasury and ultimately responsible to parliament'.[26] What Keynes and all the supporters of the arm's length principle ignore is the reality of the way in which government ideology is able to exert pressures on the thinking of the Arts Council. The flaw in their argument is the assumption that state intervention, in order for it to be such, will take the form of obvious and visible directives and that, where these do not exist, state intervention is not present. In fact, direct state intervention functions perfectly well, not least because it is able to hide behind the ruse of the arm's length principle; and the way in which it works is through individual not collective agency.

The single most effective strategy for exercising power is the deployment of significant individuals. Accordingly, government needed to do no more than select the members of the Arts Council, through the appropriate minister, who in turn appointed the officers. When it was first constituted, the Welsh Arts Council (1967) considered that its title reflected 'the measure of autonomy which Wales has always enjoyed'.[27] Yet its key positions were directly appointed by ministers of state, and WAC failed to recognize that the opportunity to appoint individuals of an acceptable persuasion, along with the power to block unsuitable appointments, is an ideal method of controlling the cultural context of theatre practice.

Raymond Williams was the first distinguished critic to challenge the notion of the 'arm's length' principle.[28] He identified the hegemonic functioning of ACGB and the *experience* of hegemony and its effects on arts practice and, also, argued that the Arts Council's description of itself as non-political is disingenuous and problematic. Whilst it may be non-*party*-political, the nature of its appointments suggests a political complexion of a very particular hue.

The aesthetic outcomes of strategic appointments are considerable in terms of the structure of Welsh theatre. Indeed, the development of standardization and incorporation is a direct consequence of the values of those individuals who have been selected to influence the movement of funds and, therefore, subsidized practices. David Adams provides an excellent account of what he calls the 'realpolitik' of Welsh theatre and reminds us that, for example, when Mathew Prichard was chairman of WAC (until 1994), he had been appointed by his cousin, Lord Crickhowell, who was then the Welsh Secretary. Prichard was also chair of the Cardiff Bay Arts Trust, vice-president of the Council of the National Museum of Wales, chairman of the Opera House Trust, a member of the Cardiff and County Club (membership by invitation only: entrance fee £810) and inheritor of a substantial fortune from his grandmother, Agatha Christie.[29]

We can safely assume that Prichard's circumstances were rather different from those of the average person living in the Valleys and yet, as chair, he was ultimately responsible for the direction of theatre practice in Wales. Even if we accept that, in reality, decisions are largely the responsibility of officers, not members, we still need to acknowledge that members are involved in determining the criteria for the appointment of officers. Moreover, when we take into account Prichard's sphere of influence, we can see that it is unnecessary for government to attempt to instruct the Arts Council on how to apportion subsidy when there is opportunity for discreet suggestions to be made without troubling the general public. In this way, the arm's length principle is nothing more than a public relations exercise which flatters the liberal intentions of the government of the day, irrespective of its complexion. The reality is that, while the public's attentions are deflected by superficial observance of a collective code of practice, the significant details of theatre practice are being refined by selected individuals in private

Whilst asserting publicly that it plays no directive role in determining what kinds of theatre practice will be incorporated, in reality government has created the context in which Mathew Prichard and the rest can dispose of funds to theatre company X and not Y. The bestowal of block grants is a direct political act which places government in close proximity to the production of aesthetic value-making. The power to set global funding totals, coupled with the knowledge that it can rely on influential individuals to ensure that those sums are spent in the preferred manner, enables government, through the Arts Council, to determine the quality of theatre practice in accordance with its own values while remaining officially neutral.

Even after devolution, there is still adherence to the idea of the arm's length principle. In the document precipitating what was purported to be the most major restructuring of ACW, *An Action Plan* (2001), Anthony Everitt and Anne Twine assert that ACW 'operates at armslength from the National Assembly'.[30] However, the content of the Assembly's report on its cultural strategy, which will be discussed later, shows the Assembly taking a more involved role than an arm's length operation would suggest.

Quality

The Arts Council's notion of quality is critical to panopticism, because the application of the concept of 'excellence' as a means of determining incorporative value is central to negotiations between the Council and its clients. The distinction between high and low standards is suggestive of an ideological transaction in which values are established to be internalized by the inmate.

An aesthetic hierarchy, as distinct from a continuum of priorities, is the chief means by which funding decisions can be made in a manner which *appears* to be fair. If, then, theatre practitioners accommodate the principles of the hierarchy, because they believe them to be in their own interests, they become self-disciplining in ways which endorse a regulated aesthetic structure. Their cooperation with inspections designed to assess quality, in the form of appraisal and performance indicators, enables the Arts Council to maintain the individual practitioner or company in a state of subjection.

It was not, though, the original intention of the Arts Council to *impose* a qualitative theatre practice on an unwilling constituency. It rather perceived its policy as being to provide the 'best for the most', as is suggested by Keynes's use of the term 'masterpieces' juxtaposed with what we would now call 'community' venues. In order to disseminate the 'masterpiece', CEMA developed methods of disqualification and invalidation, implied through what it chose to privilege. During the Second World War, for example, it sponsored theatre tours of Shakespeare to south Wales mining towns.

The striking point about CEMA/ACGB is that they seem to have believed that, until they existed, theatre practitioners/audiences had no inherent capacity to recognize quality. As the last CEMA Report demonstrates, its aims were to raise the standards of smaller repertory theatres and to improve the standards and qualifications of actors. This suggests that, in order to be a truly reforming and radical cultural project, the Arts Council needed to construct itself as *vital* to the introduction of quality. But, in doing this, it automatically invalidated many existing local (and amateur) practices.

The Arts Council's values became taken for granted as a baseline for discussions about theatre, irrespective of apparent political differences. For instance, in 1959, Richard Carless and Patricia Brewster, writing for the Conservative Bow Group, adopt Arts Council rhetoric on standards: '[The theatre] should no longer attempt to maintain outposts throughout the country, which by operating on shoestring budgets, cannot maintain desirable standards of production. Poor quality drives the public away.'[31]

There is very little in this report which had not appeared in ACGB's first Annual Report (1945–6), thirteen years previously. Carless and Brewster endorse the move towards standards, the setting up of regional centres of excellence, and the construction of a national theatre as an 'urgent priority'. The major difference is the context in which it was written; the Arts Council's report was written during a Labour government, Carless and Brewster's under a Conservative government. What this suggests is that the complexion of a government seems to make little difference to the functioning of the Arts Council because a specific understanding of what constitutes excellence became universally accepted; and, moreover, this was accompanied by a consensus that notions of quality were above, or outside of, political ideology.

In 1967, the Royal Charter omitted the word 'fine' and the Arts Council took as its objective 'the knowledge, understanding and practice of the arts'.[32] Raymond Williams observed that this apparently minor detail of altering 'fine arts' to the 'arts' in general represented rather more than convenient changes in responsibility: 'once the shift to a cultural and educational rather than financial policy had been made, quite different social relations were in question'.[33] But, despite the availability of such a critique, the Arts Council continued to promulgate its first principles.

So it is unsurprising, even a quarter of a century later, that Anthony Everitt, writing in 1993 when he was secretary general of ACGB, reviewed its priorities thus: to rededicate the arts to work 'of the highest possible quality and originality'. He defended this agenda by arguing that the largest portion of ACGB expenditure is 'rightly devoted' to protecting 'masterpieces' and keeping 'the arts of the past alive'.[34]

As further evidence of the residual relationship between post-war and contemporary thinking about quality, *A Creative Future* (1993), which claimed to speak 'for the future of the arts in England', endorsed ACGB's view of 'standards'. Its authors identified ten major principles of the arts. Number four submits that: 'Quality is the *pre-eminent* criterion for public funding of the arts. Quality is a broad term, encompassing such concepts as fitness for purpose' (my emphasis).[35] The acknowledgement that 'quality' is a broad term indicates that ACGB was prepared to admit to complexity here. However, that quality is held to be 'pre-eminent' suggests the pursuit of excellence would continue to be foregrounded.

But 'quality' does not float free of funding structures. As Baz Kershaw has argued, ACGB funding structures have been directly responsible for creating a 'poorly subsidized underclass' of theatre companies who, because of their level of funding, find it difficult to match funding criteria: '[When] theatrical "finish" . . . became an important factor in the assessment of a show's significance, this . . . became a means of ideological control . . . by comparison with ACGB revenue-funded companies [regional theatre companies] were judged to be of "poor" quality.'[36] Kershaw elucidates the interconnectedness of notions of 'quality' with levels of funding, the latter being clearly able to create a climate by which the former can develop in ways appropriate to the Arts Council's needs.

In Wales, the success of the drive towards developing ideologically produced notions of quality can be illustrated by the testimony of WAC chairman Sir Hywel Evans. In 1983 he observed that:

> In 1953 . . . the only places where you could get some real theatre in Wales were the New Theatre in Cardiff and the Grand in Swansea . . . Today, you can see high quality theatre in Mold . . . Bangor . . . Harlech . . . Milford Haven . . . Newtown . . . I would not say it was perfect theatre but . . . of perfectly good quality.[37]

This endorsement of the ACGB project reveals the extent to which its values were incorporated by WAC. There is an unambiguous definition of 'real' (high quality) theatre as referring specifically and exclusively to those practices which can be located within the context of traditional theatre buildings, and this is a notion which also carries with it the implication that Wales is an incomplete culture unless it can produce 'perfect' theatre, a concept which, revealingly, Evans assumes is unambiguous.

The thinking about quality might have been expected to change when ACGB disbanded to create an 'independent' Arts Council of Wales in 1994. Yet, even though the context for arts practice underwent a fundamental change in relationships when responsibility for funding was handed over to the Welsh Office, the conceptual framework for the arts retained the disciplinary language of ACGB: the Welsh Office's purpose was 'to encourage artistic excellence'.[38] In its document outlining what it intended as its main agenda for the year 2000 and following, ACW stated that 'at the heart of where [ACW] wants to be is a professional theatre of Wales of the highest quality'.[39]

The difficulty for ACW is that, while it may wish to be seen to be developing indigenous forms, and also to be increasing the opportunities for access to theatre practice, there is a tension between strategies adopted to ensure (Keynesian) excellence and measures appropriate to developing indigenous (community) theatre practices. A problem with notions of 'quality' is that, more than any of the other key terms used by the Arts Council which are particularly indicative of panopticism, they are acutely relative to quite deep-rooted and divisive opinions concerning matters of taste, but which masquerade as value-free standards; indeed, the crucial predicament of the designation of quality is that it confuses subjective partiality with objective worth.

Awarding subsidy on the premise that a theatre company demonstrates 'real quality' is a much more contentious exercise than the Arts Council admits. The procedure seems thorough enough: the evaluation of quality is usually the outcome of an assessment of production values (design, technical accomplishment, performance technique, subject matter, form, style, genre). But if we consider this method more closely, we can see that there are some complications, the chief of which concerns the question of referential power, or the way in which quality practices acquire critical mass.

The major difficulty here is the issue of whom the Arts Council uses to determine the presence of quality, because opinion-forming is largely created by four groups – the media, academics, Arts Council officers and theatre professionals – and although many of these are miserably remunerated, they nevertheless have significant professional status within theatre practice; so the extent to which they are actually either typical or representative of audience constituencies is at least debatable.

The crux of this matter is that audiences are not critical to the accretion of referential power. Why this is a problem relates to the way in which opinion-formers develop a structure of feeling around a play or a theatre company, which can disqualify both those who take a different critical stance and those practitioners whose work is alternative in style. Most particularly, what often happens is that certain theatre practices become authorized, while others are subtly encouraged to emulate these successful practitioners to make themselves eligible for validation. The consequence of this is that there is then a multiplicity of practices which falls outside of authorized theatre (pantomime, musicals, thrillers, two-dimensional flats used in set design, village halls as theatre venues), ostensibly because they are not of sufficient quality but actually because they do not conform to orthodox taste. It is noticeable that the perception of inadequate quality seems to correlate with the inclinations of audience constituencies comprising those who are not extensively educated in conventional terms, who do not have much money, who are unfashionable, who are working-class, who are largely female, who are elderly or who are children.

Perhaps the most significant difficulty with the Arts Council and author-ized quality is its refusal to accept any kind of relationship between popul-ism and excellence. It seems to be axiomatic that public subsidy will not be awarded to any theatre practice that is regarded as being populist. But the definition of 'populism' is often arbitrary: older, unfashionable aspects of popular culture, like Variety, for example, seem to be viewed pejoratively as populism while newer, fashionable elements, like the use of TV screens/computer technology within performance, are regarded as an imaginative inclusion of popular culture.

The problem with this perception is its qualitative separation of professionally accredited popular culture from locally evolved, 'populist' practices. This privileging of the authorized popular effectively discrimin-ates against local practices because it nudges constituencies into abandoning local popular culture purely on the basis of external aesthetic criteria. A damaging side-effect of this is the jettisoning of a range of local 'meanings', for as John McGrath asserts: 'popular culture . . . is the site of a long, on-going struggle'.[40] When professionally validated approaches to theatre production manipulate the presentation of content, local resonances can be lost in the process, with a resulting decrease in audience engagement with the theatre forms on offer. McGrath rightly observes that it is pointless to utilize local popular culture if it does not contain active meaning.[41] None-theless, he demonstrates that localism can be what gives theatre quality when he alludes to the preferences of the people of Rogart, in the Scottish Highlands, who insisted to him that local forms would be more meaningful than '"Southern" shows, no matter how theatrically excellent'.[42]

After 1994, when ACW might have revisited its thinking, far from moving away from orthodox notions of quality, ACW's *Corporate Plan 2000–2003* reiterated the 'commitment to high quality'. Moreover, this actually emulated the 'few but roses' policy of ACGB during the early 1950s in its intention to fund 'fewer companies better'.

That stance appears to be modified in *An Action Plan* (2001), by acknowledging that fostering excellence is just one option, but there is a reminder that promoting high standards is a 'fundamental' purpose of the Arts Council. Whilst the 'high arts' are viewed as part of a spectrum, rather than a hierarchy, the concept of 'bad art' is admitted, along with the notion of its polar opposite, the 'masterpiece'. However, the report underestimates the whole subjective process by which 'bad art' and 'masterpieces' are constructed.

Professionalization

Post-war professionalization exemplifies the way in which, within the Panopticon, external codes of practice are absorbed. The dissemination of professional standards by outside agencies defined what kinds of theatre were suitable for universal visibility; and, as recipients of the theatre product, audiences were then implicated in the surveillance of standards. But, in order for audiences to respond appropriately to 'masterpieces', there needed to be some mechanism which would train them to recognize acceptable standards and invalidate others. Andrew Sinclair offers evidence of educating the audience when he cites the boast of CEMA organizers that their progress with audiences in workers' hostels could be measured by the fact that 'Gradually [the audience] acquired a theatre etiquette and ceased to talk, walk about and drink tea during the performances.'[43] Keynes's stated desire was for the Arts Council to 'decentralise and disperse' and he argued for the Glasgow Citizens Theatre to be perceived as a 'model' because it used its 'own playwrights', its 'own company and an ever-growing and more appreciative local public'. In this context, he acknowledged the hopes of the Welsh Committee 'and of the stimulus it will give to the special genius of the Welsh people'.[44] But, although Keynes conceded that 'nothing can be more damaging than the excessive prestige of metropolitan standards', the evidence suggests that professionalization determined theatre practice in line with metropolitan standards. Between 1956 and 1974, the number of British regional repertory companies more than doubled from twenty-two to forty-eight, a development which Redcliffe-Maud believed produced 'standards of production which [were] as good as in London'.[45]

In 1967, the Welsh Committee acknowledged that 'new means must be found to disseminate the arts, to remove preciousness and make the arts intelligible and necessary to the majority'. But WAC, in rejecting 'the dominance of the amateur tradition' whose 'standards [have] deprived Wales of the full benefits of its own talent', ignored an important way in which the charge of 'preciousness' might have been challenged.[46] WAC could have utilized the structure of amateur performance to build a strategy for theatre which capitalized on performance traditions familiar to the Welsh. If Wales did not have a professional theatre tradition, and if, as Keynes avers, the Welsh had a 'special genius' in the arts, then it must have been a talent which was expressed through amateur practices. However, the professional strategy of the Arts Council disabled the conditions which had produced the cultural practices it was thought worth subsidizing in the first place.

ACGB's ethos produced a self-disciplining WAC, which committed itself to non-Welsh understandings of 'professionalism' at the expense of indigenous amateur traditions. The Arts Council chose to insist on professional standards which held local cultural practices in low esteem and the thrust towards metropolitan concepts of professionalism had the effect of shifting theatre in Wales away from its cultural roots. Indeed, we might argue that individual cultures like those of Wales were actually incapacitated by the spread of ACGB activity.

Yet professionalization did not necessarily develop audiences. As Redcliffe-Maud notes, despite the intensity of professional activity, 'it [could not] be said that drama [was] generally accessible'.[47] Audience figures demonstrate the impact of professionalization: ACGB admits that, by the early 1990s, 77 per cent of all adults did not attend plays.[48] Moreover, audiences were largely composed of social categories ABC1.

An outcome of the professionalizing of theatre is the disenfranchisement of the working classes and those outside urban centres. The sums devoted by ACW to Drama in the first half of the 1990s reveal that there was a considerable difference between the amounts of money devoted to theatre in Cardiff and, for example, Mid Glamorgan. In population terms, 12 pence per head of the total subvention for Drama in Wales was spent on subsidized theatre annually in Mid Glamorgan, whereas in Cardiff £3.87 per head was spent.[49] (A strictly equitable distribution would have produced spending on theatre at £1.04 per head.)

Furthermore, during 1994–5, when the Welsh Office provided a slight increase in Arts Council funding, Cardiff benefited from a 1.4 per cent increase in spending on Drama, but, in Mid Glamorgan, there was a 0.3 per cent decrease in spending. In the 1990s, therefore, the largest section of the population of south Wales, including some of the poorest sectors, received subsidized theatre worth less than 1 per cent of Wales's total theatre funding.

Long-term evidence suggests that professionalization has not succeeded in making theatre more accessible in Wales. But, despite this, ACW's initial plans for the first years of the new century perpetuated the negative effects of centralization as ACW signalled a return to ACGB's early 1950s policies of 'raising' at the expense of 'spreading': 'fewer better funded [professional theatre companies are] the key to higher quality'.[50]

The report containing objectives for 2002 implied subtle ways of ensuring professionalization, like the use of specialist officers by ACW to 'exercise artistic judgement when assessing applications'. Equally, when it confirmed that much of ACW's funding is likely to be given on a project and fixed-term basis, it draws on an important means by which the Arts Council can discipline theatre companies into doing what the Arts Council wants then to do: namely, that short-term funding is conditional and can be used in a punitive way. Although the report claims that ACW should not be in the business of monitoring revenue clients constantly and that important clients should be given funding for more than one year at a time, it also emphasizes that ACW must ensure the 'co-operation of its revenue clients' so that ACW can attain its objectives; which is a subtle way of requiring revenue-funded professional theatre companies to remain on-message.

Flagship buildings

Theatres, especially significant venues, might be understood in panoptic terms as 'watchtowers' and, therefore, as manifestations of power: the flag-ship building is a crucial means by which referential power can accrue to theatre practice. Indeed, the architecture can, in itself, stand for the high standards it is assumed are contained within. But, while the development of effective, specialized theatres would be expected as an aspect of utopian reform, the establishment of flagship theatres also offers enhanced opportun-ities for surveillance: visibility remains high where both the theatre building and the companies which perform in it are offered as models of practice.

Keynes prioritized the need for new theatre buildings, and Arts Council policy developed touring theatre based on regional repertory centres in concert with improving the facilities of theatres. What had originally been conceived of as desirable became an imperative. Many theatres had suffered from bomb damage during the Second World War, in addition to having been ravaged by the passage of time. Concern for the comfort of audiences and performers created an ideology which accepted somewhat uncritically that traditional theatre buildings contained properties essential to the delivery of high-quality theatre practice. Notions of quality and excellence included not just play content and acting, but also all the elements of production, including lighting, costumes and scenery: in this manner, community locations like factory canteens, which did not display the crucial performance indicators, were disqualified. In invalidating such venues, localized performance/audience relationships which connected with the lived experience were damaged.

In contrast to the emphasis in England on the creation of new, purpose-built theatres, like the Birmingham Rep, new theatres in Wales were sometimes converted from buildings which had a history of a community relationship/function. The Dragon Theatre, Barmouth, had been a chapel, and Theatr Fach, Llangefni, was a barn. Furthermore, in the late 1960s, WAC proposed that, where new schools or community buildings were planned, these should include opportunities for performance space. Had the Welsh Committee of ACGB extended these ideas and made them the focus of their thinking about cultural policy in Wales, this would have represented a major shift away from ACGB thinking. But WAC's general thinking about buildings demonstrated a desire to conform with ACGB standards, because the 1966 Annual Report concludes by arguing that. 'Well-equipped theatres are Wales's greatest need. Without them . . . we are bound to feel cut off from an important part of the dramatic heritage . . . the first step should be to build theatres at Cardiff and Bangor.'[51]

It is striking that the Welsh Committee used the phrase '*the* dramatic heritage' which indicates that, in Wales, the idea that there was one, unifying theatre tradition had been absorbed. Moreover, the committee's solution to the assumed isolation from the dominant culture was in mimicking the English strategy of centralization. There is a clear contradiction here between recognizing that theatre practice was not widely available and suggesting that the remedy for this was, in effect, to make it even less widely available. In determining such a large financial investment in professionally equipped theatres, the Welsh Committee ensured that less money would be available for smaller, local projects. Subsidy figures suggest that WAC's willingness to be standardized by replicating ACGB's building policy was rewarded: grants to Wales from ACGB's Housing the Arts fund demonstrated an exponential increase in 1973–4, for example, from 13.1 per cent to 31.9 per cent.[52]

What is significant about this is the extent to which building policy constructed a set of standards that could be used to determine whether a theatre practice should be incorporated. The repertory system, for instance, which developed out of ACGB's commitment to flagship buildings, is partly responsible for invalidating localized theatre practices, because the reps replaced non-specific venues.

In Wales, Clwyd Theatr Cymru (CTC) is a case in point. This theatre was built as a result of the funding made available through the Housing the Arts scheme, and it has functioned as a modern repertory theatre in line with ACGB policy. Its position became vulnerable, for a time, after the government's decision to restructure Wales into unitary authorities resulted in the loss of local authority funding. The possibility that it might have to close in 1996 became a major issue. However, the debate centred on how funding might be procured to rescue the theatre, and not on whether subsidy might be withdrawn and redistributed on an altogether different basis.

That CTC was saved from closure tells us as much about the value of flagship theatres to the international credibility of ACW as it does about the aesthetic worth of CTC and, in finding extra money for it, ACW inevitably impoverished other Welsh theatre practices. Moreover, ACW signalled its intention to enhance CTC's position as a flagship theatre by raising its national status still further. ACW stated that CTC would be supported financially and referentially as *the* English-language Welsh *National Performing Arts Company* (my emphasis), 'representing the apex of the profession'.[53] ACW also intended that resources would be concentrated on the four building-based production companies in its portfolio. Indeed, in its corporate plan, *Developing the Arts in Wales 2000–2003*, ACW argued that an important reason why ACW needed extra subvention from the Assembly was 'to achieve stability of the flagship companies'.

We might assume that venues in the Valleys which fall outside of this remit, like the Cwmaman Institute, have little prospect of achieving flagship/producing status. In revenue terms, and in contrast to CTC, the status of Valleys venues could represent the base of professional theatre. Yet, venues like the Cwmaman Institute want to compete with the flagship venues and have absorbed the idea that they can, if only they could have more sophisticated equipment. The *Report on Performance Spaces Across Wales*[54] demonstrates how venues have learned to aspire to conventional ideas about excellence and that they see this as being achievable through better technical facilities with which to facilitate 'high-quality' performances. What such venues underestimate is the extent to which high quality is a construct that relies on a critical mass accumulating around a space. For a venue like the Cwmaman Institute to become a cutting-edge arts centre, it would require a sea-change in thinking, of which there is little evidence at present.

Instead, the critical mass is collecting around the Millennium Centre for the Performing Arts in Cardiff Bay, a project which is a classic example of the flagship building. Although its progress was vexed, there was considerable pressure on the Assembly to support the Millennium Centre, which came from those who displayed the hallmarks of panoptic thinking. In an advert in January 2000, the Wales Millennium Centre proclaimed itself an international showcase to 'rival the best in the world' and stated that successful applicants (for jobs there) would need to be committed to 'establishing excellence'. Due to be completed in 2004, at a cost of £104 million, its chair said in a press release in 2002 that the Millennium Centre is 'a symbol that Wales is dynamic'.

The Wales Millennium Centre could, however, be a disaster for venues in the region because it may drive up arts investment in Cardiff at the expense of other areas. So whilst it could achieve an international profile, it may do so at a price. The Millennium Stadium has been a more successful project than some anticipated and there will be those who would point to it as evidence of the necessity for Wales to have 'world-class' facilities if it is to become a 'world-class' nation. There is, though, a considerable difference between sport and rock concerts, and formal theatre events, not least in the fact that large-scale sporting/rock events tend to be associated with a kind of 'buzz' in terms of crowds and media coverage that eludes theatre. However, with nearly 2,000 seats to fill, the Wales Millennium Centre will need to create new audiences to achieve its target of 1.75 million visitors every year.

National theatre

A single, high-status, model theatre is, with reference to Foucault, a paradigm of regulation, which controls by example the movements of disparate groups of individuals to prevent them wandering the country in random ways. As such, a national theatre is the ultimate flagship building. Its concept did not develop out of Arts Council policy: the idea for such an institution existed for much of the twentieth century. But public subsidy made it possible. Its function is to make the excellence of British theatre manifest to the world and, as a corollary to this, demonstrate something of the essence of 'Britishness'.

A national theatre is useful to tourism and to commerce, which can utilize it for corporate hospitality to encourage investment: the notion of a national theatre is, in part, connected with a commercial sense of culture as something which can be sold. Its universal visibility maximizes the potential for theatre to be seen by a wide range of individuals and organizations, and not necessarily those who are using the building specifically for the purposes of watching performance.

But this visibility also contributes to the process of promoting self-discipline because, in positioning *the* National Theatre as synonymous with high standards, there is the suggestion that its portfolio defines the standards to which theatre practice must aspire. Moreover, its location in the capital of England demonstrates that excellence is produced through centralization of resources. The concept of one, paradigmatic national theatre also accepts, uncritically, the notion that theatre practice is universal. From 1946, when ACGB was formally granted its Royal Charter, the framework for the public arts was set, and it was one which perceived theatre in just such a 'national' setting. But this centralization did not conceive of, and therefore excluded, the idea that theatre practice might have a different complexion in Wales and Scotland.

Whilst the Welsh Committee followed ACGB's lead and endorsed the need for a national theatre, this was envisaged as a National Theatre for Wales, in Cardiff. Nevertheless, it observed the same format: both 'national' theatres were to be centralized in capital cities.[55] As in England, the notion that a single, national, flagship theatre building was necessary to creating a high-status theatre practice was persistent and of long standing; in the 1930s, for instance, there had been attempts to create a Welsh national touring theatre company as a prelude to establishing a dedicated building.[56] But ACGB's drafting of the National Theatre Bill (for London) in 1949 formalized the idea of a super-flagship building, with the intention of subsuming the Welsh project.

The tenacity of the idea of a National Theatre for Wales, despite the firm commitment of ACGB to a National Theatre for Great Britain (including Wales), suggests that there was a degree of Welsh ambivalence with regard to the validity of the British enterprise. The Welsh Committee, and later WAC, appears to have negotiated a compromise between its own desire for a National Theatre of Wales, and ACGB's insistence on a single National Theatre for Great Britain. This may not have been a conscious act, but the establishment of the Welsh National Opera might be understood as a de facto national theatre project for Wales, which suited the needs of both parties.

In fact, the establishment of a WNO was achieved as much because of the commitment of ACGB as by the Welsh Committee.[57] In the early 1980s, ACGB funded WNO to a greater level than did WAC: in 1982, for instance, with £1.8 million, as compared with WAC's grant of £1.3 million. In return, WNO had to give 40 per cent of its performances in England. Nevertheless, in 1982, the chairman of WAC asserted that WNO was 'the flagship of the Welsh Arts Council'.[58] The funding of WNO points to an accommodation made to resolve the tension between Wales's interest in a national theatre of its own, and ACGB's determination to create a single, British, national theatre. By agreeing to fund WNO, additional to Wales's funding, ACGB enabled Wales to have a *form* of national theatre, funded to a level propitious to the production of excellence, while protecting the status of the National Theatre in London. By 1993–4, WNO received only 2 per cent less than the whole of drama in Wales.

The idea that a national flagship venue is essential to Welsh artistic integrity persists in some quarters, despite the evidence that such a project would demand funding that would inevitably impoverish, and therefore disqualify, other initiatives. In Wales, one reading of identity politics perceives that national identity needs to be authenticated by the establishment of (inter)national institutions. The implication of this kind of thinking is that Wales is incomplete and that, in order for it to be a 'whole' nation, it must develop the organizations which 'proper' countries have.

To that end, there is the contemporary incarnation of a Welsh National Theatre, as proposed in a consultative paper (1995) written by Phil Clark and Michael Bogdanov, and which they updated in 1999: *Towards the Provision of a National Theatre for Wales: A Federal System.* Underpinning this vision of the future is the same ideology which informs the National Theatre of Great Britain: the creation of larger audiences, the potential of an international market, the development of employment opportunities and enhancement of the infrastructure. Above all, its purpose, in Clark and Bogdanov's view, is to validate Welsh theatre through locating 'the artists of Wales on the world stage and the culture of Wales in a world context'.[59] ACW, however, distanced itself from this proposal: 'nobody yet has proved conclusively to us that something called a National Theatre of Wales will actually do better than the current provision',[60] which suggests that ACW, post-independence, might have been attempting some paradigm shifts, for this change in thinking recognizes that Wales has national theatre practices which do not necessarily need one, central building to legitimize them.[61]

Instead of developing a national theatre, either as a building or as a federation, ACW determined to 'increase funding for Welsh national performing arts companies'.[62] The last word on the idea of a Welsh national theatre, at least for the time being, seems to have come from Ceri Sherlock, the Assembly's 'arts tsar', in his *Commentary on Culture and the Arts in Wales* (2000) in which he contends that the notion of a national theatre is 'predicated on a kind of text theatre tradition of which there is no continuous or unbroken line'. Sherlock does not think that Wales should introduce a national theatre, even in federal form. Instead, he would want to prioritize our 'performative culture', companies producing Theatre for Young People, and physical and dance theatre. On the face of it, then, this seems to be a rejection of an important principle of ACGB and therefore an act of independence and a breaking with panopticism. However, the roles of both Clwyd Theatr Cymru and the Millennium Centre might position those venues as de facto national theatres. Certainly, the idea that Wales needs must have a super centre for the performing arts is hard to dislodge.

Wales and the Arts Council

The Arts Council's disciplinary power lies particularly in its ability to construct theatre practice: not merely through the sums of money it makes available, but also through its dissemination of the articles of faith to which it subscribes. In Wales, its success can be measured by its capacity to discipline and train Welsh theatre practitioners to believe that centralized objectives are in the best interests of Arts Council clients. Critical to this has been the role of successive WAC chairs who, in the guise of reform, have been able to prompt the ideological framework of WAC, and who have been crucial to WAC's perception of itself as an 'autonomous' organization, when the evidence demonstrates otherwise.

The Welsh Committee, the precursor to the Welsh Arts Council, did not have executive power because it was (merely) an advisory body; it was established in 1945 and was placed in the position of having responsibility without power. Although ACGB claimed in its first *Annual Report* that '[the Welsh Committee's] experienced recommendations [proved] helpful',[63] these were limited by their status as suggestions, because Keynes had taken executive power away from the advisory panels and the power of decision-making remained with ACGB's members and executive officers (full-time employees). The procedures and conditions of Welsh theatre practice developed in the context of ACGB's centralized actions.

The purpose of the 1967 Royal Charter was ostensibly to permit the executive control in Wales which had been signally lacking in the first twenty years of the Arts Council. But the mechanisms for executive power were effectively disabled by the nature of the chair. Whilst the 1967 Charter made the Arts Councils for Wales and Scotland discrete organizations (the Welsh Committee became the Welsh Arts Council), 'independence' did not bring with it autonomy, because it continued to be the case that the chair and members of WAC would be appointed by ACGB, with the approval of the Secretary of State for Wales; so that the conditions for autonomy were constructed by central government in a manner which would ensure that 'independent' thought was disciplined.

Raymond Williams substantiates from his own experience as a member of ACGB the view that the appointment of the chair is critical to the ideology of the Arts Council: 'not only was the broadly political character of the appointment [of chair] clear, the observable character of the Council was subtly but significantly changed [when chairs were replaced]'.[64] Williams's account of how the value systems of the chair impacted on the critical thinking and practices of the Arts Council illuminates our understanding of why and how WAC identified with an agenda which constrained its identity, as is exemplified by this apologetic account of theatre in Wales, which demonstrates the internalization of ACGB-determined imperatives relating to cultural heritage, venues, professionals and conditions: 'There is still an uneven tradition, a shortage of accommodation appropriate to the various arts, and a lack of reasonably sized professional performing companies and organizations.'[65]

The extenuating power of the chair was possible because, as John S. Harris observed in 1970, specialist advisory subject panels did not exist in Wales, as they did in England, and this reduced the resources available; there were, then, fewer individuals in a position to exert pressure on the chair.[66] In maintaining this structure, ACGB maximized the extent of its 'gaze' through the person of the chair and extended its potential to manipulate WAC's thinking, for although WAC seemed to possess the power to make its own decisions about where subsidy could be spent in Wales, Harris reminds us that WAC was subject to limitations imposed by the financial organization of ACGB, which was based in London, and by the fact that most funding was conditional on a 'project justification basis'. Raymond Williams neatly sums up the problem here, which is that 'what begins, from a Department of State, as a process of selective and administered consensus, cannot become at any of its lower levels an open and democratic public body and procedure'.[67]

The reality of management practices suggests that there was a discrepancy between WAC's belief in its own 'independence' and the coercive nature of its relationship with ACGB. But, whilst this association between the piper, the tune and the patron may be significant, it is not necessarily decisive. There have been instances when WAC attempted to shape different policies in Wales from those of England. But, where this was essayed, the evidence indicates that initiatives were invalidated by external agencies. For example, the Council for Wales's *Report on the Arts* of the mid-1960s suggested an alternative cultural policy shifting the emphasis in ACGB's articles of faith:

> the obstacles to progress towards a satisfactory scale of provision for the arts in Wales . . . [are considerable]. Yet the very absence of facilities which in other countries are almost taken for granted may present positive advantages . . . The task of building a completely new structure need not [be] unduly daunting.[68]

There are several critical points here. First, there is the acknowledgement that Wales is 'another' *country* as distinct from a region of the UK; secondly, there is the thought that the absence of 'appropriate' buildings might be an advantage; and, thirdly, there is the suggestion that a new, different structure for theatre could be possible. This implies that there were those in Wales who were prepared to think in different ways about priorities. Indeed, the Welsh Committee had already been experimenting with 'activities [which were] orientated to meet the needs of individual communities' and had explored 'new centres where Arts Council sponsored activities can take place'.[69]

The *Redcliffe-Maud Report* viewed these variations negatively. For instance, in commenting disapprovingly on Wales's use of three regional arts associations, Redcliffe-Maud seemed to fear an overly independent spirit: 'the Welsh regional associations need to work more closely with the Welsh Arts Council than they have so far done'. Moreover, bilingualism was perceived as a 'problem for the arts in Wales'.[70] Redcliffe-Maud endorsed centric-thinking and effectively provided ACGB with the argument to support universal visibility. His conclusion was that 'devolution must not be taken as far within Wales as within England' for reasons of 'language, size and other factors which distinguish Wales from England'.[71]

The *Redcliffe-Maud Report*, while appearing to demonstrate the ways in which the 1967 Charter 'strengthened' the position of Wales, actually detailed the extent to which WAC was subjected to the unifying and controlling measures of, directly, ACGB and, indirectly, the government. For example, ACGB with the 'approval' of the Secretary of State for Wales could appoint (or rescind the appointment of) the WAC Committee.[72] The position of ACGB as the 'watchtower' of Welsh theatre was epitomized by the fact that WAC was 'directly accountable' to ACGB, which took responsibility for its accounting, its premises and the sum of its grant.

The paradox of this circumstance is that, at an early stage, Wales had an opportunity to influence the whole structure of the Arts Council. Indeed, Andrew Sinclair contends that the establishment of CEMA was 'due to Welsh inspiration and English administration'.[73] He maintains that CEMA was the idea of Welshman Dr Thomas Jones. Robert Hewison suggests that this came about because 'Dr Jones . . . saw [CEMA's] work as an extension of the "social service" of pre-war Pilgrim Trust activities'.[74]

Thomas Jones (1870–1955) came from Rhymney and, in his teens, had been employed in the ironworks. By the late 1920s, he was a senior civil servant in the Cabinet Office. He was a great supporter of the south Wales settlements and made personal efforts to find funding for them. In 1930, instead of retiring, he asked to become the first secretary of the Pilgrim Trust.[75] Jones understood how patronage worked: E. L. Ellis, in his biography of Jones, shows how Jones joined the Athenaeum Club so that the Pilgrim Trust could benefit from the expertise and influence of the club's members.

By 1933, the Pilgrim Trust was making grants to the Old Vic theatre company, amongst others. Its first priority, though, was the 'relief of social misery'.[76] Hence, the settlements, which Jones thought were a form of 'cultural irrigation', were extended in Rhondda, Dowlais, Risca and Merthyr.[77] Jones believed in the local leadership of these projects and he encouraged the trust's support for arts activities, like indigenous amateur theatre productions.

In 1939, on Jones's initiative, the Pilgrim Trustees gave £25,000 to the Board of Education to support the arts during wartime and this act led directly to the establishment of CEMA in 1940 and, later, ACGB. Jones was the architect of CEMA's framework and was decisive in selecting its committee members, who were chosen in accordance with Jones's aversion to 'accredited spokesmen for established interests'.[78] As vice-chair of CEMA, Jones was its dynamo.

The terms which Jones drew up for CEMA refer to 'the provision of the widest opportunities for the enjoyment of the arts by the people, especially those who [are] disadvantaged'. He encouraged amateur activities and was opposed to the centralization of the arts. However, he also believed in the value of expert advice and in the arts attaining the 'highest standards'.[79] He was not, himself, a fan of popular culture: he disapproved of alcohol and gambling, frowned on cinema and 'was not interested in the theatre'.[80] But Jones's approach was effective because it was practical and without a 'rigid consistency of method'.[81] Ellis claims that Jones's skill lay in his ability to judge the relative merits of applications to the Pilgrim Trust.

Jones's legacy is extraordinary. The Pilgrim Trust assisted an Old Vic tour to south Wales, which was why Dame Sybil Thorndike's company could perform in the Valleys. In two years, 1.5 million people attended plays that were supported by CEMA. There is also evidence in Wales of Jones's continuing influence. For instance, the Pilgrim Trust gave the British Drama League (BDL) a grant. The BDL later mutated into the British Theatre Association; and that organization's extensive library of plays is now owned by the Drama Association of Wales.

According to Sinclair, CEMA was initially run and staffed by Welshmen. The turning point, both for Wales and cultural democracy in the UK, came when Jones's interest in indigenous culture was replaced by a Keynesian pursuit of excellence. This came about because the Pilgrim Trust, thinking that its support was no longer needed now that government was more than matching the trust's funding, withdrew its funding from CEMA in 1942. Thomas Jones resigned and John Maynard Keynes took over as chair of CEMA.[82] In effect, one Welshman relinquished CEMA to central government control, thus enabling another Welshman to promote cultural elitism; for, after Keynes's death, it was W. E. Williams who steered the Arts Council.

The promulgation of high culture coincided with a Welsh expression of different preferences. While the journalist and commentator Keidrych Rhys judged that their experiences during the Second World War inclined the Welsh towards a perception of themselves as 'a nation . . . different from England',[83] and, equally, while Wales voted decisively for a Labour government immediately after the war, Arts Council policies at this time, as applied in Wales, did not seem to correlate with public opinion. At the point when Wales indicated its political preferences and, by implication, a set of parameters for theatre practice, its structure of feeling was compromised by an altogether different way of thinking. Individuals like Huw Wheldon[84] followed Keynes's lead in professionalizing the arts, a move which was partly responsible for constructing a separation between the lived experience and theatre practice.

In a sense, Wheldon functioned as a fifth columnist (Sinclair asserts that he had a personal agenda for the establishment of the WNO) in his support for the ideas of Keynes and R. A. Butler, who wanted to 'change the vision of the early Welsh pioneers'.[85] That outlook was popular and socialist in character, in keeping with tendencies in the lived experience of Wales. But ideological perspectives coming from outside Wales dominated policy-making to encourage a metropolitan theatre practice at variance with local conditions. Nonetheless, this could not have happened without the collusory thinking of the Welsh themselves. There has to be some mechanism which enables the thinking of Dr Thomas Jones to be superseded by the Keynesian ethos, and this might be found in the shape of Welshman William Emrys Williams (1896–1977).

W. E. Williams's career was advanced by Thomas Jones. As secretary of the British Institute of Adult Education, he invented and organized Art for the People, which began in 1934: a travelling exhibition which brought the works of great artists to small towns. This scheme was partially funded through Jones's association with the York Trust. As Jones's protégé, Williams was present at the meeting which 'invented' CEMA, and Jones recommended him for appointment as a committee member of CEMA. In the early 1940s, again on Jones's recommendation, Williams became director of the Army Bureau of Current Affairs. Then, he was opposed to elitism: for instance, he believed that after the Second World War adult education would have to 'come down off its high horse and fraternize with the really common man'.[86]

Robert Hewison argues that Williams's philosophy of the arts was 'part of the demonology of the right'.[87] Yet Williams was on poor terms with Keynes, who decimated the funding of Art for the People. Hewison indicates how Williams, despite a modest background, came to be 'one of the most powerful cultural mandarins in the country',[88] for he was secretary general of ACGB from 1951 to 1963. However inconvenient it may be to recognize this, the principles of incorporation – quality, professionalization, flagship buildings and centralization, which have been damaging to a distinctively Welsh theatre practice – were influenced by a Welshman, albeit one born in Manchester.

As Williams became more powerful within ACGB, his views increasingly displayed a belief in contestable value judgements; Hewison accounts for Williams's ideological shift by arguing that he strengthened the Arts Council's function as an arm of the establishment in return for an increase in his own power (he was knighted in 1955). He quotes Williams as asserting that '[ACGB] should . . . [focus] on the maintenance and enhancement of standards',[89] which is somewhat inconsistent with his former strategy of making art widely accessible. Williams shows how far he had moved away from the popular when he argues that: '[It would] be better to accept the realistic fact that the living theatre of good quality cannot be widely accessible and [ACGB should] concentrate [its] resources upon establishing a few more shrines like Stratford.'[90]

Both Robert Hewison and Andrew Sinclair, in their major books on the Arts Council, detail Williams's autocratic tenure, during which ACGB established its articles of faith connected with quality and high standards;

and it was those values which encouraged Wales into developing an arts practice inconsistent with the lived experience. Moreover, under Williams's secretary generalship, Wales did not even achieve its own 'shrine', but rather languished under the twin burdens of 'inadequate' professional standards and an absence of shrine-worthy venues.

This indicates that professionalization and a particular notion of 'high' standards were not inevitable, but rather the consequence of one set of imperatives being followed rather than another. The reasons for this are connected with the way in which power structures have operated to promote Keynesian notions of 'excellence' as having *intrinsically* greater worth than practices associated with cultural democracy. Ultimately, W. E. Williams identified, in a hegemonic sense, with an elitist concept of 'art' instead of Dr Thomas Jones's more egalitarian idea of cultural practices.

Panopticism, hegemony and class

Thus far, the argument has suggested that the Arts Council functions as a 'watchtower' observing, training, controlling and disciplining theatre practitioners; and, in response, theatres/practitioners have internalized the procedures of production to construct the kinds of theatre the Arts Council encourages. But this expression of panopticism might also be understood as an aspect of hegemony, in the sense that 'the true condition of hegemony [takes the shape of] effective self-identification with the hegemonic forms'.[91]

The advantage of the concept of hegemony is that it explains the way in which the recipient of theatre practice, the audience, experiences a dominant culture; whereas the notion of panopticism provides a helpful account of the way in which power structures operate on theatre practitioners to encourage collusion, self-discipline and self-identification.

There is also a class dimension to this. Foucault specifically discusses the importance of the Panopticon to the bourgeoisie as a device for extending its control over the penalized subject; and we might also view the Arts Council in this light, particularly if we take into account the class backgrounds of the chair and members. Raymond Williams points to the way in which representatives of an informal ruling class were given positions of power to make executive decisions about the arts, and the titles of the individuals who have occupied the chair of WAC since 1946 confirms this: *Lord* Harlech, *Sir* William Crawshay, *The Marchioness* of Anglesey, *Sir* Hywel Evans.[92] Whilst it may be true that these people were selected as individuals, their ability to represent directly the people of Wales must be doubtful. Williams argued that ACGB was essentially a ruling class acting on behalf of the established upper and middle classes, 'thus [the government] can give Lord X or

Lady Y both public money and apparent freedom of decision in some confidence . . . that they will act as if they were indeed State officials'.[93]

The *Minutes of Evidence* of the Committee on Welsh Affairs (1982) demonstrate how such an informal ruling class has exercised power over theatre practice. Although the role of officers, as professionals, is to provide specialist advice to members, Council members have been prepared to reject officer recommendations. For instance, during the early 1980s, WAC members overturned a drama committee decision by giving more money to the Sherman Theatre than the committee had agreed should be given.[94]

One reason why this is of concern becomes apparent if we take into account class differentials as they relate to theatre practice. Figures show that, in November 1997 in Wales, 26.4 per cent of play-attenders were from socio-economic groups AB, 32.7 per cent from C1, 20.9 per cent from C2 and 20.1 per cent from groups DE.[95] This points to at least some discrepancy between the social class of some of the chairs of the WAC and that of the average play-attender in Wales, an incongruity which may well have some bearing on the inability of the Arts Council within Wales to divest itself of disabling, dominant modes of thought.

Independence of thought and the Arts Council of Wales

In April 1994, ACGB formally ceased to exist and the Arts Councils of Wales, Scotland and England became three separate bodies, each with a Royal Charter. The difference between these and the 1967 Charter is that ACW was no longer responsible directly to a larger, centralized Arts Council, but rather to the Welsh Office, which arrangement was replaced by the National Assembly for Wales (NAW) in 1999.

An outcome of the severance of ACGB was the production of a wealth of documentation from the several Arts Councils, affording a glimpse into the mindset of each. Yet the published material disclosed a singular sensibility and a remarkably coherent, unified set of objectives, despite the fact that these manifestos were prepared for different countries with variations in class distribution, political complexion, and so on. The pattern of stated principles defines the condition of panopticism – self-discipline, the internalization of the 'gaze', conformance with preferred structures, hierarchies and procedures. ACW's appropriation of ACGB's orthodox terminology suggests that it has internalized the Arts Council's values. Hence, it might be argued that ACW was allowed to become independent because it could be relied upon to replicate the doctrine of incorporation.

WAC's *Blueprint for the Nineties* (1993) illustrates the extent to which WAC's thinking before devolution was, essentially and substantially, ACGB thinking. ACGB's statements are taken from a range of sources and it is not argued that ACGB handed WAC a set of imperatives. But, as can be seen from Table 6, the WAC *Blueprint for the Nineties* reflects ACGB thinking to a considerable degree. In practice, this amounts to an 'archive of rules', which provides further evidence of the way in which ACGB has functioned as a hegemonic agency. What it suggests is that the Arts Council in Wales has internalized a centralized, metropolitan set of structures to such an extent that it cannot imagine how an authoritative reconfiguration of principles might be essayed. Whilst ACW perceived itself as autonomous, its adoption of the conceptual framework within which ACGB operated indicates that it was unable to distinguish itself in any meaningful way from ACGB; and, as Raymond Williams asserts, the state of being hegemonized is characterized by 'effective self identification' with the manifestations of cultural dominance.[96] Instead of evolving a differentiated theatre practice, the major outcome of deliberations relating to an independent ACW was confirmation of the centrality of the playwright[97] and of professional theatre, which was acknowledged as 'the prime interest of ACW Drama Board'.[98]

Table 6.
Comparison of WAC's priorities and ACGB's objectives

WAC's priorities	ACGB's objectives
Support for the arts of the past	Promotion of the arts of the past[b]
Increased access to the arts	Access[c]
Improvement of arts education	Increase of audiences through education[d]
Upgrading of arts buildings	Need to 'commission new buildings to the highest standards'[e]
Enhancement of Wales's international standing in the arts	Importance of international exchange[f]
Increase of investment in the arts from a wide range of agencies[a]	Growth of arts economy, and improvements to efficiency and the quality of the service[g]

a) WAC, *Blueprint for the Nineties* (Cardiff: WAC, January 1993), 2–3.
b) *ACGB Annual Report* (1992–3), 30–1.
c) Ibid., 4–5.
d) Ibid.
e) Lord Palumbo, *ACGB Annual Report* (1991–2), 3.
f) Anthony Everitt, *ACGB Annual Report* (1991–2), 4–5.
g) Anthony Everitt, *ACGB Annual Report* (1992–3), 4–5.

ACW's statements in the second half of the 1990s suggested that theatre practices associated with cultural democracy would be accommodated by the Lottery department, where long-term revenue funding is avoided, leaving ACW's Drama Board to promote 'high quality artistic leadership and direction'.[99] ACW reiterated that the key to the future of the arts in Wales is the provision of 'a high quality of experience' and, whilst it acknowledged that this must be judged by context and objectives, it nevertheless assumed that the funding of theatre practice could be premised on the basis of a broad agreement of what constitutes quality, a point of view it shared with the ACGB of the 1940s.[100]

ACW's capacity for self-discipline was further substantiated by the content of its *Corporate Plan 1997–2000*. Despite some shifts in emphasis, many of ACW's priorities constructed post-independence were familiar from the *Blueprint for the Nineties* (WAC, 1993), which was produced before the separation of the Arts Councils. For example, we might understand the policy of developing mainstream audiences across Wales as a form of support for the arts of the past.[101] The plan also reprised ACW's commitment to increasing access;[102] to the development of arts education;[103] to the upgrading of arts buildings;[104] to promoting opportunities for Welsh artists abroad;[105] and to maximizing the opportunities for private fundraising.[106] Interestingly, this set of principles bore a marked resemblance to ACE's manifesto published a month earlier.[107]

The publication of the *Corporate Plan 1997–2000* preceded a maelstrom in the arts in Wales, one which occasioned what seemed to be major changes in the structures, procedures and practices of Welsh performance. However, whilst there were some resistances to the panoptic model I have been describing, there was nothing like the reorganization that was claimed for the period. Indeed, although the packaging altered, the devil was in the detail and much of the reorientation actually reinforced those tenets of belief that I identified earlier as being indicative of panopticism.

In the decade between 1992 and 2002, some thirty reports, papers or documents were published on theatre/performance in Wales. These were mainly ACW documents, but they also included written interventions by, amongst others, the Parliament for Wales Campaign, the Institute of Welsh Affairs and the National Assembly of Wales. ACW alone produced fourteen documents which contained actual policy details. I have not included in this audit the number of fairly substantial written responses made by groups and individuals, like Wales Association for the Performing Arts and Voluntary Arts Wales, for instance, but the sheer volume of words produced during this period suggests that there was something rotten in the state of the arts in Wales.

There had been systemic difficulties in Wales for the best part of twenty years – the term 'crisis in Welsh theatre' was already being used in 1998 –

but what triggered the uncontainable opposition was, first, the draft and, then, the finalized version of the ACW Drama Strategy (1999). In 1998, there had been concerns for the future of experimental and innovatory theatre and also for middle-scale touring. By 1999, though, the focus had shifted to Theatre-in-Education (TiE) (also understood as Theatre for Young People (TYP) in this context) and new writing. This was because ACW had announced that it was to reduce the number of TYP companies from eight to five; and also that a single organization for new writing was to be established, whereas there had previously been three major organizations. In both cases, existing companies had to apply for 'their own jobs', as it were; being unsuccessful would mean the end of the company.

It was, perhaps, the failure of one TYP company, Gwent, to retain its funding which led more than anything to the ensuing furore, when the local MP, Llew Smith, presented an Early Day Motion in the House of Commons. Other Welsh MPs also openly criticized ACW in the House of Commons. Then a range of other organizations joined the commotion: the Writer's Guild condemned the ACW Drama Strategy, as did the Independent Theatre Council. The *Western Mail* and the BBC gave Welsh arts more coverage in a few months than they had done in previous years put together; and HTV made a programme on the TYP situation. The resignation of Joanna Weston, then ACW's chief executive, was called for on an almost daily basis. Finally, in late 1999, the Assembly's Post-16 Education Committee (which was then responsible for the arts in Wales) called on ACW to provide an explanation of its Drama Strategy.

In fact, the opposition to ACW was not as clear-cut as it might have appeared and theatre organizations were not quite as united in solidarity against ACW as they seemed to be. In 1998, the year before the real difficulties emerged, ACW had published *Building a Creative Society: A Consultation Paper on a Strategy for the Arts in Wales*. This was ACW's largest ever consultation exercise with over 2000 documents distributed and more than twenty meetings held. ACW claimed that the project showed that the majority of members of the Welsh arts community were in favour of change, which gave the ACW the mandate to introduce the changes contained in the Draft Drama Strategy of 1999. However, ACW stated at the time that it had received 220 responses to *Building a Creative Future*, which represents just 11 per cent of the 2000 documents distributed. So it is unclear who the majority were who were in favour of change and how the ACW knew that they were (and, moreover, what the changes were that they wanted).

On the evidence of the Drama Strategy for Wales (June 1999), the substantive change was to be the number of companies receiving subvention; the implication is that those who had demanded change were primarily concerned with the effects on themselves of consistent underfunding. Hence, ACW had little choice but to reduce the number of clients in order to provide the remainder with the increase in funding which would be necessary to produce the 'high artistic quality'[108] that ACW regarded as central to its vision. It might be argued, then, that those companies who claimed the necessity for funding increases in the financial climate, as it was then, pushed ACW into endorsing retrogressive policies, namely those concerned with excellence, attracting the 'cream of the profession', supporting building-based production companies, delivering 'the highest professional standards', developing high-profile 'national' performing arts companies, promulgating the notion that Clwyd Theatr Cymru represents the apex of 'artistry', and with ensuring that 'quality professional productions' are offered to smaller communities.

Given that ACW found it difficult to disregard the thinking it had inherited from ACGB, we might imagine that the advent of a Welsh Assembly with its new powers would make it possible for a very different approach to the arts to be introduced in Wales. Throughout the late 1990s, ACW was the major player in the arts in Wales, because local authority funding declined by 33 per cent between 1996 and 1999. In late 1999, however, the Assembly began to take an active role in arts advocacy and policy-making, which it did in two ways initially: by instigating a review of the arts and the Arts Council; and by appointing an 'expert adviser' on the arts.

This resulted, in 2000, in the publication of the *Wallace Report* (a management review of ACW) and *A Culture in Common* ('a proactive policy for the arts'), along with Ceri Sherlock's *Commentary on Culture and the Arts in Wales*. However, shortly before *A Culture in Common* was published, the Assembly disbanded the committee which had commissioned it – the Post-16 Education and Training Committee – and established a new cabinet position of Minister for Culture, Sport and the Welsh Language, with an accompanying committee. That new committee published *Creative Future: Cymru Greadigol* (a Culture Strategy for Wales) in January 2002, the purpose of which was to refine the thinking contained in *A Culture in Common* and to produce a 'clear vision'.

All of these initiatives promised a radical departure in thinking. Indeed, the *Wallace Report*[109] began with the phrase 'MAKE IT NEW'. But the detail did not support the fresh start that was envisaged. Although Wallace found that ACW had not managed its circumstances well and that what was needed was a new spirit of openness and partnership, the report endorsed ACW's systems. Its recommendations that ACW use regional committees, centralize strategy-making, strengthen links, review monitoring procedures, reduce paperwork, increase feedback, introduce three-year funding agreements, improve appeals procedures and methods of policy-making were about good housekeeping rather than radical thinking: using regional committees was a return to how things had been before 1994.

This practice of introducing illusory change continues. ACW's review of its procedures and practice seems to be a departure from the past and the *Arts Development Strategy 2002–2007* was intended to mark a new beginning for ACW. However, analysis of the detail reveals that the new strategy attempts to produce change without accomplishing a real difference. It brings to mind the Who song 'Won't Get Fooled Again', in which we are invited to 'meet the new boss: same as the old boss'.[110] The so-called *new* strategy bears the hallmarks of panopticism, traps the Welsh subsidized performance sector into repeating the principles of the past and provides further illustration of the way in which older precepts are embedded in policies that claim to be a major re-evaluation.

Key to this was the appointment of Anthony Everitt as ACW's consultant. Although ACW may well not have had any deliberate intention to do so, in appointing Everitt it enabled external values to be parachuted in to a different lived experience during an exercise that was supposed to be about separating from the past. Everitt's suitability for this task was debatable. As secretary general of ACGB in the early 1990s, he had been responsible for negotiating the devolvement of many arts organizations to the Regional Arts Boards, in line with the *Wilding Report*'s requirements. (Richard Wilding, who at the time was head of the Office of Arts and Libraries, was asked to write the report by Richard Luce, then Minister for the Arts. The *Wilding Report* (1989) recommended increased decentralization and led to the replacement of the Regional Arts Associations with a smaller number of Regional Arts Boards, and a reduction in the number of clients dealt with centrally by ACGB.) Robert Hewison reminds us that Everitt's resignation in 1994 had been 'widely called for': during Everitt's tenure, Hewison argues, ACGB had 'lost the confidence of both the government and the arts constituency'.[111]

Intriguingly, the basic principles of the *Wilding Report* seem to have found their way into Everitt's proposals for ACW – devolve, reduce administration, centralize the development of international links and the responsibility for 'national' companies, and develop a long-term vision. The priorities stated in Everitt's 1991–2 ACGB *Annual Report* (support for the individual artist, education in the arts, dissolving the 'artificial' barrier between the amateur and the professional, renewing the stock of buildings, international exchange, detailed monitoring of outcomes and performance indicators, transparency) are contained within Everitt's proposals for ACW. It seems passing strange that what was considered appropriate for Great Britain, as a whole, could still be deemed suitable for an independent Wales, when the importance of its arts autonomy had been recognized by the partition of 1994 (an act which Everitt had prepared).

Everitt's strategy reviews seemed to coincide with an increase in government funding. When he was at ACGB, between 1990 and 1993 there was a 26 per cent increase of funding. In Ireland, the delivery of his review corresponded with an increased government grant for the arts. The Welsh Assembly announced a 23 per cent increase in subvention a few months before the publication of Everitt's *Five Year Arts Development Strategy 2002–2007*. In Northern Ireland, Everitt's review accompanied an increase in funding of £337K. In return for that additional funding, certain aspects of restructuring are delivered, like delegating funding to the regions, introducing 'far-reaching' consultation and setting new priorities, normally to do with access, excellence, the growth of the arts economy and introducing greater methods of efficiency. In every case, enhanced funding follows a period of underfunding. It is as though government makes the arts pay a price for better subvention; and a review followed by restructuring is part of that, whereas better funding might, in and of itself, solve difficulties without a review.

Everitt seems to have the right profile for conducting ACW's strategy review. He has written a number of publications on arts and cultural policy, has advised the Hong Kong Arts Development Council, the Irish Arts Council and the Arts Council of Northern Ireland; and he is a former director of East Midlands Arts. However, Everitt's CV also makes him an inappropriate choice because he is a professional, international consultant and certain principles seem to find their way to whichever organization Everitt is reviewing. In Northern Ireland, he recommends integrating Lottery funds with art-form departments, as he does in Wales.[112] His report for the Irish Arts Council defines as being important for the Irish what he also considers crucial for the Welsh – the introduction of multi-annual funding, the Arts Council to become a development agency. In broad terms, it is reasonable that the Welsh and the Irish could warrant similar treatment. But the reality of the two countries – in economic terms alone – is such that you would also expect there to be significant differences in arts strategy.

A key feature of Everitt's approach is the 'thorough' research exercise. The Irish report (*The Arts Plan: 2002–2006*) refers to draft consultation papers, 190 written submissions and the arrangement of meetings. In Wales, too, views were sought, meetings held, consultation delivered. Nevertheless, we should note that ACGB's *A Creative Future* (1993) emerged out of 'the largest ever [consultation exercise]' and Everitt was at the helm when it was prepared – a vast national research exercise which resulted in a weighty report from which no discernible benefit seems to have emerged.

Everett can say, rightly, that full consultation has taken place and ACW will point, again correctly, to the lengthy consultative process. The problem, though, is the concept of consultation. Everitt's reports for the variously disposed Arts Councils all extol the necessity for transparency, but without considering what this really means. The crucial concern is not whether 300 people respond here or 500 people offer their views there, but how, exactly, you do something with the testimony of the consulted. As we have seen, the numbers of those responding to requests for consultation can be relatively small – a minority, even – and this could be because some arts organizations consider that it is not worth the amount of time it would take to make a response, given that what they have to say does not seem to count for very much.

If you know how the Arts Council works, it would be possible to write the main objectives Everitt's report identifies without a consultation exercise. This is because of the effects of panopticism: we all know the 'menu'. Thus, it was never likely that objectives for Wales might include, for example: 'it is recommended that Clwyd Theatr Cymru should be privatized. Henceforward, Ystradgynlais Miners Welfare Hall will receive revenue funding of £1.5 million per year.'

The problem of consultation is that it does not necessarily carry with it a mechanism for incorporating different perspectives. In fact, in Wales, there was a range of dissenting views and Everitt was told about this by members of the Welsh arts community; but it is hard to see how those opinions were accommodated by the final report. For instance, in February 2001, WAPA wrote a letter to Everitt. In it, WAPA said that they were unconvinced that much would be achieved by yet another reorganization, because the problems faced by ACW were caused by 'a lack of competence, professionalism and vision'. WAPA also referred despairingly to the numerous previous occasions when the remit of ACE had been discussed, without much having changed, and argued that decentralization could be problematic.

An even more stringent view was proffered by VAW, who stated in their letter that they felt Everitt's paper lacked an 'understanding and appreciation of Welsh politics and culture'. Even more troubling, VAW contended that Everitt's process ignored the Assembly's examination of Welsh arts and culture. VAW pointedly introduced the idea of 'colonialism' into the debate and also took issue with the idea of regionalization and with the tension between excellence and access. In truth, ACW was already talking about regionalization before Everitt was appointed (in line with the *Wallace Report*). But, in appointing Everitt, ACW had a consultant whom they must have known was supportive of regionalization.

The *Five Year Arts Development Strategy* is, however, just one of two adjacent frameworks for performance practices in Wales. The other is the Assembly's Culture Strategy for Wales, *Creative Future: Cymru Greadigol* (2002). ACW regards this document as being a cousin to the Everitt and Twine report. However, while it was noted in their *Action Plan* (2001) that ACW 'operates at armslength from the National Assembly', the content of the Assembly document suggests that it has rather short arms. *Creative Future* expresses a clear cultural ideology. Oddly, though, despite pointing out that cultural facilities should be accessible to all, irrespective of gender, ethnicity, sexuality and so on, the then Minister for Culture in Wales, Jenny Randerson, omits mention of the crucial category of class, and this even though she asserts that culture cannot be disaggregated from the 'rest of living'. *Creative Future* does not, however, manage to reconcile 'equality of access' with its aspiration to 'sustain the highest standards in . . . the professional arts' and, in this, it reiterates those values which have been predominant in the arts since the Arts Council's inception. This report might have been published at any time and in any place in the UK during the last fifty years, because its first principles are those common to most of those who produce reports on the arts. Although *Creative Future* supports the idea of using culture to help community development, it also endorses 'competitive' cultural enterprises.

Creative Future is a statement of preferences or desired shifts of emphasis. It is also a reminder that the Assembly has overall responsibility for the arts and that the Arts Council is an Assembly-*sponsored* organization, which reinforces the idea that ACW is not at much of an arm's length from the NAW. Moreover, the Assembly's intended mode of working is decidedly reminiscent of the panoptic model: the idea of 'monitoring', for example, raises concerns. Indeed, there is a clear indication that the Assembly is playing the same game that the Arts Council has long played, which is about giving increased subvention in return for the adoption of appropriate behaviour. Hence, the Assembly indicated that it had budgeted for a 35 per cent increase in funding to ACW between 2000 and 2004, in return for which ACW had to restructure.

That said, the Assembly's recognition that organizations other than ACW need to be involved in policy-making could help to curb ACW's monolithic tendencies. Equally, the Assembly's acknowledgement of arts practices like the Penrhys project may result in shifts in funding which might not have happened in the former ACW climate. But the Assembly's insistence that ACW's restructuring be 'cost-neutral', coupled with its keen interest in the value of the arts to employment and the economy suggests that its belief in the capacity of the arts to fill cultural 'gaps' is as much 'economic' as it is to do with social equity and community well-being: the performing arts as a useful tool for pacifying and moderating troublesome behaviour.

The problem of *Creative Future* is that it does not acknowledge the difficulties of reconciling what are different ideologies within the Assembly's strategy. When it states that providing a link between the public and the arts 'does not always mean giving the public exactly what it knows it wants' it has not fully thought through what gaining 'the widest popular support for the arts' actually means in practice. The development of complementary relationships between professionals and amateurs and community organizations is fine in theory but deeply problematic in practice, because these different groups do not always speak the same language. It is particularly telling that the Assembly says there must be more effective support for professionals to ensure that they produce 'high quality results', because this use of nebulous vocabulary returns us to the original principles of ACGB in another time and another country.

The Assembly's statement that Wales must have a mixed theatre economy of local theatre companies and flagship companies might well perpetuate current difficulties. Although the intention to ensure that Lottery-funded venues have sufficient revenue funding could make a difference to venues like the Cwmaman Institute, *Creative Future*'s determination to provide Wales with 'high quality theatre' leaves us no further forward because the nub of the issue remains – how you reconcile limited subvention with calls on funding. It is fairly inevitable that flagship companies will command the lion's share.

Where there could be a deviation is in the greater involvement of local authorities who, it is intended, will develop cultural policies. How these could work in tandem with the Arts Council's new five-year plan is debatable, though. The synthesis of local, regional and national cultural strategies begs some questions, particularly when the 'national remit' companies are supposed to play an important role in implementing policy. The idea of 'practical cooperation' between national and community companies perpetuates the idea of a hierarchy between the two. There still seems to be the idea that there is 'art', on one hand, and 'community regeneration' on the other. When *Creative Future* says that the image of Wales must be one of 'excellence' we are reminded of exactly the kind of thinking that Keynes encouraged the Arts Council to adopt at its inception. Given that the Assembly has said that it expects the ACW to 'support the values, priorities and objectives of the Welsh Assembly Government', we can imagine how things might develop. The attempt to reconcile excellence and participation is likely to be a fraught one.

Creative Future is not as thoughtful as *A Culture in Common* (2000), the earlier Assembly report out of which *Creative Future* developed. *A Culture in Common* argued that all publicly funded institutions should 'promote indigenous talent' and acknowledged that Wales had, in the past, accepted the 'dominant models of theatre' in England. It also observed that the conventional notion of a 'national theatre' was inappropriate for Wales. Most significantly, it conceded that 'excellence' is a 'slippery' idea and that high quality should emerge out of 'grass roots' activity: 'Wales should strive for excellence in the arts, but must know in what context value might be measured.' The report's most radical conclusions were that reform could not be left to 'existing Arts Council personnel' and that the idea of a Royal Charter for ACW was outmoded. This report is perhaps the best document for clearly expressed critical thinking about the arts in Wales that has been published. Nevertheless, it still adhered to the idea that national remit companies should 'set standards for national creativity' and 'extend their presence throughout Wales', a belief that is consistent with the notion that theatre companies cannot set their own standards without being authenticated by official organizations.

The undercurrent of radicalism was further substantiated by Ceri Sherlock (the expert adviser appointed by the Assembly). In his *Commentary on Culture and the Arts in Wales* (2000), Sherlock endorsed the need for a 'radical agenda' and argued that we should *start* from the grass roots. He believed that Wales was experiencing a 'paradigm shift' when 'stifled voices are at last heard'.

Sherlock acknowledged that there had been 'hierarchies of values' and his solution was to establish Cymru'n Creu, a forum intended to 'stimulate critical debate and discussion' and conduct research. This might have been the means by which the 'stifled voices' could have been heard. However, membership of Cymru'n Creu suggests that it could become another society for the unofficial Welsh arts freemasons, where the usual suspects will hold forth.

The problem would then remain how to integrate different points of view and, particularly, to extend decision-making mechanisms in any meaningful way. Sherlock noted that advice from expert panels was frequently disregarded by ACW. Equally, he recognized that local authorities have had a relationship with the Arts Council that was 'poor to non-existent'. Furthermore, he observed that the division between the Artform and Access departments at ACW led to marked differences between professional and community arts. There is, though, no guarantee that Sherlock's proposals would ameliorate these difficulties, especially given that Sherlock himself accepts that the earlier consultation process 'appeared to be cosmetic'. So might this one.

If you argue, as Sherlock does, that not everything can be funded, then you are positioning yourself alongside the early ACGB members and saying that choices must be made while tacitly refusing to make those choices. So, although Sherlock acknowledges rock music, storytelling and so on, he is also saying by default that demotic forms such as these will, when push comes to shove, lose out in the funding stakes; and this is where the problem has always been. What do you fund? If this, then not that. Sherlock's, and the Assembly's, reiteration that not everything can be funded perpetuates the current and historic difficulties. So much for a paradigm shift, especially when we realize that *Creative Future* in refining *A Culture in Common* quietly jettisoned the more radical ideas, like rescinding the Royal Charter. Above all, the Assembly did not ultimately foreground the two areas which would have produced a radical difference. It did not insist that notions of excellence be abandoned altogether and it did not ensure that ACW was re-organized by an innovatively constituted, objective task force. Instead, ACW's reform was influenced by one of ACGB's former commanders.

The model of the Panopticon has been used here to describe the way in which theatre practice becomes incorporated: panopticism, in common with incorporative procedures, structures, controls, disciplines and captures theatre by defining the terms of engagement. The Panopticon as metaphor offers a way of examining the development of disciplinary procedures by the Arts Council. This is not to say that ACGB made a deliberate and conscious choice of adopting a panoptic framework. On the contrary, my argument is that the Arts Council was (and is) a utopian project designed to liberate theatre practices from the very real constraints of material poverty. In theory, its ambitions were (and are) egalitarian. But it is difficult to achieve equality of opportunity in practice.

Panopticism is an adjunct of organizational structuring and is a direct consequence of inadequate funding levels: panopticism and hegemony are functions of having money. The organizing principle underpinning the use of disciplinary procedures is that chaos can be controlled by imposing a structure. Panopticism is not an abstraction, therefore. It can be seen in *action* when the Arts Council normalizes, categorizes, professionalizes and disciplines through its policies in practice. It sets 'standards', identifies 'excellence', develops systems of inspection, assessment and appraisal, and extends the reach of 'the gaze' by ensuring the complete visibility of theatre processes and performances.

The permeation of this gaze can be detected in the outcomes of the relationship between the Arts Council in Wales and the former ACGB: WAC/ACW identified with an external set of procedures for systematizing theatre practices, and accommodated what is, in effect, cultural intervention. But it did so believing that this was in its own best interests. For this reason, WAC/ACW assimilated the language of ACGB and perceived itself as having an 'uneven' tradition, and a lack of 'good size' professional touring companies. It followed England's lead in siting theatres in 'important centres': in Cardiff and Bangor, for example. But buildings produce particular forms of theatre, and the space demands certain kinds of responses. Architecture is not innocent of ideology. Most significantly for Wales, the Arts Council has been responsible for defining who holds executive power, and for appointing those individuals who influence the decision-making process.

Panopticism does not, in itself, discriminate between the English and the Welsh. Its outcomes are distributed across a cultural continuum, and can be discerned in who sees theatre, where they see it, whom and what they see, and the way in which theatre companies work. It creates the hierarchy of space that privileges the National Theatre over a village hall, and London over the Rhondda. It encourages performers to believe that success is syn-onymous with, say, a season at the RSC. The aesthetic expands or contracts to fill the spaces offered by venues, and constructs definitions of small-, mid- and large-scale touring. Performance practice – company structure, management and training – is constrained by the conditions of funding because accountability (visibility) involves submitting to a system of surveillance (appraisal). In becoming part of the funding system, theatre companies collude with panopticism; and it is in this way that the Arts Council shapes the imaginative world of the nation.

Whilst this construction of theatre practice can be observed throughout the UK, it has, however, had a particular impact in Wales. The main reason for this lies in the effects of categorization. In order to be *seen* to distribute subvention fairly, the Arts Council developed a system of categories, or disciplines. But these have been responsible for excluding dramatic forms which fail to conform, and it is the exclusions which have defined Wales as a nation without theatre traditions. In conventional Arts Council terms, therefore, Wales can be seen as a 'void'. Consequently, global totals of public subsidy have been used to compensate for the perceived lack of a theatre practice instead of enhancing the practices which might, under a different system of categorization, have suggested themselves as worthy of funding; and it is those *other*, unincorporated theatre practices which are particularly reflective of much of the lived experience in Wales.

In 1959, the Welsh Committee of the Arts Council apologized for the fact that 'there is a strong native tradition of drama, but virtually no professional theatre'.[113] If this statement is compared with ACW's 1996 boast that 'Wales has developed a professional theatre which is a source of pride',[114] it supports the idea that a panoptic strategy of establishing mechanisms for the external discipline of standards created a professional theatre practice in Wales at some expense to indigenous performance traditions.

There appear to be few signs of new thinking: ACW's *Corporate Plan 2000–2003* intended 'to target areas of low provision', like Objective One areas, to develop 'closer links between artists, producers and the audience' and target arts development in areas of low opportunity. However, the funding for this seems to have been earmarked out of the Lottery, although there was talk in some quarters of placing the Coliseum, Aberdare, on revenue funding. Until, or unless, the Arts Council can imagine revenue-funded venues with producing companies being positioned in the south Wales Valleys change will be limited.

ACW says that its role, in common with other Arts Councils, should change from direct provision to strategic development. But, in order to determine tactics, it would need to tackle the residual problem of reconciling 'excellence in the professional subsidized sector' with support for arts in the community, particularly in view of the Millennium Centre build and its future (economic) relationship with community halls, not to mention larger professional venues. The question of how orthodox notions of quality can be married with indigenous means of access and participation is pressing, given that by 2000 the C2DEs were still in the minority of play-attenders.[115]

The balance of money between different kinds of performing arts groups remains telling in terms of how power is subtly exercised to ensure that the first principles of the Arts Council (and, therefore, of panopticism) are achieved. Table 7 shows how money is used to support the ideals of quality, professionalization, flagship buildings and national theatre, even when ACW advertises in its annual report (2000–1) the promotion of participation and encouragement of diversity.[116] Global totals and differentials point to inequalities.

There are, of course, several ways of examining the figures and you could argue that the Sherman, for example, given what has been said earlier about its use of orature, is not absoutely incorporative of the ideals outlined above. Nevertheless, the emphases created by general funding differentials are revealing. The total sum proposed for Clwyd Theatr Cymru and the mainstream companies was £2 million. But the figure proposed for the TYPs was only 46 per cent of that; and the total proposed for community arts was just 24 per cent of that for CTC and the mainstreams. Yet the TYPs and community arts are more likely to be able to play a significant role in promoting participation, because they are closer to the 'grass roots' than CTC and the mainstreams.

Table 7.
ACW subsidy figures for theatre 2001–2

Actual figures spent[a]

Wales's national performing arts company (Clwyd Theatr Cymru)	£1.1 million
Mainstream performing companies (Torch Theatre, Theatr Gwynedd, Sherman Theatre)	£847,900
TYPs (8 companies)	£938,000
Production companies (5)	£505,400
Projects – Drama (2000–2001)	£88,700

Projected figures[b]

Performing arts community touring (Night Out scheme)	£101,900
Community arts (targeting areas of low provision)	£501,600

a) As detailed in *ACW Annual Report* for 2000-1.
b) In *Developing the Arts in Wales 2000-2003*, draft ACW Corporate Plan for 2000–3.

Table 7 shows the scale of financial changes that would need to be made before performance practices coming out of the grass roots could be funded at a level comparable with that of the companies with a national remit. It is one thing to say that access and participation will be important. It is quite another to subsidize them in such a way that they can produce conventional notions of high quality which would make them eligible for equal funding. It is all very well to boast that Blackwood Miners Institute would receive a 37,5 per cent increase. But when that increase represents a total grant of only £20K, that is a tiny amount compared with CTC's income.

The developments considered after the March 2001 report perpetuate the tension between quality, access and participation. It is promising that Objective One project development support will be forthcoming, that there will be Valleys audience development initiatives, that ACW will develop local authority partnerships and that there will be enhanced community theatre and touring. However, it is inauspicious that revenue support to community arts clients will be increased by only £250K.

The March 2001 report envisaged that checks and balances could be created by introducing greater transparency and, indeed, it is this openness that both the Assembly and the Arts Council believe can mitigate against the conservatism discussed above. However, as with the notion of consultation, transparency can be ambiguous in practice. The idea of open council meetings, for instance, is useful only if witnesses can make interventions. It is also one thing to send reports to clients, but another to introduce mechanisms by which they (and non-clients) can challenge them. Members' names can be published but that does not mean that the way in which they are appointed will be democratic. Transparency is a somewhat slippery notion, particularly if the ACW is to be the 'final court of appeal' and especially since that Council will be reduced in size: an even smaller and more select group will decide who is worth what. Besides, organizations can be adept at cosmetic, strategic transparency while making the real decisions in corridors.

There will be those who think that this is a cynical point of view. But what is needed is more cynicism, by which I mean that accepted standards should be interrogated and discarded and, like the original cynics, we should mount a principled 'opposition to conventional forms and usages'.[117] We have not been sufficiently restive with the received conventions of the Arts Council. The problem is that to be so, and thereby to acquire creative freedom, performance practitioners would need to be much more self-determining; and that might necessitate working outside the Arts Council's remit, with all that implies.

The point during the Second World War when responsibility for the organization of popular concerts in factory canteens was transferred from CEMA to ENSA was, in retrospect, a watershed for the performing arts in the UK, and in Wales especially, because it meant that a major decision about the function of ACGB had, in fact, been taken without any real debate. In effect, indigenous, working-class culture was removed from the remit of state-subsidized arts practice.

Yet the idea that certain considerations needed to be made in Wales was recognized, although not formalized, from an early stage. Hence, Thomas Jones's stance in the 1930s that surplus chapels ought to be transformed into community centres is an expression of the belief that culture should be an organic development out of what is already there in the community. But although important critical thinking was available, the gatekeepers, curators and benefactors chose to ignore it. Basically, and as far as Wales is concerned, they listened to the wrong people.

4

Colonizing the Mind: Antipathies, Polarities, Incompatibilities and Contradictions

The problem of theatre in Wales is that critical opinion pressurizes us into believing that quality and excellence are inherent in some performance practices but not in others. In this chapter, I am going to look at examples of opinion-forming and referential power to suggest how certain kinds of theatre have come to be privileged during a process which amounts to a 'colonizing' of the mind.

The awarding of prizes, which is an aspect of referential power, has long been a feature of Welsh theatre. In the early twentieth century, competition adjudicators influenced the development of Welsh playwriting by rejecting certain plays and, by implication, playwrights. Emlyn Williams, for instance, did not win a prize at the 1923 Eisteddfod with a new play of his.[1] Whilst the development of the Arts Council distanced theatre practice in Wales from the crude processes of adjudication and, therefore, in theory allowed for a more open means by which critical opinion could evolve, new methods of legitimization – the awarding of prizes – materialized. Some of these have been official, while others have been more subtle; nevertheless, the judgement that a piece of theatre has quality has been made by comparatively small groups of individuals serving as de facto adjudicators. These gatekeepers, curators or custodians of theatre in Wales include Arts Council officers and members, local authority arts workers, academics, theatre reviewers, critics and authors, theatre practitioners themselves, and those who write reports on productions and theatre companies for the Arts Council. Between them, they create the critical approbation that gives a piece of theatre 'referential power'.

The estimation of critical worth is, to some extent, the viewpoint of a relatively narrow corps of specialists in the field. Yet its estimations of value can have a powerful influence. One difficulty is the way in which gate-keepers achieve their positions. At times, it can appear that referential power has been vested in the hands of individuals who have been helped to acquire status by having connections to others with rank in the arts.

It might have been expected that the advent of the Arts Council would have limited the opportunities for canvassing and networking. What the Arts Council was meant to do was replace the 'missionary positions' of arts funding – benefaction, patronage and sponsorship – with more disinterested approaches. However, patronage, and its potential for exercising referential power, remains a possibility and the success of theatre practitioners may be contingent on their developing the right kind of connections.

In Wales, before the 1940s, the economic role of the patron was crucial because there were not many individuals with money and an interest in Welsh theatre. Olive Ely Hart suggested in 1928 that 'in the matter of patronage, Wales [was fortunate] in having a group of literati wise enough to assist development without forcing modes or dictating policies'.[2] But, no matter how beneficent such patrons were, they encouraged theatre which reflected their view of the world, and the point of the Arts Council was to introduce more impartial methods of funding. However, ACW's panoptic procedures enabled theatre practices to acquire referential power in ways that are just as partial as those associated with the benefactors, patrons and adjudicators of yesteryear. This is evident from the fact that public funding is largely conditional on whether a theatre practice has been legitimized by those with referential status.

Legitimization has had the effect of segregating theatre into two distinct categories: the 'significant' and the 'peripheral'; and binary thinking of this kind dominates debates about Welsh theatre.[3] On one side is the logocentric mainstream, with its adherence to the playwright, written text and a canon of writing; and with its ideology that theatre is an art form which derives from an authoritative centre, that the professional actor is an uniquely skilled individual whose abilities empower the text to speak through her/him, and that what Welsh theatre needs most is to be exposed to the greatness of the classics. Another manifestation of the mainstream is what ACW used to call 'developmental' theatre for, although theatre companies of this complexion like to perceive themselves as a radical alternative to written-play theatre, their means of production are often very similar. Moreover, in Wales the 'developmental' has acquired a large measure of referential status.

The playwriting and developmental approaches to theatre appear to have bifurcated around 1980 when Eugenio Barba's Danish company Odin Teatret gave workshop-demonstrations in Wales to professional theatre practitioners. Since then, Welsh theatre seems to have been engaged in a debate, although it is not as formal or as coordinated as that term might suggest, over the advantages of one methodology over the other; and it could be argued that this discourse, which is essentially about referential power, has contributed to creating a debilitating block in the performance culture: one which might be described generally as centring on a (false) dichotomy between a logocentric approach and a physical-visual one.

Outside those two main strands of 'formally-written' plays, on one hand, and the 'developmental', on the other, is a third category embracing a range of 'community' theatre practices. I would argue that it is forms of theatre associated with that term 'community' which lack real referential power. Intrinsic to debates about Welsh theatre is a hegemony in which certain values are understood at a deep level to have superiority over others: namely, that theatre with established referential power takes precedence over indigenous, popular performance practices of the kind that are often connected to 'community' theatre. Wales has evolved a hierarchy of theatre and performance forms; what is promoted as being of unarguably high quality is far more contentious in reality. What I am going to do now is attempt to show how referential power is bestowed and acquired through those three categories of theatre I have identified.

Plays, playwrights and playwriting

At the end of the twentieth century, ACW's 1999 Drama Strategy appeared to initiate a new phase in the dialogue about the value of the playwright. However, current debates about playwriting in Wales are not so very different from those taking place the best part of a century ago. Olive Ely Hart contended in the 1920s that Wales is a country particularly receptive to 'the play' because 'Welsh audiences [have been] trained for generations in the art of listening to the spoken word',[4] a view which is shared by many contemporary theatre practitioners.

The idea that the Welsh are especially responsive to the written play has been widely disseminated through three particular notions, which typically constitute the material and the means by which referential power has been exercised; and status is usually conferred or solicited through evoking one or more of them. When, for example, the Sherman Theatre issued a response to the Drama Strategy it encapsulated such historical debates about playwriting in Wales by referring to these three issues: first, the question of whether writing is a 'craft', as opposed to an 'art', second, the idea that Welsh theatre must be statemented by measuring it against the canon of other European countries (non-European cultures do not tend to prioritize dramatic literature); and, third, the assertion of a need for a Welsh replication of metropolitan, London-based centres of writing, especially new writing, like the Royal Court theatre.

The ideology behind new writing is that it is perceived as having a critical role to play in helping the Welsh to find out who they are and in creating a conduit to international referential power. For instance, playwright Tracy Spottiswoode, in an open letter to Joanna Weston, endorses the idea that a vital purpose of playwriting is to project a Welsh voice on to the 'world stage'. Yet, achieving that would necessitate supporting the existing hierarchy of referential power. Whilst acknowledging the role of TYP companies in supporting new writing, Spottiswoode demonstrates how deeply ingrained is the notion that commissioning sources confer status on the play. So commissions from the 'community' sector are regarded as being of less value because its productions are not going to be performed at prestigious theatres like the Royal Court.

The discourse of playwriting is part of a continuum that has its immediate antecedents in an earlier, discarded raft of detractors, like Dedwydd Jones who, in his series of *Black Books* in the 1980s, lambasted WAC for its attitude to Welsh plays in the English language.[5] In common with present-day play advocates, Jones believed that 'the end-product of drama is plays';[6] and that playwrights are the 'front-line troops of the theatre'.[7] Jones's view was shared by Carl Tighe, another playwright, who reviewed theatre in Wales in the 1980s. Tighe believed that Welsh play wrights could not get performed on the main stages if their work was too local; but he also contended that 'the writer in Wales has no tradition, nothing out of which to develop, nothing to fight against and nothing to disagree with'.[8]

That opinion would have surprised not only Olive Ely Hart, who published her Ph.D. thesis on Welsh, English-language new playwriting in 1928, but also some of the playwrights she wrote about. For instance, Merthyr-born J. O. Francis might have found Tighe's view odd, given that his (Francis's) play *Change* (1912) was all about reacting against one's background. Moreover, as one of a number of interesting playwrights working in Wales at that time, Francis might have been disappointed that Tighe had not thought that Francis and his peers were contributing something by way of a modest tradition. As Hart shows, Francis's work marked the start of an interest in Welsh drama from outside Wales.[9] However, knowledge of that interest and of the body of work that engendered it seems to have been mislaid within the Welsh playwriting culture. This is unfortunate, because we could otherwise draw two inferences: first, that the claim that Wales has not had a tradition of (new) playwriting is somewhat misplaced; and second, if it has not, this does not prove anything in terms of cultural stature.

Reading Hart's thesis now is instructive because it shows that contemporary dialogue about new playwriting in Wales reiterates what was being said seventy-five years ago. Hart argued that Welsh theatre could develop only if its 'body of professional playwrights of no mean order' were given either theatres to provide 'native, professional [productions] for their plays', or travelling companies who could offer the same function, which is pretty much the current consensus.[10]

The attitudes of the playwrights whom Hart cites prefigure present views. Caradoc Evans, for example, foresaw that Welsh playwrights would be pushed towards universalism, while Richard Hughes commented, presciently, that Welsh drama was going to be difficult to develop because of the problem of persuading the Welsh that 'one good company is better than three mediocre ones'. D. T. Davies contended that the value of playwrights was in their expressing the dissatisfaction of a younger generation. Davies felt, in common with other playwrights of the time, that plays could not be performed properly by amateur theatre companies because they had neither the interpretative tools necessary to understanding what a play is about, nor the team skills vital to a good performance. All the writers who corresponded with Hart believed that Welsh casts were vital. But these playwrights also believed that the future strength of Welsh theatre lay in developments which, it could be argued, have done much to compromise theatre in Wales, namely a professionalized system and a Welsh national theatre.[11]

Hart concludes her thesis by referring approvingly to a prestigious production of Ibsen's *The Pretenders* (1863), which was due to be performed in Wales in 1927. Paradoxically, given that Hart was writing in the 1920s, she took a less narrow view from that espoused by Terry Hands, amongst others. Hart, rather than using Ibsen's oeuvre as a stick with which to beat the Welsh on the grounds that they do not have such a dramatist and are not, therefore, fit to take their place on the world theatre stage, observes that Ibsen was a particularly apt model for Wales because 'Wales, like Norway, must discover or re-capture a mode of expression peculiarly and significantly her own'.[12] It is not a simulacrum of either Norway or Ibsen that Hart recommends; rather, it is to encourage the idea that it is important for a country to create its own differentiated and particular theatre practice using the play-text as but one means of achieving that. When Hart and the playwrights to which she refers talk about theatre, they admit only of the play-textual model. They were, however, cognizant of experiment, even if they conceived of its happening within the play-text; so their thinking was not as bipolarized as that evinced by many current critics.

It sometimes seems that there is an over-readiness to separate the written play from the developmental. Jeni Williams, for instance, argues that there is a 'determinedly avant-garde and academic consensus . . . against text-based theatre'. But her point that 'a theatre "tradition" which omits the practice of writing risks disappearing into unrecoverable myth' is one which, in reality, few would disagree with.[13] Nor would there be much argument with her view that 'intelligent writing needs to be seen and valued as integral to an intelligent and questioning theatrical practice'.[14] In fact, playwriting actually receives more attention than its worried advocates admit; it is telling that the longest and most expensive book on Welsh theatre is about four playwrights: *State of Play* (Gomer, 1998).

The opinions expressed by the Sherman, Tracy Spottiswoode and Jeni Williams share certain characteristics that are particular to the promotion of the playwright and playwriting and which illustrate the movement of referential power through the culture. Although their views come from different directions – a theatre venue/company, a freelance playwright, and an academic and critic – they demonstrate how prevailing opinions develop through a process akin to osmosis. Underpinning their judgements is the belief that an exemplary body of dramatic literature is essential to any cultured society, a belief that has much in common with imperialist attitudes. The subtext of the view that has been absorbed is that Wales has no 'canon', therefore it has no approved sense of itself.

Wales's only hope of creating a 'history and theatrical identity' is 'through new writing', as Krishnendu Majumdar puts it in an article in the *Guardian* (14 March 2001). Majumdar indicates that Wales is the 'poor relation' because it has no suitable institution to present new playwrights and there fore has difficulty in 'expressing its identity through theatre'. Indeed, the health of theatre in Wales is often equated with the number of new plays produced; a somewhat crude index, perhaps, given that there were eighteen commissions for new plays from theatre companies in Wales in 1998–9, for instance.

Majumdar's assumption is that Welsh theatre lacks credibility because it is absent from the mainstream: a '[run] in the West End [would legitimize] Wales'. Yet this ignores the possibility that purposeful detachment from the English mainstream might be a more effective way of expressing Wales's identity than a season in the West End. Moreover, whenever the question of the 'canon', and Wales's apparent lack of one, is raised, it seems to be forgotten that there have indeed been Welsh playwrights who have had the kind of success in the West End which carries with it the potential to acquire classic, referential status; and yet that still does not seem to have legitimized plays from Wales. During the 1930s, the Welsh made inroads into the West End and Emlyn Williams, especially, was a hugely successful, famous and wealthy playwright. A more recent example of a Welsh playwright who has been admired in the English mainstream is Peter Gill: he is Welsh and working-class, has been described as 'one of [British] theatre's best-kept secrets' and his play *The York Realist*, which received excellent reviews in 2002, was performed at the Royal Court in an English Touring Theatre production directed by Gill himself.[15] But what needs to be remembered is that metropolitan, bourgeois referential power will tend to supersede regional critical opinions so that the capacity of a Welsh play to achieve canonical status will be limited by strategic judgement. Hence, the plays of Williams and Gill, *inter alia*, even were they to have canonical potential, might well be denied that status for very complex political reasons which have little to do with aesthetic quality.

The evidence does not support the notion that London theatre runs would necessarily provide Wales with the canon of plays that some have argued are essential to the promotion of Welsh theatre. But the idea of an authorized Welsh 'canon' encapsulates the difficulty with orthodoxies in relation to writing. One particularly pernicious thought, for example, is that Wales has a problem because it does not have a playwright of stature, like Henrik Ibsen, around which to build a theatre culture. This view has been advanced by Terry Hands, amongst others, and it has been rightly criticized by the playwright Dic Edwards for its unproblematized use of an 'English' theatre model.[16]

Edwards sensibly refocuses the issue of playwriting towards material concerns about nurturing playwrights in a country that has experienced financial deprivation. The economics of playwriting may be more decisive than is often acknowledged and discussion about the pecuniary context of writing could well be more productive as a means of challenging the conventions of referential power than debates about playwriting as an art-form. A commission to write a play is worth around £5,000 in Wales and, as the Sherman Theatre stated in 1999, most writers in Wales cannot make a living out of theatre writing alone. Despite the formation of a discrete company – in 2000, a new company, Sgript Cymru, became responsible for commissioning, developing and staging new plays in Wales – the only category of theatre to be cut as part of the Drama Strategy 1999–2000 was New Writing. According to research conducted by Tracy Spottiswoode, Sgript Cymru's budget represented just 4 per cent of the total Drama budget in Wales.

So perhaps it is the economics which accounts for the fact that, in David Adams's opinion, Wales 'is still not producing the playwrights . . . willing or able to interrogate contemporary culture'.[17] What we need to consider, then, is the extent to which writing plays might be an activity performed by those who can 'afford' to write or who have the potential to acquire referential status.

The avant-garde, the developmental and the experimental

It could be argued that, during the 1990s, developmental theatre enjoyed the highest international referential status of companies from Wales, a position which can be traced back to the work of two particular companies. By the late 1970s, Moving Being and Cardiff Laboratory Theatre had already established a presence in Welsh theatre practice. In the 1979 *British Alternative Theatre Directory*, Moving Being described itself as a 'theatre of mixed means . . . to locate ideas of the body and its being in the world' and this foregrounding of 'the body' typifies the approach of what later became known as the 'developmental' theatre companies in Wales.

They emerged at regular intervals throughout the 1980s and were influenced by a mélange of ideas drawn from earlier theatre practitioners, like Antonin Artaud and Jerzy Grotowski; from American experimental theatre, like the Living Theatre; from artists, like Salvador Dali; from philosophers, like Roland Barthes and Jacques Derrida; and from dance companies, like DV8. But there were other influences, including martial arts and Japanese theatre. For many of the developmental theatre companies, the medium was itself political and their various challenges to the hegemony of the play-text constituted acts of political opposition comparable with the content of plays emanating from the 'alternative' theatre spectrum. An example of this objection to the conventional play is encapsulated in an article by Mike Pearson, formerly artistic director of Brith Gof, entitled 'The script's *not* the thing'.[18]

By the 1990s, 'developmental' theatre companies in Wales had achieved a profile which appears to support the view that written plays were being marginalized. David Hughes, writing in 1996, contended that it was the international touring of companies like Volcano which had enabled Welsh theatre to 'mature'.[19] Hughes further suggests that in the 1990s the experimental groups constituted the real National Theatre of Wales.[20] Brith Gof, he asserts, brought theatrical methods from 'all over the world to *challenge*' Wales (my emphasis), which suggests that developmentalists intended to be deliberately provocative.[21] Such an internationalist methodology, continues Hughes, enabled Welsh theatre to develop out of 'parochialism'. Consequently, Welsh theatre '[could] now proudly turn back to Europe and offer itself as a body of mature work by matured companies'.[22] Whereas Olive Ely Hart claimed that it was years of listening to sermons that made the Welsh especially receptive to the play text, Hughes now argued that: 'The Welsh audience through years of careful exposure to the terms of this experimental work . . . can understand in ways which are . . . difficult for those with entrenched views on what constitutes theatre.'[23]

Hughes's writing exemplifies the means by which referential power is transmitted. His belief that developmental theatre was the 'real' National Theatre of Wales was one which was shared by a significant cohort of influential gatekeepers. It is possible to demonstrate how referential power is distributed by tracking some of those gatekeepers. In this instance, we can do so by using developmental theatre as our starting point, although the exercise could just as well be carried out in the context of playwriting. If we begin randomly with David Adams (although, again, the starting point could be with any one of a number of individuals), simply because he has been the most prolific theatre critic in Wales, we can gain some idea of how opinions about theatre are disseminated and, further, how a structure of feeling about particular kinds of theatre gains momentum.

One of the most lauded Welsh theatre companies working in the broad area of the developmental is Volcano. Indeed, in ACW's Drama Strategy document of 1999, Volcano was identified as the only 'experimental' company to which ACW intended to give three-year revenue support. Such was ACW's confidence in the company that in 2000–1 it granted the company £100K, which represented a 60 per cent increase. Moreover, ACW's *Five Year Arts Development Strategy 2002–2007* endorsed Volcano's status as a revenue-funded organization.

This recognition for the company, which started working professionally in 1987, contrasts sharply with their position in 1991–2, when ACW gave the company just £16K, the smallest sum awarded in the category of Development Production Companies and Projects. Several other companies in that category no longer exist, including Moving Being which had received the largest sum. The intriguing aspect of this is how Volcano's and Moving Being's positions were, in effect, reversed; and this is where a consideration of referential power becomes relevant.

Volcano themselves were obviously aware of the usefulness of referentiality because, in an early application to WAC, they cited one of David Adams's reviews of their work in which he stated that the company was 'one of the hottest properties in the emergent new Welsh theatre'.[24] In his 1990s reviews for the *Guardian* Adams repeatedly enthused about Volcano: 'this [is an] amazing company . . . Until you have seen Volcano you have not really seen dangerous theatre';[25] Volcano's new production is 'gobsmacking';[26] and Adams's account of Volcano in his monograph *Stage Welsh* is unequivocally admiring.

In order to understand referential power, we need to examine how Adams's opinion of Volcano could be ventilated in circumstances which would enable a correlation between a structure of feeling about the company and funding levels to be established. Now, I am not saying this is how Volcano came to achieve status, because the exact process is necessarily speculative. Rather, I am going to try to show how referential power works by using Volcano and David Adams as a case study.

As has been demonstrated, Adams wrote enthusiastically about Volcano's work and did so in the *Guardian*, a national broadsheet with, arguably, the best arts coverage in Britain. He has also written in the *Western Mail*, the *New Welsh Review* and has contributed to books. Hence, his views have had the opportunity to circulate amongst a readership which includes other gatekeepers. But he was also in a position to influence funding, for he was a member of WAC's Drama panel in 1991–2, when Volcano were first gaining a toehold on the funding ladder.

It is worth noting the names of some of the other members of that panel: Hazel Walford Davies, Jamie Garven, Ceri Sherlock and Jane Davidson. Garven is a respected professional theatre director working with a range of different companies; Sherlock was eventually appointed the Welsh Assembly's 'arts tsar'; Jane Davidson served on WAC's/ACW's main council committee, was chair of ACW's Drama Board in 1995–6, and is currently Minister for Education in the Welsh Assembly. (It is also worth mentioning that Janek Alexander, who as director of Chapter Arts Centre was supportive to Volcano and has even directed some of their work, was a member of ACW's Dance panel in the mid-1990s. Equally, Sybil Crouch, who was encouraging to Volcano in her capacity as manager of the Taliesin Arts Centre in Swansea, was later chairman of ACW.) As for Hazel Walford Davies, since 2000 she has been an ACW council member, appointed by the National Assembly, and was also chair of the Literature panel for a period. Indeed, her biography in the 2000–1 ACW *Annual Report* is an index to the functioning of referential power because, in addition to her ACW commitments, she was a Senior Lecturer in Theatre Studies at the University of Wales, Aberystwyth (and is now at the University of Glamorgan); and, amongst other activities, she is a fellow of the Welsh Academy and a member of the Editorial Board of the *New Welsh Review*.

So, what begins with David Adams as an articulated enthusiasm for a theatre company can become, at a later stage, a structure of feeling or, even, an orthodoxy because of the way in which personal recommendation is able to evolve into referential power through an incremental process of collective opinion-forming. By virtue of her affiliations, Hazel Walford Davies, alone, can disseminate a structure of feeling through academics, Arts Council members, members of the Welsh Assembly, playwrights, critics, actors, theatre companies, students, journalists and members of the media. Connections thus established can resonate over a very long period of time and manifest themselves in a variety of ways, including job appointments and other professional engagements. Nine years after Adams and Davies were colleagues on the WAC Drama panel, they were to be found co-authoring an article in *NWR* on 'Theatre as an interface between Wales and the world'.[27]

'Only connect', E. M. Forster memorably urged; and, indeed, the study of referential power in Wales is extraordinarily akin to the Hollywood game of 'Six Steps to Kevin Bacon', where participants have to draw the connections in film between any given actor and Kevin Bacon. In a small nation, it is not difficult to identify who has been in contact with whom and, therefore, suggest how prevailing opinions might be spread. The Volcano nexus is just one example but, even here, we can discern connective tissue between particular individuals and, more importantly, between key institutions and organizations as individuals work their way through Welsh agencies of power. It is perhaps the case that arts activities across all countries and cultures function through a network of connections, and there may well be advantages to that. My point is that the effects of 'networking' could also be detrimental.

In the case of Volcano, referential status was achieved because a critical mass gathered around them. Conversely, this is also why companies like Moving Being disappear, as can be seen from the words of Nic Ros, a member of ACW's Drama Board in 1994–5 and a Lecturer in Drama at the University of Wales, Bangor. In the *New Welsh Review* in 1997, he explained that Brith Gof's funding was decreased because of 'growing ACW disatisfaction with the company's work'. Instead, 'the development of . . . exciting companies . . . [needed] to be prioritised . . . companies like Volcano'.[28]

The structure of feeling in Wales supported Volcano. However, had the company been subject to another order of referentiality, matters might have been different. In fact, contrasting views of Volcano were available. Ian Shuttleworth, writing in the *Financial Times*, described *The Message* as a 'disappointing hotchpotch';[29] and Lyn Gardner of the *Guardian* (which had largely dispensed with reviews of productions in Wales by the late 1990s) pronounced that *Moments of Madness* was lacking in 'theatricality'.[30] Moreover, although Volcano had acquired a reputation as Wales's leading international theatre company, foreign reviews could also be antipathetic, as in the case of a Russian critique which described the company as 'pretentious and feeble'.[31]

Additionally, when critiques of their work were made within Wales, as when Caitlin O'Reilly described *Vagina Dentata* as 'the worst of the avant garde',[32] Volcano were allowed to respond in a manner which implied that the company occupied a special territory beyond criticism. In his reply to that review, Paul Davies dismissed O'Reilly's prose as a 'jumbled collection of half-baked, ancient, academic terminology'. Moreover, Davies was himself in a position to add to Volcano's referential status by writing articles for the *New Welsh Review*.[33]

During the 1990s, *NWR* played a key role in encouraging structures of feeling about theatre. The most obvious incident of its privileging the gatekeepers involved Michael Baker, then ACW Drama director, who was allowed to review David Adams's book, *Stage Welsh*.[34] But the most telling example of the functioning of the gatekeepers was when Hazel Walford Davies dedicated *State of Play* to one former Drama director of ACW, Michael Baker, and the book was then reviewed in *NWR* by another – Gilly Adams.[35]

The majority of articles appearing in the *New Welsh Review* from the mid-1990s were written by individuals who were hospitable to, or workers in, developmental theatre. However, these contained ideas which had been gaining in currency over some twenty years. Like the playwriting 'group', the 'developmentalists' created a set of reference points which helped the spread of referential power through the growth of a common, approved language. Both the playwrights and the experimental theatre practitioners were being urged to look towards Europe. But while the former were encouraged to turn to Ibsen, the latter were pointed towards Eugenio Barba. What commentators like David Hughes ignored, though, was that there was a growing body of opinion which held that the 'developmentalists' were just

as entrenched in their views about what constituted theatre as the adherents
to the written play. Hughes's contention that '[Theatre companies] striving
to find new languages, hybridizing their theatrical and cultural forms . . .
have emerged as having the voice which Wales seems to understand' was
coming increasingly under suspicion.[36]

It perhaps did not help the cause of developmental theatre that some of its
cohort seemed to be interested in promoting ideas about theatre without
knowing much about the Welsh lived experience. For instance, Gordana
Vnuk, former theatre programmer at Chapter Arts Centre, in an interview
in the *Western Mail* in 1999, opined that the 'innovative arts' is where the
'future belongs' for Wales. Yet, during an interview with Heike Roms when
Vnuk was first appointed, Vnuk had admitted that she '[didn't] know a lot
about Welsh theatre'.[37] Although Chapter rightly seeks to consolidate its
considerable international reputation as a flagship for the contemporary
arts, its aim of promoting 'the best performance from Wales' may not have
been ideally served by a programmer who had limited knowledge about the
culture within which the arts centre is located, and who might therefore
have experienced difficulties in providing effective mediation between inter
national product and local constituencies.

After the Drama Strategy, developmental theatre experienced some
changes in profile. Brith Gof and the Magdalena project lost their revenue
status, while other companies were made increasingly reliant on project
funding. Of the developmental companies, Volcano alone was promoted and
awarded three-year funding. Critical reactions to these changes centred on
the idea that *because* it seemed to be devaluing the experimental, the Arts
Council was, therefore, artistically conservative.[38]

The flaw in the thinking about developmental theatre, as it presented itself,
was that terms like 'experimental' and 'innovative' were used in a very
generalized way to refer exclusively to theatre companies which drew on
particular, non-naturalistic, European traditions of making theatre; and the
implication was that those who engaged with the written play and the playwright were not experimental and innovative. Jeni Williams went so far as to
criticize what she saw as a 'Stalinist rejection . . . of the creativity that expresses itself in written language while valuing . . . that associated with the
eye'.[39] Like David Hughes before her, Williams suggests that what Welsh
theatre needed to do was grow up; but while Hughes defined mature theatre
as the developmental, Williams implied that grown-up theatre is that which
incorporates the written text – a polarization of the arguments, which positioned playwriting and performance-making at opposite ends of the theatre
spectrum.

This reductiveness is partly accounted for by the looming presence
throughout the 1990s of that bogus term 'physical theatre', the use of which
led to discursive culs-de-sac. Theatre practitioners used it to camouflage

some very flaccid thinking. But, because Wales had experienced a vibrant developmental theatre culture, the term 'physical theatre' acquired some resonance there.

Both the advocates of the written play and the protagonists of the develop‑mental seemed to share a belief that the prime purpose of Welsh theatre is to develop a *mature* theatre practice that is capable of challenging the people of Wales and leading them away from parochialism. Where they are different is which art-form they think is best suited to achieving this. Fundamentally, however, they are on the same side because their attitudes towards the political and ideological relationships between performer, production and audience have marked similarities.

Raymond Williams considered that the paradox of the avant-garde is that, like the bourgeois theatre, which it claims to challenge, it denigrates the human condition by representing it as a 'fragmented ego in a fragmented world'. Far from challenging audiences, in Williams's view the avant-garde reduces the 'scale of human possibility and human action'.[40]

The means of production amd the indicative drama

The problem of the avant-garde, as far as Raymond Williams was con‑cerned, is that it does not often attack the dominant means of production (and the fact that few critiques and analyses of theatre investigate this is, I would argue, the nub of the problem with the referential status of most theatre practices). There is, therefore, a big difference between cod-alter‑native and genuinely oppositional theatre practices. The developmental often tries to legitimize itself by laying claim to progressiveness and new‑ness. However, as Williams argues, the emergent is 'not identical with the innovatory'.[41] In his opinion, the authentic emergent is characterized by 'new meanings and values, new practices, new relationships'.[42]

Although developmental companies positioned themselves as being experi‑mental, for the most part experiment was confined to the style, form and content of the piece of theatre itself, rather than to the means of production. The developmental has been absorbed into the dominant in ways that would have seemed unlikely twenty years ago. As a result, experimental perform‑ance-makers and adherents of playwriting have much more in common with each other than they seem to think.

In Wales, what ought to be of concern to those with referential power is not whether or not the written text is valuable, or if a piece of theatre is innovative, but how that theatre practice might be capable of challenging the prevailing means of production. Many theatre companies in Wales (and in the UK, as a whole, it must be said) have been cautious about trying different and radical methods of production, by which I mean the way in which a company organizes itself and establishes its own lived experience in the larger social context within which it is located. (Paradoxically, Volcano had one of the most interesting ways of working; as a workers' cooperative, the company did, indeed, challenge the conventional means of production. But few commentators took account of this, preferring to concentrate on the company's form and style.)

Practical logistics, along with economic imperatives, pressurize theatre companies into operating in certain ways. Road links influence the location of companies, for instance; so companies gravitate towards centres like Cardiff, rather than, say, Bedlinog. Equally, by being based in Cardiff, theatre companies benefit from networking with all those other organizations, as well as fellow theatre companies, that are based there. But it is not just about location. The means of production also affect the length of time a company can spend preparing and rehearsing a project, and the number of perform-ances which needs to be given and where the touring schedules take a production. Hence, given the usual constraints, it is not financially viable for a theatre company to break with the conventional means of production.

Moreover, it is difficult for a new theatre company to emerge with a way of working that reconfigures the usual means of production because, once one company is *in situ* with a particular niche-market, any new company can only succeed by replacing the existing company; and, generally, the Arts Council tends to continue to subsidize the already known because they have acquired referential power. The problem then becomes: how do the emergent emerge and how does a theatre company attack the means of production and prevail-ing opinions?

The link between playwriting the text and developmental playmaking is that both are, to use Raymond Williams's terminology, 'indicative drama': that is, they tend to describe the world as it is. They don't hypothesize by employing the 'subjunctive', by asking: 'what if this happened?'[43] Because *hypothesizing* theatre has not been widely available in Wales, the collective sociohistorical and cultural experience of Wales has not been adequately explored. Contingent and suppositional theatre, at least in terms of content, would be one way of developing a challenge to the dominant means of production. This brings us to the work of the 'community' theatre companies of Wales, who have attempted to create a theatre practice that amalgamates the writer with the physical-visual and also reconfigures the means of production; but who have not, generally, enjoyed the kind of referential status that I have been discussing up to this point.

TYP and 'community' theatre

Raymond Williams maintained that theatre needs to be developed from 'where reality is being formed, at work, in the streets, in assemblies'.[44] Although the nomenclature of Wales's community theatre companies has changed over the years – community touring, Theatre-in-Education, Theatre for Young People – such companies are characterized by a willingness to work where, they would argue, 'reality is being formed'.

In the rest of the UK, many TiE companies lost their funding during the 1980s and 1990s, and Wales is unique in having a network of eight theatre companies dedicated to working out of and with specific communities: indeed, Dic Edwards has described the TiE movement in Wales as 'the strongest in Britain and perhaps globally'.[45] The fact that most TYP companies, as the TiE and community companies are now generally known, are not based in Cardiff, but in smaller locales, such as Llwynypia, Abergavenny and Llandrindod Wells, is worth noting in any discussion of the relationship between theatre and the lived experience.

Like the playwriting traditions and the avant-garde, TiE is regarded as an import; Gill Ogden contends that TiE was originally an 'English' form. However, she also says that it has been transformed into a Welsh practice through its application.[46] But, unlike other forms of theatre, TiE has seldom been given referential status in the form of reviews or features in the media, despite the fact that, in Ogden's opinion, TiE has produced some of 'the most innovative and dynamic experimental theatre' in Wales.[47]

Here, though, lies one of the predicaments of theatre taxonomy in Wales, because understandings can be fluid. David Hughes, for instance, cites Brith Gof and other experimental groups as also having tried to '[make] work for and with the people of the rural communities and small towns'.[48] Accordingly, there is a complex situation where experimental companies produce theatre that is intended to engage with the lived experience; and TiE companies develop theatre that relates to the lived experience but which is also experimental. (This is comparable to the playwriting/developmental discourses, referred to earlier, where playwrights write plays which may also be experimental, and experimental companies may make performances using a written play-text.)

Both developmental practitioners and the advocates of playwriting have expressed reservations about the influence of community touring on theatre practice in Wales, particularly in relation to the establishment of a dominant aesthetic. Mike Pearson, for instance, averred that the scope of Welsh theatre was constrained by the fact that, 'all of theatre practice in Wales was being defined [in the 1970s and 1980s] by what you could get in the back of a Transit van'.[49] Meanwhile, the play-writers have suggested that, although TYP companies have been an important source of commissioning new writing, TiE productions have sometimes suffered from an impoverished and limiting use of language because plays can be subject to the collective, devised process.

Even from within community theatre, comments show that there are tensions over what theatre of this kind should be doing in terms of form and strategy and that, moreover, TiE contains within it the same arguments over aesthetics that bifurcate the play-writers and the play-makers. In one of the most insightful essays ever written about theatre in Wales, Greg Cullen raises some critical issues while reflecting on his experiences as writer-in-residence at Theatr Powys, one of Wales's longest-established community companies. Cullen crystallizes the difficulties of developing playwriting that engages with the lived experience when he argues that: 'hiring writers who . . . wish . . . to write about ideas misses the point . . . to tour a community with theatre which does not make sense to it is a fatuous exercise.'[50] His beliefs refocus both the play-writers' and the play-makers' arguments because what he touches on is the crux of the matter, which is that engagement with the community comes first and that all else is subservient to and dependent upon it. If this becomes the writer's basic premise, then this is bound to have considerable and determining consequences for the aesthetic. As Charles Way, another play-wright who has been widely performed by community companies, observes: playwrights in Wales write 'for audiences that don't share the same concerns as the audiences that frequent the Royal Court', an opinion that contrasts sharply with the view that Welsh playwrights ought to want to write plays that are targeted at the Royal Court.[51]

Community theatre companies can also have complex problems in challenging the dominant means of production. At one end of the spectrum, Gwent Theatre was able to capitalize on its relationship with the local community when, after working for more than twenty-five years in south-east Wales to provide artistic and cultural events for the people of Abergavenny and its environs, the company's future was threatened with the potential loss of its ACW franchise. The community actively supported the campaign to protect the company because, as Caroline Sheen, one of its youth theatre alumni, commented: '[Gwent] Theatre is an integral part of the Gwent community'.[52] At the other end of the spectrum, though, reports from behind the scenes of community companies show that those who work in community theatre in Wales are by no means as committed to a different ideology as might be thought. Greg Cullen reveals that, in reality, the members of Theatr Powys had few links with its community and scant social knowledge of the local people during the 1980s.[53] For many of the actors, he argues, working in a community theatre company was just a career move. This manifested itself in 'the superior sense of good taste that some [company] members felt they held over their audience'.[54]

Greg Cullen and Charles Way are both playwrights, albeit ones who approach writing in a different way from that of many of the new writers. So Cullen's conclusion that, in Wales, it is 'the work of writers . . . [that] has been most undervalued' is predictable. Cullen and Way share the views of the advocates of playwriting towards the developmental in Wales. Cullen considers that 'experimentation [has been] uncritically encouraged'[55] and Way observes that '[it has been said] that narrative theatre [is] dead', although he adds that he has 'yet to see the corpse'.[56]

The reason why Greg Cullen's essay is significant is because he talks about community theatre in aesthetic as well as sociocultural terms, whereas the standing of community theatre has often been compromised by the perception that it exists outside of referential power: few TiE productions have acquired critical status in Wales, let alone elsewhere. When reviewers cover community theatre, there is often a sense of their being patronizing. Although the reality is that many community theatre practitioners are divisible into play-writers and play-makers, reviews tend to treat community theatre events as though they were commendable only for their social use (and, likewise, reviews of 'proper' theatre productions do not tend to touch on anything outside of the aesthetics).

Take, for example, a critique of a project produced by Small World with intergenerational communities in Ely, Cardiff. Jeni Williams's review is clearly not meant to be qualified. Yet, when she says that Small World are 'exemplary practitioners of *community* theatre' (my emphasis), this can be read as a reminder that what Small World do is not theatre per se. Indeed, she goes on to substantiate that impression by arguing that this kind of theatre is not 'theatre in the sense of a defined and sophisticated end product and should not . . . be judged . . . like . . . pieces written for the professional theatre: the value of this kind of theatre . . . lies in its ability to change individual lives'.[57]

Williams wants to be laudatory; nevertheless, the reason why there is an unhelpful binary system of theatre in Wales is partly because community theatre has been shunted into a critical siding. The subtext of how we talk about it implies that it is away from, yet also beneath, referential power: some lesser species of theatre that is outside of strategic formation, that occupies a branch of social welfare which, like an incontinence sheet, provides a basic service. To say that the chief value of this kind of theatre lies in its capacity to change lives is to place an enormous burden on community theatre, which no theatre company ought to have to accept. It is extraordinarily divisive to argue that one kind of production can be evaluated by assessing its use of structure, form and images, and so on, whilst another is to be tested on its capacity to alter people's lives. Steve Davis, artistic director of Spectacle, argues rightly that community theatre is effective when 'it is first and foremost good theatre'. Moreover, he contends that there is no reason why, given a level critical playing field, community theatre could not enhance Wales's reputation on the international stage. As he says, the work of Joan Littlewood, Welfare State International and 7:84 all derived from community contexts and yet have had international success.[58]

Evidence suggests that the subliminal idea that community theatre, and
its variations, is not 'proper' theatre has had an influence on funding
decisions. Joanna Weston asserted that ACW's funding of projects that
ensure access to all members of the community is '*alongside* its firm commitment to excellence' (my emphasis).[59] Community practices are, then, parallel
to, but not synonymous with, excellence. Weston's attitude has an ante-
cedent in Roy Bohana's view (Bohana was deputy director of WAC/ACW
between 1982 and 1995) that standards 'cannot be secured by ill-equipped
teams of strolling players performing one-night stands in village halls'.[60]

Moreover, the notion that community theatre, and its variations, occupies
a critical no-man's land is substantiated by the findings of an internal audit
report by PricewaterhouseCoopers in August 2000, which stated that a major
reason why the TYP review was disastrous was that ACW had not identified
the objectives of TYP in Wales, including those to do with audiences, spaces
and methodologies.

That being so, there is a further consideration to be made about the
subtext of the Arts Council's attitude to community theatre. ACW's explanation for the TYP franchises was that it wanted to honour a 'long standing
commitment to increasing the proportion of funding to . . . the South Wales
Valleys . . . the decision to base three . . . new companies in the valleys
recognised the additional community benefit of having producing arts
companies resident not just visiting these areas'.[61] Yet, if ACW acknowledges there is a problem with the location of theatre companies and also
that touring has political implications, we might wonder why the 'proper'
theatre companies, as it were, were not encouraged to be resident in the
Valleys. One inference which might be drawn is that forms of theatre which
tend to be perceived as lacking in referential status are good enough for the
working classes.

The theatre practices outlined thus far are not the only approaches to
community theatre, however, for there are examples of theatre which have
attempted to attack the means of production and which tap in to the local
lived experience while also trying to establish their own production values.
There is, though, a big difference between the way in which Ewart Alexander
has written plays for Ystradgynlais, for example, and the way in which much
TiE is produced: not least because Alexander is actually from Ystradgynlais.[62] Secondly, his views about theatre challenge some of the basic
assumptions that characterize the dominant thinking. For instance, he
argues that 'Wales is just not big enough to sustain a constant number of
worthwhile plays'; he also thinks that some individuals are too hasty in
calling themselves playwrights, just because they happen to have written one
or two plays. As for the 'developmental', Alexander asserts that 'too often
the so-called innovative is at best only novel'.[63] His contention that 'there
has been too much dependence on Arts Council funding at all levels of

drama production in Wales to the detriment of quality' is important.[64] Instead of relying on subsidy, which might well carry with it pressures and limits, Alexander's play for the local community found different forms of finance and these, along with some of its production methods, represent a way of developing different means of production. Institutions and organizations already existing in the village were utilized; amateurs and professionals were joined together in a hybridized practice; and local community groups themselves contributed to the finances of the project, collectively and severally. Ewart Alexander's composite methodology in Ystradgynlais achieves a means of reconciling concerns about 'standards' with a theatre practice which emerges out of the lived experience, but which is brave enough to eschew the usual conventions of referential status.

Liminality and occupying boundaries

Although it assumes great importance, the reality of referential power/status is that even those who enjoy it have fundamental differences. The evidence of the arguments indicates a deep fissure in Welsh theatre. Paul Davies of Volcano makes a very salient point about the polarities, and perhaps even incompatibilities, of Welsh theatre:

> what the 'grassroots' or communities want, and what the Assembly and its Arts Agency hopes to deliver may, in practice, be very different. It is at this fundamental point of difference that we might discover that our culture holds a lot less in common than we had originally envisaged.[65]

Davies is probably right that Welsh theatre and performance culture is never going to resemble the United Colors of Benetton. The difficulty, however, is that the possible accommodation of different views about theatre in Wales is, at present, handicapped by systems of subsidy which load the dice in favour of some kinds of theatre and not others, so that what happens in the 'grass roots' is hampered by its taking place in a less propitious context than that which has referential power. The problem, therefore, is to ameliorate the difficulties that binary thinking causes through strategies that could develop liminality.

There are three meanings of the term 'liminal'. It can refer to a transitional stage, or to being marginal and insignificant, or to occupying a position on a boundary or threshold. The idea of Wales inhabiting a frontier, or border, between settled and unsettled territories of performance practice is intriguing. If we imagine theatre/performance in Wales as being in a state of transition between the established orthodox and radical parochialism, then we need to consider how to 'decolonize the mind' of Welsh theatre to achieve a different mindset. What we need to do, therefore, is examine ways of refusing our consent.

In John Hodge's filmscript of Irvine Welsh's novel *Trainspotting*, the central character, Renton, has this to say:

> I hate being Scottish. We're the lowest of the fucking low, the scum of the earth, the most wretched, servile, miserable, pathetic trash that was ever shat into civilization. Some people hate the English, but I don't. They're just wankers. We, on the other hand, are colonized by wankers. We can't even pick a decent culture to be colonized by. We are ruled by effete arseholes. It's a shite state of affairs . . .

Renton's peroration is also very applicable to Wales because it does not treat its subjects as victims but, rather, makes them responsible for their collusion with panopticism and with strategies that have been employed to block their own indigenous performance practices. Instead of being junior partners in our own disempowerment, the alternative is to evolve distinctive tactics for theatre-making which resist orthodoxies. Some organizations have already been doing that and I would like to turn now to a major example of contestation.

Methods of resistance: the website

The Theatre in Wales website is, perhaps, the most important example of resistance to orthodoxy.[66] It was created by Keith Morris in Aberystwyth in 1996 and has become a major theatre resource. It contains news, features, details about venues, companies and performers, a play archive of all the 672 new productions by Welsh companies since 1991 and reviews of current productions. The website acts as an egalitarian method of 'networking' because it passes on information about events and puts people in touch with one another for professional purposes. Morris has also edited, with Gill Ogden, a reference book.[67]

The website receives no funding and functions through its unpaid contributors. Because of its financial status, the website is 'free of editorial control and can be a disinterested channel' of expression. It does, though, 'reserve the right to remove anonymous messages and any others of a defamatory nature', more on which later. Of course, the website is available only to those who have access to a computer and to the internet, both of which are expensive to set up in the home; so there is a financial constriction on who can access the website, which restricts its availability, even though it is possible to gain access to the web through public organizations.

Nevertheless, the Theatre in Wales website is one of the most productive means by which cultural democracy can be developed in Wales. This is because you do not need an invitation to join in the discussion. Furthermore, although anonymity is frowned on, it is possible to speak without revealing yourself. The website's Forum is a real mechanism for debate and the dissemination of information. Indeed, Keith Morris acknowledges that the 'occasional Deep Throat in the corridors of power' has disclosed details. Whilst it is difficult to prove that putting such information in the public domain has affected decision-making, there is no doubt that the website's capacity to remind those in power that certain details are known acts as a check on potential action. Given the named replies to the Forum, it is clear that, *inter alia*, the chairman of ACW reads the site, as do many directors of theatre companies.

Contributors to the website will often contextualize points of view that might otherwise be taken at face value if they appeared through the usual channels. For instance, Roger Tomlinson put forward some criticisms of the website on the grounds that, in his view, the forthrightness of the debate against the Arts Council would make Welsh theatre practitioners look unseemly. However, his position was called into question when Janek Alexander, director of Chapter Arts Centre, informed the website that Tomlinson had 'neglected to say that his organisation . . . [was] one of the winners in the [ACW] Drama Strategy'.[68]

Before the advent of the website, it was often difficult to obtain information and to participate in the discourse of theatre in Wales. Finding details was time-consuming and, sometimes, they were protected or controlled by interested parties. But by September 2002, for example, there were 117 items on the website on the Drama Strategy and 233 on ACW.

Also important is the opportunity, for those who might otherwise be excluded from arts fora, to express a point of view. The website Forum tackles a range of subjects including, for instance, the Millennium Centre for the Performing Arts, alternative reviews of play productions, and, of course, the Arts Council. Exchanges are immediate, random, unmediated and unexpurgated. Individuals are able to contribute at all hours of the day. At times, usual conventions of address and, even, of courtesy are discarded. Contributions can be misspelled and ungrammatical. The discourse is allowed to find its own level without being chaired and disciplined and part of its value is that 'webversation' seems to produce a kind of disembourgeoisement that challenges pomposity and intellectual arrogance in a way that does not happen at conferences and meetings. It can be brutal and rude, but it also makes explicit the subtext of attitudes which, before, were only revealed through chance encounter or behind closed doors. Such terms of engagement have been important for the website. Keith Morris has, in fact, exercised censorship and erased some correspondence, but not without a debate in which it was clear that not everyone agreed. Some demurred at the use of 'bad' language, while others thought that content should be subject to restraints.

That debate inadvertently brought out some important issues which perhaps would not have been revealed through the conventional review process, like the competitive nature of the Welsh performance world. The website has highlighted the hostilities of theatre in Wales – 'Underneath all the politics and general nastiness is there still any real passion for theatre?', asked one contributor.[69] It could be argued, though, that the website has served a useful purpose in exposing the existence of such resentments. There was criticism, for instance, of the way in which Gwent Theatre organized their campaign to have their grant reinstated by complaining about aspects of their 'rival' Theatr Iolo's profile and also of Spectacle's perceived reluctance to speak out against Gwent's possible demise.

The opportunity to make theatre tensions public is one of the website's most important roles. It is crucial that the half-submerged frictions are allowed to surface and be acknowledged. The history of theatre in Wales is the history of who has had the power to influence the attitudes that have shaped the configuration of theatre forms and practices – dispositions which have been at the roots of why, for instance, theatre company X and not Y has been awarded subsidy. By enabling the undercurrents of attitudes to be expressed, the website brings them to a point where they can be properly identified.

This is illustrated by an anonymous outburst on the website on 17 April 2000:

> Terry Hands [artistic director Clwyd Theatr Cymru] . . . what do we get . . . a three part epic of a sub-standard Welsh novel . . . how bloody patronising . . . has the Torch [theatre] finally and thankfully burnt out? . . . Talk to any actor in Cardiff and what they really want is Phil Clark [artistic director of the Sherman] to be finally given the push . . . Frank Vickery, that sub-standard, am-dram valleys playwright . . . Jeff Teare [former artistic director of Made in Wales] . . . has done nothing to enhance Welsh writing . . .[70]

Although this is old material, I have quoted from it at length because the correspondent's message points to an important basic principle. While you might want to dismiss the content as a rant, the points s/he makes have been made by others, except that they have been expressed in the language of formal criticism. (It is unusual to find all these attitudes coming from one, single source.) Beneath the conventions of formal discourse and behind the façades of orderly procedures, the real thought processes and attitudes which have shaped the Welsh theatrical/performance landscape can be similar to those of the ranting correspondent cited above. The difference is that the ranter probably is not in a position to match funding to her/his predilections, whereas some of the more decorous are; and we should all have some concerns about that.

Another important issue is that of the role of theatre criticism. The website has established opportunities for the reviewing of plays to be egalitarianized, which is a good development. It is not entirely convincing that theatre reviews, in general, are either desirable or useful, but it is at least sensible to open up the room for writing them. In Wales, the power to make public statements about theatre has been limited to a very narrow constituency. David Adams, the major reviewer of Welsh theatre, has, rightly, criticized the 'paucity of informed criticism'.[71] However, while suggesting that the difficulties of the drama strategy could have been ameliorated by the public's participation in debates about the culture, Adams also states that matters would have been different if the people of Wales had been 'given the opportunity to *witness* the arguments of *informed and professional* critics' (my emphasis).[72]

The problem with Adams's position is that it is part of the panoptic method of approach described in chapter 3. Witnessing an argument is not at all the same thing as participating in it. We have to wonder what the definition of an 'informed and professional critic' is: presumably, not the website ranters; or those others who, we assume, need to learn from professional critics what kinds of theatre it is appropriate to believe in.

The process of reviewing is akin to that of 'orientalism' as defined by Edward Said: 'the Orient is *controlled* by making statements about it, teaching about it, describing it' (my emphasis).[73] As Said also reminds us, the power to block 'narratives . . . is very important to culture and imperialism, and constitutes one of the main connections between them'.[74] The nature of theatre reviewing is beset by difficulties to do with the imposition of value judgements – the blocking of narratives – masquerading as well-informed *knowledge*.

The importance of the Theatre in Wales website is that it has enabled a wider range of voices to be heard in the critique of play production, and this has led to some robust exchanges. In one such exchange, contributor Stanley Leary challenged Jeni Williams's views and, in doing so, revealed a certain bias in her thinking. Leary's comments on *Hamlet*, directed by Firenza Guidi of Elan, registered 'a profound disappointment in the "quality" of the [production]', which he thought was 'arrogant and naive'.[75] Jeni Williams disagreed with his critique, but, in acknowledging that she '[thinks] highly of Ms Guidi's work', confirmed that she is guilty of the 'partisan effusiveness' that she claims to want to avoid.[76]

What this episode reminds us is that, no matter how 'professional' play reviewing is, it is still a value judgement and, as such, should not carry with it the capacity to create the referential power that productions and theatre companies acquire, a factor which is more influential in the awarding of subsidy than we perhaps care to acknowledge. The website is an important means by which the strategic formation of theatre hierarchies can be reconfigured.

Reconstruction and regeneration

One way of moving forward is, paradoxically, by being more mindful of the past. We have not been particularly good at learning from Welsh theatre history — unsurprisingly, perhaps, when we consider how often Wales has been told that it does not have a theatre tradition worth mentioning. As Olive Ely Hart observed in the 1920s: the drama of Wales 'may prove to be the channel best fitted to link the culture of the past with the life of the present'.[77]

But decolonizing the mind relies not just on acknowledging the fallacies that have accreted during the historical processes of the development of referential power, or on reimagining the assumptions of theatre practice, but also on evolving different ways of working. Some Welsh theatre workers are already thinking along these lines. Paul Davies, for instance, argues that '[the] relationship [that theatre companies have] with the public, and the public sphere itself, may be the critical test by which [their] practice is communicatively ordered'.[78] The notion of pluralism is critical, it seems, to some visions of future practice; Krishnendu Majumdar contends that, 'for Welsh theatre to truly thrive, we have to be comfortable with multiple Welsh identities'.[79]

What I would argue is that an embedded relationship with the public, of the kind that is implied by Davies and Majumdar, can best be developed by discarding orthodox approaches to critical thinking about theatre. So that, instead of locating theatre as an art-form, we might find helpful the attitude of, say, the Shakers, who believed that form followed function and therefore that 'art' was (merely) a by-product of usefulness. (Friedrich Engels modelled the ideal commune on the Shakers.) They also believed in simplicity and in a lack of artifice; the style of a piece of furniture developed organically out of its intended use. Hence, it was beautifully made *because* it was entirely functional. If the item did the job, it was, *ergo*, an excellent artefact. We could do a lot worse than apply this thinking to theatre/performance practice. It is worth noting that, before the seventeenth century, the 'artist' was regarded as an artisan. According to *The Oxford Companion to Art* (1992), before the sixteenth century painting, for example, was thought of as a specialized manual craft. During the Middle Ages 'artists' were even regarded as 'mechanics'. Raymond Williams in *Keywords* (1983) claims that the term 'artist' was, from the sixteenth century onwards, used to describe 'any skilled person'. He argues that 'the emergence of an abstract, capitalized **Art**' was a nineteenth-century development. Indeed, as Williams observes, most sciences were regarded as arts before the eighteenth century. His explanation for the changes in usage lies in the development of 'art' as a commodity.[80] My own point is that our general understanding of theatre/performance as 'art' might be unhelpful and a return to accepting the performing 'artist' as a skilled worker or artisan could be more productive, not least because, as Terry Eagleton has contended in *The Ideology of the Aesthetic* (1990), '[when art is] sequestered from all other social practices, [it becomes] an isolated enclave within which the dominant social order can find an idealized refuge from its own actual values of competitiveness, exploitation and material possessiveness'.[81]

But thinking anew is not just about function and form, it is also about money. The kind of codependency that has grown up between the Arts Council and theatre companies is debilitating. Paul Davies, again, makes a sound point when he asserts that 'arguments for theatre mean interacting with the actual world', with, for instance, 'the low level of earnings for most performers'. His observation that 'market is a word that seems very difficult for those in the arts in Wales to pronounce' is particularly apposite.[82]

Both the income of performers and the ways in which they engage with the 'market' might be improved by exploring alternative methods of funding; and here is a good example of where it might be helpful to look towards the history of Welsh theatre, because there is evidence of interesting methods of funding being used before the existence of the Arts Council by the amateurs. During the early part of the twentieth century, for instance, each member of the Little Theatre, Aberdare, contributed 6d a week. By 1936, audience members bought season tickets for 7s 6d and paid by instalments through collectors who called door to door. Tickets for individual shows were also sold in this way. Up to the 1940s, a welfare levy was collected from miners' wages at the local collieries, part of which was used to subsidize the Coliseum, Aberdare. Of course, this was before the creation of the Arts Council and the amateurs had no alternative but to be creative in finding money. But there are those who have argued for similar methods to be used today.

In 1984, Owen Kelly contended that theatre companies should create a need for what they produce, so that communities would want to pay directly for theatre. Kelly maintains that artists use the excuse of requiring state funding to disguise their fear that audiences will not pay for their services and he cites the early trade unions, who raised their own funds despite working out of a background of poverty. His basic position is that real cultural democracy can be achieved only through a financial commitment of the kind operating in the early co-operative societies. Indeed, he goes so far as to say that arts projects should not take place if the state funding they accept forces them to compromise their ideals. Projects should therefore, he concludes, be funded from multiple sources. Most controversially, he believes that workers should cease to see themselves as needing the security of a salary.[83]

The Arts Factory in the Rhondda, the Cwmaman Institute and Ewart Alexander's community production in Ystradgynlais are examples of finding ways of shifting the emphases of funding so that there is less reliance on the usual Arts Council channels and more inclusion of community-raised funding. But it is, admittedly, more difficult for the traditional notion of professional theatre companies to operate in that way, which might suggest that we need to reconsider the conventions of the theatre company: perhaps, even, along the lines of orature where performers are not permanent, full-time professionals, but combine performance with other earning activities. Perhaps, also, we need to examine how theatre companies could develop as cultural agencies, where their own theatre practice is subsidized by the other activities they generate.

Theatre practitioners should have the power to determine their own performance practices in joint, equal and democratic collaboration with the diverse communities which produce the lived experience that surrounds them. We do not know what that kind of theatre would be like, because theatre companies have been so subject to the limits and pressures engendered by divers gatekeepers, curators, benefactors and patrons who, in a multiplicity of mainly well-meaning ways, push us all into producing and admiring performances we do not necessarily care for all that much. Some terrific theatre companies in Wales atrophied because they were compromised by the need to acquire referential status. We have perhaps lost sight of the fact that taste is not a methodology.

5

Conclusions: Changed Priorities

The central argument contained in this book is that the Arts Council exercises a disciplinary power which homogenizes and standardizes theatre practices. Indicators of quality and value have been developed that appear to be equitable and universal but which are, in reality, selective, metropolitan, bourgeois ideas of excellence. Audiences in Wales, irrespective of language differences, have tendencies in relation to class orientation, cultural practices, political beliefs and national identity that are particular and distinctive. Because of this, Welsh audiences can be disenfranchised from dominant theatre practices (the incorporated) when the connections between the lived experience and indigenous performance practices (the unincorporated) are underestimated. Additionally, the Arts Council's panoptic procedures might seem to promote theatre-as-product, rather than as a set of processes, which positions theatre within a capitalist mode of production in contradistinction to the means of production typical of many indigenous performance practices.

The power of theatre subsidy

The Arts Council has established an archive of rules which privileges certain kinds of theatre: for instance, revenue-funded companies have more status than project-funded companies. Because the Arts Council controls the money supply, it has been able to manipulate the organizing principles of decision-making and this has captured and disabled indigenous Welsh theatre practices.

At times, though, spending appears to suggest that Wales has been over-subsidized in comparison with England, information which serves the purpose of neutralizing potential Welsh complaints. In the mid-1990s, for example, ACE spent the equivalent of £0.55 per head of population on Drama, while ACW spent £1.04.[1] But a different picture emerges when the number of theatre companies per head of population is examined. In England, there was at that time one theatre company for every 68,000, whereas in Wales, there was one theatre company for every 85,000 people.[2] It is clear, then, that an examination of subvention on its own produces a complex reading and total revenue sums do not allow for a complete analysis. Despite that seemingly generous subsidy, Wales is still less well-served, in terms of its provision, than is England. David Newland, formerly director of VAM and currently ACW South Wales director, has compiled a set of statistics on how Wales's spending on the arts compares with that of the UK as a whole which suggest that devolution has made matters worse financially and that it is England which has benefited from the separation.

Table 8.
How Wales's arts spend compares with the UK

	Wales	England	Scotland	N Ireland
Arts Council direct grant-in-aid[a] 2000–1	£13.7m	£336.5m	£26.4m	£5.7m
Direct grant-in-aid per head	£4 65	£6.73	£5.18	£3.40
Arts Council direct grant-in-aid[a] 2001–2	£14.7m	£347.8m	£30.3m	£7.4m
Direct grant-in-aid per head	£4.99	£6.95	£5.93	£4.40
% increase in 2001–2	7	3.2	12.9	26.5
Index (i.e. for each £1 spent in England)	72p	£1	85p	63p

I am indebted to David Newland for allowing me to use these figures, which were compiled by him.
a) Excluding operating costs and lottery costs.

As can be seen from Table 8, Wales has been spending far less per head on the arts than England. Moreover, and as David Newland observes, during the next few years England will also benefit from increased spending of some £25 million in relation to the *Boyden Report*. Even though the National Assembly for Wales announced in 2002 a spending increase on the arts of 23 per cent, Wales is still developing from a lower economic base.

But the problem of theatre in Wales is not just about money. It is also that ACW has espoused dominant bourgeois modes of thinking, which suggests that it satisfies Raymond Williams's criterion for the 'true condition of hegemony': that is, 'effective self-identification with the hegemonic forms'.[3]

The power of the Arts Council to determine what is seen in the theatre has depended on its capacity to link subsidy to definitions of excellence; and this has been supported by executive power, which has rested in the hands of a class and intellectual minority-elite (a 'selectorate') whose dispositions have privileged professionalized buildings over localized practices. Welsh theatre might, even, be said to have been structured to be inferior, because Wales has had a different experience of theatre practice from that of England and could not therefore match the criteria for incorporateable quality. Wales has enjoyed a strong amateur tradition, has not had a system of repertory theatre buildings comparable with England, has displayed an ambivalence towards every attempt at creating a unified 'national' theatre and has evinced a predilection for popular, localized performance strategies. Instead of capitalizing on these cultural conditions, the Arts Council has instead appeared to establish a theatre practice out of keeping with the reality of the lived experience in Wales.

The shaping of a centralized reality

The discrepancy between the lived experience and theatre practice is illustrated by the geography of theatre production in Wales. In 1994, the year that ACW became independent, some 50 per cent of WAC subsidized theatre companies were based in Cardiff, whereas only 4.3 per cent of theatre companies were based in Mid Glamorgan. Independence did not, however, appreciably alter that position. By 2001, 42 per cent of theatre companies were based in Cardiff and 3 per cent were in what used to be known as Mid Glamorgan.[4]

Centralization is a function of hegemony, which assumes that theatre practice is best organized at a pivotal point from which appropriate theatre product is distributed, thus ensuring that dominant standards are maintained. Although it could be argued that touring theatre militates against that state of affairs – since it is peripatetic, it matters little where it has been developed – this idea needs to be problematized, because touring theatre is also capable of delivering a centralized consciousness which produces definitions of reality outside of, and perhaps disconnected from, the audience's understandings of reality. Theatre practice cannot be indigenous and distinctive unless it emerges out of the full range of available, local cultural practices.

ACW's *Five Year Arts Development Strategy 2002–2007* makes much of the fact that the Arts Council is decentralizing, or devolving decision-making, as ACW terms it. However, whilst this strategy seems to represent change, that does not mean it will actually make a difference. For instance,

ACW states that it will appoint a National List of Advisers who will assess applications for funding, which gives it ample opportunity to ensure that approved 'experts' deliver the right kind of 'good quality product' that ACW continues to insist upon. It asserts that the basis of its strategy will be 'open dialogue with artists and arts organisations', yet no mention is made of a similar relationship with audiences. Most revealing is the sentence, 'where feedback indicates that changes need to be made, *ACW* will consider how best to make those changes' (my emphasis). Hence, ACW remains the arbiter of best practice. What appears to be a radical reorganization of the Arts Council may, in fact, be a rephrasing of the same first principles that have dogged the history of the Arts Council. It is, for instance, unnecessary to claim that accessibility to the arts needs to be increased, per se, because what some constituencies would define as the 'arts' – pub bands, say – is already easily accessible, albeit unsupported by public subsidy. Tellingly, the Development Strategy identifies what it really means by 'accessibility' when it makes special mention of the term 'mainstream professional theatre' in this context. Even after extensive reorganization, disciplinary procedures remain embedded in ACW's objectives: the idea of training for the community arts sector, for example, raises questions about the way in which training can be used as a means of insisting on a particular way of seeing theatre; and, in stating that funding will be given to organizations that 'contribute to the development of the Strategy', ACW subtly reminds potential applicants that funding will be dependent on producing the kind of theatre that ACW wants.

Welsh identities

Welsh theatre in the English language is widely perceived as being subsumed by the greater category of 'British' theatre. This ignores, though, that in order to define what Welsh theatre is in the English language, it is crucial to acknowledge its range of constituent voices. Part of reclaiming indigenous theatre involves resisting the idea that the English language inevitably homogenizes cultural identity; and recognizing the importance of class is critical to this.

The fact that Welsh plays in English are increasingly hard to promote suggests that what we are seeing in Wales is the widening struggle of metropolitan, middle-class theatre to charm and convince audiences. Attendance at incorporated theatre practices, in both Wales and England, is primarily the preserve of social groups ABC1, an audience that is in decline. Professional practitioners will have to admit, therefore, that they need the support of greater numbers from groups C1, C2 and D. In Wales, which has been shaped to a considerable extent by the working classes, theatre that is targeted at the middle classes, even if subliminally, is inevitably a practice which excludes a significant, informing constituency and which will disenfranchise many local constituencies from formal theatre practice.

The predicament is how Welsh theatre practice can include the working classes, whose popular culture has been unincorporated. In particular, the important question is how Welsh theatre procedures can be decolonized; and of crucial significance in this context is the whole area of the identification of worth, which is tied up with self-confidence. There is cause for optimism in the English-language cultural sea-change that has taken place in Wales and the nature of this transformation is encapsulated in a quote from the play *House of America* (1988). Ed Thomas's central characters, Sid and Boyo, reflect on the lack of Welsh heroes and, in doing so, exhibit the low self-esteem of a south Wales damaged by the failure of the 1984 miners' strike:

> SID: [Elvis] was the king, but look at Wales, where's its kings, where's our
>   heroes? . . . one answer, mate, we haven't got any.[5]

At the time when the play was originally written, Sid's words were reminiscent of Bertolt Brecht's aphorism: 'Unhappy the land that has no heroes . . . No, unhappy the land that needs heroes.'[6] More than a decade later, Welsh rock musicians, for instance, have been successful at raising the profile of the working classes of Wales and boosting the self-confidence of people in the Valleys; and this has added to the means by which the Welsh can articulate a sense of identity.

The dilemma for the English-speaking Welsh (as distinct from the pejorative 'Anglo-Welsh'), however, is how English-language theatre might articulate a specifically Welsh cultural identity, a difficulty which is compounded by warnings against romanticizing the past or of using nostalgia to drive narrative content. There is perhaps too much contumely attached to the informal list of banned clichés of Welsh identity markers – miners and pits, the figure of 'Mam', single mothers living desperate lives on housing estates, ageing, narrow-minded chapel-goers and the young unemployed dreaming of escape to London or America.[7]

Professional theatre practitioners in Wales have been too quick to dismiss local and national structures of feeling and over-eager to embrace accounts of atomized or non-stereotypical Welsh identities and, consequently, they have often produced theatre which fails to draw compelling ideas about Wales together through popular performance strategies, using archetypes in the context of familiar congregation. Most theatre practitioners would wish to avoid the easy stereotyping of Welsh culture, as displayed in the Hollywood versions of *How Green Was My Valley* and *The Corn is Green*. But a reluctance to examine the material of stereotypes may prevent Welsh theatre from exploring archetypes which provide the 'detail' necessary to discern meaning, rather than the detail which merely gives 'colour'.[8] The fear of incorporating the imagery of imperialist discourses is, itself, an outcome of imperialism.

If English-language theatre in Wales is to develop a distinctive complexion and move away from being 'a million miles from the values and agendas of most Welsh people, who spend little, if any, time contemplating their own Welshness',[9] then it can do so only by developing a *practice*, rather than a range of *products*, which emerges out of a negotiated structure comprising a localized producing company working directly with its constituency. The (postmodern) move towards presenting individuals (characters) as complex and multifaceted is admirable, but to ignore their relationships with economically determined class structures is an evasion of the realities of the lived experience in the Valleys. There is a *shared* experience of Welsh working-class life which has been underexamined in the context of theatre.

The south Wales Valleys

Theatre practice in Aberdare and the Valleys serves as a key to understanding the wider context of theatre in Wales, because it provides a particularly useful example of the unincorporated. The history of theatre practices in the Aberdare area shows the real impact of the Arts Council's disciplinary procedures on indigenous, working-class performance traditions in Wales and also demonstrates the way in which public theatre subsidy has functioned to disenfranchise large sectors of the general public. Such disempowerment is a by-product of professionalization; a fairly rigid model of excellence in theatre has been responsible for marginalizing those amateur performance traditions which connect the local lived reality with its representation through theatre. Moreover, the strategies of professional theatre tend to be significantly at variance with modes of production in the Valleys. It is not an accident of geography that Tower Colliery, near Aberdare, is the only deep mine in Wales that is owned and run by a collective. Tower's achievement is indicative of a local structure of feeling which ought to be instructive for theatre practice in the Valleys. Where production and consumption are integrated, as in the working practices of Tower, there is more of a will and commitment to succeed. Tower's distinctive mode of production could offer a new model for theatre practice in Wales: namely, that it can be localized by using its own producing companies, modes of production and signifying buildings.

For this reason, the architecture of the Coliseum might actually be seen as an advantage, rather than a problem, and the Cwmaman Institute could be considered deserving of revenue funding. Yet, these kinds of theatre spaces, which are inscribed with a multiplicity of local meanings, have no formal, in-corporated, status in the world of the Arts Council. In 1998, they accounted for exactly nought per cent of ACW's main drama funding,[10] Although the Cwmaman Institute received in that same fiscal year a Lottery award of £1.8 million, its theatre practices are of relatively low status, which makes it difficult for the institute to fulfil the criteria for incorporateable quality.

We have had over fifty years of public funding for theatre through the Arts Council, more than thirty of them with an Arts Council specifically for Wales, and yet Aberdare is barely better provisioned from the public purse, to which it contributes, than it was half a century ago. The description of Cwmaman by an arts consultant as a 'dead end' is telling, as it epitomizes what the Valleys seem to mean to many of those involved in professional theatre.[11]

Defining terms

The explanation for the self-identification of Welsh theatre practitioners with external, hegemonizing concepts about theatre lies chiefly in their endorsement of terms and definitions. Effective decolonization involves rejecting unproductive and irrelevant notions of theatre. But professional theatre practitioners in Wales are some distance from evincing independently evolved thought; the available, published material suggests that concepts about theatre practice dating back to the early part of the twentieth century have not been properly interrogated. Value-laden political assumptions have been accepted uncritically and continue to inform discourses about Welsh theatre. Yet in order for theatre procedures in Wales to develop independently, terminologies relating to quality would need to be reconfigured. These include consideration of the definition of professional theatre practice, what constitutes indigenous performance, the use of the term 'parochial' to de-stabilize the integrity of localized theatre, the idea of 'community theatre' in a Welsh context, and understandings of the relationship between cultural democracy and the role of the audience in the means of production.

A re-evaluation of the terms 'amateur' and 'professional' is crucial. Although Welsh cultural practices have tended to revolve around amateur traditions, the Arts Council has downgraded 'amateurism' and fetishized the professional. Amateur theatre practices have therefore been held under suspicion to the extent that they are often seen as inherently risible. The amateur and the professional have developed as separate, distinct entities, as though contact between the two would dissipate the integrity of the other. While there are valid economic and creative reasons for theatre practitioners to be paid as professionals, the formal location of professional theatre practice within the economic modes of production has had the effect of placing amateur theatre practice outside the economic superstructure and, consequently, on the margins of what is recognized as theatre practice. This closure has produced an unequal distribution of power between the amateur and the professional, so that professionals tend to perceive themselves as bringing something of value to the amateur, but not that the amateur might bring something to the professional. Performance efficacy in Wales could well evolve out of the dynamic of an amateur/professional hybrid in the context of a new concept of the 'producing' company.

The notion of what, exactly, constitutes an indigenous theatre tradition is obviously problematic. There is, first, a difficulty in the concept of time, that is how long a tradition needs to have existed before it can be said to have credibility. Then, secondly, there is the question of whether, in order to be considered Welsh, a tradition must have originated in Wales or can simply occur in the country. We might argue that, since theatre is a human construct, it cannot be said to be innate anywhere. Discourses on theatre in Wales tend to agree that there has not been an indigenous tradition of theatre; but this is to oversimplify the history of Welsh theatre. Cecil Price has provided evidence of a tradition of professional theatre in Wales for over 400 years. But the accepted reading of the import of this is that this tradition was a largely English cultural practice and cannot, therefore, be described as indigenous. This, though, ignores whole areas of cultural participation and dismisses the idea of cultural exchange. Price shows that several theatre companies had long periods of tenure in Wales – the Melville family in Swansea, the Stanton company at Wrexham and William Haggar through-out the coalmining areas of south Wales – and it is important to consider how such companies might have been influenced by their Welsh audiences as much as they influenced their audiences. Moreover, Price suggests that, as early as 1503, a Welsh company of actors was performing in Shrewsbury, which indicates that the theatre traffic, although limited, was moving both ways. So it is not necessary for Welsh theatre practitioners to feel obliged to 'invent' or 'imagine' new theatre practices simply for the sake of it, when there is the history of one to reappropriate on their own terms, if they so choose.[12]

The issue of 'parochialism' is an important aspect of this debate. The fear of theatre practice being narrow and inward-looking, particularly at a time of increasing internationalism, is well-founded. But centrally produced, national touring theatre is equally problematic. To some extent, this is a difficulty of language: parochialism is localism in the pejorative. The point, though, that local theatre practices may have difficulty in developing uni-versally understood meanings is well made by Baz Kershaw, who argues that 'contextuality . . . offers serious disadvantages to the achievement of a more general efficacy'.[13] Disapproval of localized theatre practices in Wales revolves around the view that plays needs must deal with the big issues in a wider context; so the depiction of 'provincial' narratives is attacked for its smallness. This ignores, however, the capacity of metaphor and allegory to travel and for the finely observed detail of small, local narratives to hold transferable signs and symbols meaningful to audiences other than those for whom the text was originally prepared. In Wales, parochialism is often also used interchangeably with nostalgia and sentimentality, terms improperly deployed to denigrate any use of the past. The contention is that, unless theatre provides a negative critique of events from history, it must, therefore, be sentimental. There is, however, a considerable difference between *yearning* for the past and *investigating* it.

Raymond Williams argued that 'community' is one of the most complex words in the English language, so it follows that 'community theatre' must also be one of the most complex terms in the vocabulary of theatre practice. Persistent underfunding of community arts projects often disables community theatre practices; and the poverty of the practice then conditions an aesthetic which compares unfavourably with the Arts Council's criteria for quality. Community theatre in Wales has become synonymous with the small, the powerless, the transitory and the unglamorous and this is perceived as having determined a distinctive and dull aesthetic. But, just because levels of funding seem to have constructed a stereotype of community theatre style and form in some instances, this does not mean that the notion of 'community theatre' per se is necessarily limiting. There is no unbreakable rule that community theatre cannot position itself in a conventional theatre space, or that it is imperative that it is peripatetic, or that it must always devise its play-texts. What matters about community theatre is its function within a defined community and its modes of production. Accordingly, community theatre companies could also be defined as experimental theatre companies, whereas the Arts Council and many theatre practitioners have a tendency to think that these terms are mutually exclusive. There is no logical reason why the Cwmaman Institute, for instance, could not be imagined as a developmental theatre venue.

If the notion of 'community theatre' is complex, understandings of 'cultural democracy' are even more so, for they question the whole commodity culture of the Arts Council. I have argued that one of the most significant outcomes of the imposition of disciplinary procedures is the development of theatre as a standardized product. Consequently, the democratic integrity of theatre practice relies on the willingness of professional performers to connect theatre productions with their audiences: unless grants are specifically tied to a theatre company's relationship with a constituency, there is no economic or aesthetic necessity for the audience to be included in the creative process. Of course, its gaze and response can be productive of meanings which 'complete' the process of theatre as art. But this traditional understanding of the relationship between methods of production and modes of consumption does not imagine the radical intervention of the 'gaze' in the production process itself. The problem of cultural democracy is that, while it is deemed to be an integral aspect of the aesthetic of community theatre, it is not understood to be a function of product-orientated theatre companies, irrespective of whether they are mainstream or developmental, fixed or touring.

The Arts Council and many professional theatre companies have a vested interest in obstructing certain modes of production. Funding is premised on the assumption that a production will occur at a pre-arranged time and place and under agreed circumstances. If it does not, it cannot be made to be visible, a fundamental requirement of panopticism, and therefore neither can it be regulated.

Cultural democracy necessarily involves intervention taking place throughout the whole creative process, even if that means disrupting the procedure or destroying the product. This is, however, an ideology which is fundamentally different from the Arts Council's. The bourgeois, metropolitan provenance of the Arts Council has led it to take a classicist approach to developing theatre; so it wants to create beautiful artefacts of lasting value.

For cultural democracy to work, though, professional theatre practitioners would need to be self-abnegating to the extent where they would be prepared to risk wrecking their own professional status. That means relinquishing their traditional, directive roles as missionaries, curators and gatekeepers (that is, as functionaries of externally devised, panoptic or disciplinary procedures) and, instead, developing a theatre practice which draws on models of relationships from within the local lived experience. The problems of not doing so are neatly summed up in *The Art of Regeneration*:

> Unless [arts] projects involve, and win the support of local people, they cannot be sustained over time. External solutions frequently produce only resentment and hostility . . . Planners [define the terms of engagement]. But they [do not always] see the town through the lived experience of its residents . . . They are limited by professional constructs.[14]

This Comedia report gets to the heart of the matter and its particular value is in treating the 'professional constructs' of the Arts Council as unproductive. Quality is not, then, about high product standards, whatever those are, but about developing a theatre practice whose identity is created by 'drawing on the unique nature of a place and its people'.[15]

The strategies of cultural democracy are incompatible with the Arts Council's 'archive of rules' concerning quality, where quality is the pre-eminent criterion for funding.[16] Whilst the Arts Council has acknowledged that quality is a broad term and accepts that there must be fitness of purpose, there is a widespread understanding of what 'quality' actually means in practice: that is, a piece of theatre which has 'high production values'. The problem is that these are selective value judgements masquerading as universal standards. It is in this sense that the notion of quality is hegemonic because it imposes one concept of order on what is assumed to be the natural chaos of unregulated, unincorporated theatre practice. Panopticism, or surveillance, is then a means by which quality and order can be ensured in an otherwise dangerously anarchic moral universe. It is for this reason that professionals are essential to the good governance of theatre, because they can, at the least, be relied upon to fulfil the terms of the contract and complete the product which, alone, testifies to the value of art.

Were the Arts Council to abandon its procedures relating to standardized performance indicators, which are the chief means by which panopticism functions, an altogether more effective and enfranchising climate could develop. The present system values and protects the well-disciplined. Hence, funding will be 'rationalized' by excluding those whose quality is indeterminate in Arts Council terms. Standardized notions of quality serve the interests of those who are theatre literate; so the middle classes and the educated are served well, or better, by incorporation, because it both fulfils and reinforces their expectations about theatre practice.

In a cultural democracy, fitness of purpose would be the *only* indicator of quality. Accordingly, we could conceive of the Blaengarw Community Play as having greater quality than a production by Clwyd Theatr Cymru, and Arts Council funding would be commensurate with that perception. The whole structure of funding would change to enable theatre in Wales to be reflective of the Welsh people, a radically different and differentiated practice from that which it has now.

Arts Council disciplinary procedures have led to definitions of 'quality' being used which are actually notions of art and not of performance efficacy. In Wales, where the evidence of socio-economic conditions, cultural practices and language differences supports the idea that Wales is another country, the *same* notions of art are used to appraise theatre practices emanating from a *different* lived experience.

To define art is to define reality. The description of a play, or a production, as 'good' or 'bad' is a value judgement indicative of the terms of reference of the adjudicator, and when such judgements are made in the context of funding decisions, the reality of subsidized theatre practice becomes dependent on selective notions of good or bad art. The project of cultural democracy is, therefore, the reclamation of definitions of reality from what Owen Kelly describes as 'the great tradition of European art', the Arts Council's promotion of which, he argues, is a form of imperialism.[17] The challenge to imperialist structures in Wales could include an understanding that Wales might develop performance practices different from those which have emerged in the context of a British or English tradition: practices which might not even resemble a European or American theatre tradition, but which might share impulses with African or Indian performance practices. If English-language theatre in Wales is understood as orature, rather than as an art form, perhaps its future could be imagined as *distinctively* Welsh.

The difficulties of theatre outlined in this book seem often to have been caused by different constituencies trying to converse without a common language and the resulting communication breakdowns have been somewhat disruptive. For the future, it would be good to see Welsh performance practitioners, whatever their preferences, being free to amaze with their *own* daring.

Notes

CHAPTER 1

[1] Gwyn A. Williams, *When was Wales?* (London: Penguin, 1991), 291.

[2] Ibid., 294.

[3] Social grade definitions taken from ACGB, *Extracts from 1991 RSGB Omnibus Survey: Report on a Survey of Arts and Cultural Activities in Great Britain* (London: ACGB, 1991). A is upper middle class, B middle class, C1 lower middle class, C2 skilled working class, D working class and E those at the lowest subsistence level.

[4] Dai Smith, *Aneurin Bevan and the World of South Wales* (Cardiff: University of Wales Press, 1994), 136.

[5] John (Pendar) Davies wrote accounts for the local paper about Aberdare's history from the 1860s to the 1930s, including theatre and performance practices. See Cynon Valley History Society, *Old Aberdare*, vol. 8 (Neath: Gwasg Morgannwg, 1997), 82–94.

[6] Pendar, in Cynon Valley History Society, *Old Aberdare*, ed. J. Mear, vol. 5 (Mountain Ash: D. J. Pryse, 1988), 35.

[7] Ibid., 37–8.

[8] Meic Stephens (ed.), *The Oxford Companion to the Literature of Wales* (Oxford: Oxford University Press, 1990), 152–3. (Hereafter *OCLW*.)

[9] Pendar, in *Old Aberdare*, vol. 8, 86.

[10] D. L. Davies, *A History of Cwmaman Institute* (Mountain Ash: D. J. Pryse & Son, 1994), 29.

[11] Geoffrey Evans, 'The amusement of the people: popular entertainment in Aberdare before moving pictures', in Cynon Valley History Society, *Old Aberdare*, vol. 7 (Cardiff: Chas Hunt & Co., 1993), 48.

[12] Pendar, *Old Aberdare*, vol. 5, 36.

[13] Smith, *Aneurin Bevan*, 70.

[14] Evans, 'Amusement of the people', 48–51.

[15] Ibid., 58.

[16] Ibid., 53–5.

[17] *Old Aberdare*, vol. 8, p. 86.

[18] Davies, *History of Cwmaman Institute*, 43.

[19] From an original document dated 20 November 1903, ARL, Cat. No. WH1/7/1.

[20] Aberaman Public Hall and Institute, 12 April 1910, ARL, Cat. No. WH1/7/6.

21 Author unidentified, 'Foundation to learning laid eighty years ago', *Aberdare Leader* (5 August 1982).

22 Davies, *History of Cwmaman Institute*, 24–5.

23 Jack Jones: see *OCLW*, PP. 308–9. Jones (1884–1970) was a novelist and playwright.

24 Jack Jones, 'Old engine shed that became a theatre', *Weekly Mail* (10 April 1939), ARL, Cat. No. D1/9/26.

25 Report on the Little Theatre in *Western Mail* (20 February 1931).

26 See D. R. Davies, 'Talk on dramatic society', *Aberdare Leader* (15 December 1977), ARL, Cat. No. D1/9/28; *The Little Theatre, Aberdare, Coming of Age Celebrations 1931–1952* (Aberdare: Electric Press, 1952); Jones, 'Old engine shed'; and 'Aberdare's British drama triumph', *Express* (5 June 1947).

27 Editorial, *Aberdare Leader* (4 December 1980).

28 Letter to the author, from Gwyneth Jones, Hon. Secretary, Aberdare Little Theatre (Trecynon Amateur Dramatic Society), 22 September 1998.

29 Ibid.

30 The Settlement opened in 1936 and was designed as an educational and cultural centre for the unemployed. In the mid-1930s, one in three people in Aberdare was unemployed or a dependant on an unemployed person. Source: Cynon Valley History Society, *Aberdare Pictures from the Past*, vol. 2 (Cardiff: D. Brown & Sons, 1992), plate 57.

31 Details taken from a handmade poster held at ARL, dated 25 February 1937. The performance took place at the Workmen's Hall, Trecynon, the precursor to the Coliseum.

32 Unnamed correspondent, *Western Mail* (3 May 1947), ARL, Cat. No. WH6/1.

33 ACGB, *Annual Report, 1966 1967*, section on 'Wales', 41.

34 Gilly Adams, 'The cultural health of the nation: the arts and a Welsh parliament', in John Osmond (ed.), *A Parliament for Wales* (Llandysul: Gomer Press, 1994), 237.

35 Quoted by D. R. Davies, in 'The Coliseum', *Aberdare Leader* (30 August 1979).

36 Ibid.

37 *Aberdare Leader* (27 November 1937), ARL, Cat. No. WH6/1, 1937–51.

38 Revd Cynog Williams, *Aberdare Leader* (21 October 1939), ARL, Cat. No. WH6/1, 1937–51.

39 See *OCLW*, 188.

40 E. Eynon Evans, *Cold Coal: A Drama of Welsh Life* (London: Samuel French, 1939).

41 Ibid., 51.

42 Ibid., 61.

43 Ibid., 21.

44 Jack Jones, *Aberdare Leader* (27 November 1944), ARL, Cat. No. WH6/1.

45 Ibid.

46 D. R. Davies, *The Minute Book*, 18 February 1948 to 9 March 1955. These are Davies's handwritten minutes of the Coliseum's committee meetings, ARL, Cat. No. WH6. The Coliseum committee 1948 comprised: NCB reps (7), miners' reps (6), Entertainments committee (co-opted) (7), Opera sub-committee (12), variety contests sub-committee (8); 40 members in total.

47 14 September 1962, ARL, Cat. No. WH6/2.

48 D. R. Davies, chairman of the Coliseum's Theatre Management Committee, original manuscript of a talk on the Coliseum, given at the Library, Aberdare, 24 March 1980, ARL, Cat. No. WH6/4.

49 *The Fifth CEMA Report, 1944–1945* (London: CEMA, 1945), 13, refers to 'the shortage of buildings' suitable for presenting theatre and to the 'co-operation' of 'theatre owners in small towns'. CEMA describes the pressing need for new, appropriate theatre buildings. Hence, we can understand its use of the Coliseum in the context of a national shortage of theatres.

50 Ibid., 13.

51 Advertisement in *Aberdare Leader* (28 July 1945).

52 Davies, *The Minute Book*, 31 May 1948.

53 Then Arts Council Officer for Wales.

54 *The Minute Book*, 13 April 1948.

55 Haydn Davies, *Western Mail* (8 September 1954).

56 This term is used now to refer to those plays which are deemed to have achieved 'greatness'.

57 D. R. Davies, 24 March 1980.

58 Andrew Sinclair, in *Arts and Cultures: The History of the Fifty Years of the Arts Council of Great Britain* (London: Sinclair-Stevenson, 1995), 67, avers that Huw Wheldon and Dr Wynn Griffiths, officer and chairman of ACGB's Wales Office, had a hidden agenda to establish a Welsh National Opera, from 1947.

59 *The Minute Book* records that the invitation was dated 6 April 1948.

60 Quoted by D. R. Davies, 30 August 1979.

61 F. G. H. Salisbury, *Daily Express* (9 November 1932), ARL, Cat. No. WH6/1.

62 Tom Phillips, a remark attributed to 1946, quoted in *Aberdare Leader* (24 March 1980), ARL, Cat. No. WH6/3.

63 D. R. Davies, manuscript of a talk, 24 March 1980, ARL, Cat. No. WH6/4.

64 Quoted by D. R. Davies in an 'Ordered Report', dated 1959 (no day/month recorded), of the British Drama League Finals – the BDL was an organization devoted to amateur drama – the first to be held outside England. ARL, Cat. No. WH6/2.

65 Quoted by D. R. Davies, 'From adversity to accolade for amateur players', *Aberdare Leader* (12 February 1981).

66 14 September 1962, ARL, Cat. No. WH6/2.

67 Ibid., Howell Palmer, the Operatic Society's ticket secretary.

68 4 December 1980 – an editorial leader commenting on the fact that only 86 people had attended the opening night of the Phoenix (amateur) Players' production of *The Tempest*.

69 J. T. Davies, *Aberdare Leader* (15 September 1962).

70 21 October 1966.

71 ACGB, *Annual Report, 1965–1966*, 41.

72 ACGB, *Annual Report, 1966–1967*, 41.

73 Bill Dufton, in ACGB, *Annual Report, 1969–1970* (WAC section).

74 The Questors Theatre (founded in 1929) is described as 'the UK's most famous am dram' company in *McGillivray's Theatre Guide, 1996–1997* (London: Rebecca Books, 1996), 272.

75 Graham Laker, 'Avoiding the mistakes of the 1970s', Theatre in Wales website, originally published in *New Welsh Review*, 39 (winter 1997/8). (Hereafter *NWR*.)

76 'Foundation to learning laid eighty years ago', *Aberdare Leader* (5 August 1982).

77 The purchase of the Coliseum was made possible with the help of a grant from the Welsh Office's Valleys Regeneration Fund as part of a strategy, supported by WAC, of restoring several Valleys venues. The Coliseum was substantially renovated and reopened in April 1992. Further renovations took place in 1994–5 and the building opened again in April 1995. As part of the rebuilding, the auditorium was reduced to 617 seats.

78 Pat Murphy, former Deputy Director of Leisure CVBC, in a recorded interview with the author at Mountain Ash Town Hall, 22 September 1995. From 1996, CVBC became RCT.

79 Eric Hitchings, in a report to CVBC's Leisure Services Committee, 19 May 1995.

80 Martyn Green, in a recorded interview with the author, 21 September 1995.

81 Valleys Arts Marketing, *The Coliseum, Aberdare: Three Year Plan 1995/6–1997/8*, draft, not for publication (Aberdare: VAM, 1995), 17–18.

82 Film has not been included for analysis and these figures should be understood in the context of a deliberate 50/50 split between theatre/live events and film. The 1949–50 figures are wholly based on live events. The figures are represented as a percentage of total live programming; figures for amateur and professional work are represented as a percentage of the category under which they appear.

83 The figures for 1949–50 have been obtained by analysing the Coliseum bookings sheet for this year, the only one extant in its entirety: ARL., Cat. No. LC 791. The figures for 1992–5 have been obtained by analysing eleven programmes from this period. Each programme covers two–three months.

84 This excludes the film programme. In autumn 1998, the Coliseum offered 16 live performances. In every example, the figure used excludes film and music. The percentages represent the proportion of theatre productions to the total number of live, performance events.

85 Saturday 10 October 1998.

86 VAM, *Databox Analysis 1997/98: The Coliseum Theatre, Aberdare*, ed. Lynfa Protheroe (Aberdare: VAM, 1997), 6.

87 Ibid., 12.

88 Roger Tomlinson, *The Initial Report on the Beaufort Research Results* (Cardiff: Welsh Arts Council, 1993). In this report, Tomlinson states that 'attenders at the arts include a higher percentage of women, are somewhat older, have a higher standard of education . . . and are up market of the population' (4). Horup (VAM, 1997, 6) provides more recent figures, also using Beaufort Research, and shows that arts attenders are 'likely to be female, aged 55 and over [and] from ABC1'.

89 In October 1998, RCT decided to transfer the Coliseum from the Leisure Services Department to the Education Department.

90 Figures extrapolated from a sample of five, two-monthly Coliseum programmes between August 1999 and November 2000.

91 The Coliseum's programme, 'What's On!', December and January 1998/99.

92 Alun Lewis (1915–44).

93 Gwladys Lewis, *Pleasant Place* (Godreaman, 1934). There is a printed copy of the play in ARL.

94   Davies, *History of Cwmaman Institute*, 60.
95   Ibid., 94.
96   Brenda Culliford, late Secretary of the Cwmaman Institute Theatre Group, in a letter to the author, 8 October 1998. The group gave its last performance at the Old Hall on 19 September 1998. It closed for two years while redevelopment and refurbishment were carried out with the aid of Lottery funding. The bar reopened in the summer of 2000 and the theatre in 2001.
97   VAM, *Cwmaman Public Hall and Institute: Study to Examine Potential for Development of Cinema and Theatre Programme*, ed. Angela Tillcock (Aberdare: VAM, 1995), 13. The estimate is 3261 attendances; the total population of Cwmaman, according to the 1991 census, is 10,310.
98   Ibid., 28.
99   Brenda Culliford. Average attendance: 200 per night; total capacity: 344. We need to be cautious with the Cwmaman figures as they have not been independently audited and no formal research data exists on typical live attenders.
100 Brenda Culliford.
101 6 July 2000.
102 Source: 1991 census.
103 Tillcock, *Cwmaman Public Hall and Institute*, 28.
104 There is a useful explanation of labour power and the labour process by T. Bottomore, L. Harris, V. G. Kiernan and R. Milliband (eds), *A Dictionary of Marxist Thought* (Oxford: Basil Blackwell, 1988), 265–70.
105 Raymond Williams, *Towards 2000* (London: Chatto & Windus/The Hogarth Press, 1983), 197.
106 Peter Zadek, quoted by James Woodall, in an interview about Zadek's production of *The Merchant of Venice*, *Independent* (29 August 1995).
107 Owen Kelly, *Community, Art and the State* (London: Comedia, 1984), 50.
108 Ibid., 133.
109 Raymond Williams, *What I Came to Say* (London: Hutchinson Radius, 1990), 60.

CHAPTER 2

1   23.6%, according to the *Digest of Welsh Statistics* (1994).
2   See Katy Bennett, Huw Beynon and Ray Hudson, *Coalfields Regeneration: Dealing with the Consequences of Industrial Decline* (Bristol: Policy Press and Joseph Rowntree Foundation, 2000).
3   Ibid., 5.
4   Raymond Williams, *Towards 2000* (London: Chatto & Windus/The Hogarth Press, 1983), 196.
5   Tony Thompson, *Observer* (1 April 2001).
6   David Gow, *Guardian* (28 June 1995).
7   Michael Prestage, *Observer* (18 June 1995).
8   Jamie Wilson, *Guardian* (18 June 2001).
9   Ben Summerskill, *Observer* (22 July 2001).

10 Anna Meredith, *Western Mail* (17 April 2000).

11 Wilson, *Guardian*.

12 *Western Mail* (magazine) (30 October 1999).

13 Diana Coole, 'Is class a difference that makes a difference?', *Radical Philosophy*, 77 (May/June 1996), 17.

14 Gordon Marshall, *Repositioning Class: Social Inequality in Industrial Societies* (London: Sage, 1997), 61.

15 David Adamson and Stuart Jones, *The South Wales Valleys: Continuity and Change, Occasional Papers in the Regional Research Programme* (Trefforest: University of Glamorgan, 1996), 26.

16 Figures based on the 1991 census: A 0.78%; B 9%, C 13.6%.

17 Adamson and Jones, *South Wales Valleys*, 2–3.

18 Bennett et al., *Coalfields Regeneration*.

19 John Harland and Kay Kinder (eds), *Crossing the Line. Extending Young People's Access to Cultural Venues* (London: Calouste Gulbenkian Foundation, 1999), 26.

20 Adamson and Jones, *South Wales Valleys*.

21 Usage: leisure centres 41%; public houses 56%; night clubs 21%; wine bars 10%.

22 John Edwards, *Talk Tidy: The Art of Speaking Wonglish* (Cowbridge. D. Brown & Sons, 1985), 46.

23 Kwesi Owusu, *The Struggle for Black Arts in Britain* (London: Comedia, 1986), 127–150.

24 Ibid., 132.

25 Ibid., 139.

26 Ibid.

27 In the *Guardian* (15 November 1997), Lyn Gardner describes how the actress Zoë Wanamaker stopped a performance to reprimand the audience for whispering. Gardner argues that it is only since the nineteenth century that audiences have been quiet.

28 Gwyn A. Williams, *When was Wales?* (London: Penguin, 1991), 225.

29 'Communication is community', *Bare Boards* (Blaengarw: Valley and Vale, 1994), 8.

30 Raymond Williams, *Drama in a Dramatised Society* (Cambridge: Cambridge University Press, 1975), 10–11.

31 ACGB, *49th Annual Report, 1993/94* (1994).

32 Figures calculated from the ACW's *Annual Report 1999–2000, Towards a Creative Wales*. Valley and Vale's subvention of £100,855 was spread across six different categories of funding and Clwyd Theatr Cymru's £1,080,670 across two.

33 This title was also used by the Manic Street Preachers for their 1996 album.

34 Patrick Jones, 'Everything must go', in *Fuse* (Cardiff: Parthian Books, 2001), 139.

35 From the official programme for *Everything Must Go*, Sherman Theatre, Cardiff, 1999.

36 For a good account of the 1960s Welsh rock bands, see Deke Leonard's books: *Rhinos, Winos and Lunatics* (Bordon: Northdown Publishing, 1996); and *Maybe I Should've Stayed in Bed?* (Bordon: Northdown Publishing, 2000). See also Dan Matovina's *Without You: The Tragic Story of Badfinger* (San Mateo, CA: Frances Glover Books, 1997).

37 All quotes from musicians taken from the author's recorded interviews with a series of Welsh rock musicians from September to November 2000.

38   According to ACW's *Beaufort Welsh Omnibus Survey: Arts Trends in Attendance and Participation* (Aberdare: VAM, 2000), 79.

39   Basingstoke's MP is Andrew Hunter, who was deputy chairman of the Monday Club, a right-wing organization which supports voluntary repatriation of ethnic minorities. More than 20,000 people in Basingstoke voted for him in the 2001 general election.

40   Gwyn A. Williams, quoted by Anne Showstack Sassoon (ed.), *Approaches to Gramsci* (London: Writers and Readers Publishing Cooperative Society, 1982), 213.

41   Raymond Williams, *Problems in Materialism and Culture* (London: Verso, 1989), 39; and *Marxism and Literature* (Oxford: Oxford University Press, 1992), 115–17.

42   I am indebted to Lynfa Protheroe of VAM for her help in providing me with the detailed figures she prepared for the *Databox Reports 2000–2001*, in particular those for the Coliseum Theatre, the Blackwood Miners' Institute and the Beaufort Theatre.

43   In 2000–1, Blackwood filled 35% of its seats and Beaufort 40%.

44   VAM, *Blackwood Miners' Institute Databox Report, 2000–2001*, 6.

45   In 2000–1, the total average number of attendances was 214 for professional and 415 for amateur events.

46   See William Ebor (ed.), *Men without Work: A Report Made to the Pilgrim Trust* (London: Cambridge University Press, 1938).

47   Ibid., 305.

48   The Arts Factory was featured on a BBC Radio 4 programme, *Changing Places*, in 2001.

49   Tim Dwelly, *Creative Regeneration: Lessons from Ten Community Arts Projects* (York: Joseph Rowntree Foundation, 2001).

50   Dic Edwards in 'Theatre as forum', a discussion with Hazel Walford Davies, *NWR*, 31/viii (1995–6), 81.

51   Ibid., 79.

52   Dic Edwards, *The Shakespeare Factory, Moon River: The Deal and David*, ed. Brian Mitchell (Bridgend: Seren, 1998).

53   Bennett, *Coalfields Regeneration*, 23.

54   http://www.knowhere.co.uk/3191_goodbad.html

55   Dai Smith, *Wales: A Question for History* (Bridgend: Seren, 1999), 24.

56   Ibid.

57   The term 'effective' is being used here to delineate the alternative to the notion of 'quality' as understood by the Arts Council.

58   Baz Kershaw, *The Politics of Performance: Radical Theatre as Cultural Intervention* (London: Routledge, 1992), 21–9.

59   Owusu, *Struggle for Black Arts*, 128.

60   Ibid., 130.

CHAPTER 3

1   Figures provided by ACE's Press Office on 5 July 1995.

2   Owen Kelly, *Community, Art and the State* (London: Comedia, 1984), 43.

[3] Michel Foucault, 'The eye of power', in Colin Gordon (ed.), *Michel Foucault: Power/Knowledge* (London: Harvester Wheatsheaf, 1980), 147.

[4] Ibid., 156.

[5] Ibid., 158.

[6] Ibid., 164.

[7] Michel Foucault, 'Panopticism', from *Discipline and Punish*, in Paul Rabinow (ed.), *The Foucault Reader: An Introduction to Foucault's Thought* (London: Penguin, 1991/1984), 206.

[8] Ibid., 208–9.

[9] CEMA was founded in 1940.

[10] It had, however, been subject to pressures, censorship (direct and covert) and legislation. In medieval times, it was the clergy which regulated performances, by refusing to allow entertainments that it considered blasphemous to be performed within the Church. But the clergy's role was replaced, or added to, by the monarch and the court. During the reigns of Edward VI, Henry VIII and Mary, plays were censored and active steps were taken to control theatre practices. After 1469, the profession of entertainer was regularized when Edward VI introduced a guild to limit entry to the minstrelsy; an Act of Parliament was passed by Henry VIII in 1543 which banned the mention of doctrinal issues in plays; and, in 1559, Elizabeth I passed a Proclamation which banned plays that discussed religion and politics. This was developed by the establishment of the Revels Office, whose job it was to examine plays for unacceptable material, a function which later formed the basis for the office of the Lord Chamberlain. Sometimes, royal patronage has been used to override the more conservative elements of society, as when Royal Letters Patent were issued in 1574 to allow the Earl of Leicester's men to perform in London, against the wishes of the Burghers. But the monarchy was largely in favour of theatre, providing it could control content. During the Interregnum, however, between 1642 and 1660, Cromwell closed all theatres and plays were allowed to be performed only in schools. Charles II restored public theatre, although he passed the 1660 Monopoly Act which restricted the performance of serious dramatic work to only two theatres in London, known as the Patent Theatres. During the eighteenth century, obvious control of the theatre passed from the monarch to Parliament and to the government. Walpole introduced the Licensing Act of 1737 to remove politics from theatre and, particularly, to prevent playwrights from satirizing his administration. It was this act which formally extended the Lord Chamberlain's office to include the direct censorship of theatre. The Theatres Act of 1843 replaced the 1737 Licensing Act and led to a series of regulations about theatre buildings and the licensing of plays. During the nineteenth century, the Lord Chamberlain's office made extensive use of an Examiner of Plays, so much so that, by 1907, there was an active campaign by some theatre practitioners to remove formal censorship of the theatre, because the Lord Chamberlain could refuse to licence plays for public performance. In 1968, an Act of Parliament finally removed the Lord Chamberlain's power of censorship over theatre.

[11] Rabinow (ed.), *Foucault Reader*, 212.

[12] Ibid., 193.

[13] Ibid.

[14] Ibid., 199.

[15] The section on Wales from *The Arts Council of Great Britain Report, 1965– 1966*, 8–9.

[16] Rabinow (ed.), *Foucault Reader*, 19.

[17] Ibid., 205.

[18] Robert Hewison, 'The Arts Council of Great Britain 1946–1994', *49th Annual Report and Accounts, 1993–1994* (London: Arts Council of England, 1994), 36.

[19] Lord Keynes, 'The Arts Council: its policy and hopes', reprinted from *The Listener* (12 July 1945).

[20] *The Fifth CEMA Report* (1944–5), 32.

[21] Ibid.

[22] Hewison, 'Arts Council of Great Britain', 36.

[23] Ibid.

[24] ACGB, *First Annual Report, 1945–1946*, 37.

[25] Lord Redcliffe-Maud, *Support for the Arts in England and Wales* (London: Calouste Gulbenkian Foundation, 1976), 31.

[26] Keynes, 'Arts Council'.

[27] The section for Wales in *The Arts Council of Great Britain Report, 1967*, 41.

[28] Raymond Williams, 'The Arts Council', *Political Quarterly*, 50/2 (April–June 1979), 159.

[29] David Adams, *Stage Welsh: Nation, Nationalism and Theatre: The Search for Cultural Identity* (Llandysul: Gomer, 1996), 36–7.

[30] Anthony Everitt and Anne Twine, *Restructuring the Arts Council of Wales: An Action Plan* (Cardiff: ACW, 2001).

[31] Richard Carless and Patricia Brewster, *Patronage and the Arts* (London: Conservative Political Centre on behalf of the Bow Group, 1959), 110.

[32] *The Royal Charter for The Arts Council of Great Britain* (1967).

[33] Williams, 'Arts Council', 163.

[34] Anthony Everitt, 'Priorities for Patronage', *Guardian* (22 May 1993).

[35] Howard Webber and Tim Challans, *A Creative Future: The Way Forward for the Arts, Crafts and Media in England* (London: HMSO, 1993), 28.

[36] Baz Kershaw, 'Building an unstable pyramid: the fragmentation of alternative theatre', *New Theatre Quarterly*, 36/ix (Cambridge: Cambridge University Press, November 1993), 343–4.

[37] House of Commons, Minutes of the Committee on Welsh Affairs, Session 1981–1982, *Minutes of Evidence: Welsh Arts Council, Wednesday 19 May 1982* (London: OHMS, 1982), 17–18.

[38] The Welsh Office, *Departmental Report 1995: The Government's Expenditure Plans 1995–96 and 1997–98* (London: HMSO, March 1995), 49.

[39] ACW, Artform Development Division, *Draft Drama Strategy for Wales: Consultation Paper* (Cardiff: ACW, 21 January 1999), 3.

[40] John McGrath, *The Bone won't Break: On Theatre and Hope in Hard Times* (London: Methuen Drama, 1990), 57.

[41] Ibid., 65.

[42] Ibid., 72.

[43] Sinclair, *Arts and Cultures*, 34.

44 Keynes, 'Arts Council'.
45 Redcliffe-Maud, *Support for the Arts*, p. 116.
46 The section for Wales in *The Arts Council of Great Britain Report, 1967*, 41.
47 Redcliffe-Maud, *Support for the Arts*, 117.
48 Figures taken from ACGB's *47th Annual Report and Accounts, 1991/2*.
49 Figures obtained from ACGB *Annual Reports* in the 1990s.
50 ACW, Draft Drama Strategy for Wales, 1999, 2.
51 The section on Wales in *The Arts Council of Great Britain Report, 1965–1966*, 42.
52 Minutes of the Committee on Welsh Affairs, 11.
53 Draft Drama Strategy for Wales, 1999, 4–5.
54 Claire Jenkins for Cymru'n Creu, October 2001.
55 The section on Wales in *The Arts Council of Great Britain Report, 1965–1966*, 43.
56 Cecil Price, *The Professional Theatre in Wales* (Swansea: University College Swansea, 1984), 40.
57 Minutes of the Committee on Welsh Affairs, 17.
58 Ibid., 21.
59 Phil Clark and Michael Bogdanov, *Consultative Paper on a National Theatre for Wales* (July 1995), 3.
60 Michael Baker, former Drama Director of the Arts Council of Wales, quoted by Peter Morgan in 'Theatre in Wales: noises off', *NWR*, 29 (1995), 60.
61 This case is well made by David Adams in *Stage Welsh*.
62 *Developing the Arts in Wales 2000–2003*.
63 ACGB, *Annual Report, 1945–1946*, 5.
64 Williams, 'Arts Council', 160.
65 The section on Wales in *The Arts Council of Great Britain Report, 1967*, 41.
66 John S. Harris, *Government Patronage of the Arts in Britain* (Chicago: University of Chicago Press, 1970), 57.
67 Williams, 'Arts Council', 162.
68 The section on Wales in *The Arts Council of Great Britain Report, 1965–1966*, 41.
69 Ibid.
70 Redcliffe-Maud, *Support for the Arts*, 47.
71 Ibid., 48.
72 Ibid., 85.
73 Sinclair, *Arts and Cultures*, 27.
74 Robert Hewison, *Culture and Consensus: England, Art and Politics since 1940* (London: Methuen, 1995), 34.
75 E. L. Ellis, *T.J.: A Life of Dr Thomas Jones, CH* (Cardiff: University of Wales Press, 1992), 330.
76 Ibid., 338.
77 Ibid., 341.
78 Ibid., 435.
79 Ibid.
80 Ibid., 538.
81 Ibid., 435.
82 See Hewison, *Culture and Consensus*, 37, and Sinclair, *Arts and Cultures*, 36.
83 Keidrych Rhys, quoted by Sinclair in *Arts and Cultures*, 64.

[84] Then Arts Council Officer for Wales.
[85] Sinclair, *Arts and Cultures*, 36.
[86] Ellis, *T.J.: A Life*, 443.
[87] Hewison, *Culture and Consensus*, 41
[88] Ibid., 79.
[89] Hewison, *Culture and Consensus*, 80.
[90] Ibid.
[91] Williams, *Marxism and Literature*, 118.
[92] Minutes of the Committee on Welsh Affairs, 2.
[93] Williams, 'Arts Council', 165.
[94] Minutes of the Committee on Welsh Affairs, 26.
[95] Brigitta Horup, *Arts Attendance and Participation in Wales, June 1993– November 1997* (Aberdare: VAM, 1997), 14.
[96] Williams, *Marxism and Literature*, 118.
[97] ACW, 'Consultation paper 3', July 1996. In June 1996, ACW's Drama Board issued a series of discussion documents: 'Planning for the millennium'.
[98] ACW, 'Consultation paper 4', section 1. 2.
[99] ACW, 'Planning for the millennium', June 1996, section 2. 5.
[100] ACW, *Building a Creative Society: A Consultation Paper on a Strategy for the Arts in Wales* (Cardiff: ACW, May 1998), 6. This publication followed on from a major re-structuring of ACW: from December 1997, Drama was subsumed by a new Artform Development Division.
[101] ACW, *Corporate Plan 1997–2000* (Cardiff: ACW, November 1996), 30.
[102] Ibid.
[103] Ibid., 22.
[104] Ibid., 12.
[105] Ibid., 24.
[106] Ibid., 25.
[107] ACE, *The Policy for Drama of the English Arts Funding System* (London: ACE, October 1996).
[108] ACW, Drama Strategy for Wales, June 1999, p. 2.
[109] The *Wallace Report* was written by Richard Wallace, a retired civil servant from the Welsh Office.
[110] The Who, 'Won't Get Fooled Again'.
[111] Hewison, *Culture and Consensus*, p. 265.
[112] The Arts Council of Northern Ireland, *The Arts: Inspiring the Imagination, Building the Future* (2001).
[113] Sinclair, quoting from the Report of the Welsh Committee, 1959–60, *Arts and Cultures*, 121.
[114] ACW, Drama Department, 'Consultation paper 4', 'A strategy for middle scale drama programming', July 1996, section 2. 4.
[115] Valleys Arts Marketing, *Beaufort Welsh Omnibus Survey*, November 2000, 26.
[116] Unless otherwise stated, these figures are contained in the ACE press release of 20 March 2001.
[117] See Simon Blackburn, *Oxford Dictionary of Philosophy* (Oxford: Oxford University Press, 1996) 87.

CHAPTER 4

[1] Russell Stephens, *Emlyn Williams: The Making of a Dramatist* (Bridgend: Seren, 2000), 53.

[2] Olive Ely Hart, *The Drama in Modern Wales: A Brief History of Welsh Playwriting from 1900 to the Present Day. A Thesis* (Philadelphia: [privately published], 1928), 15.

[3] Elan Closs Stephens acknowledges the existence in Welsh theatre of 'camps' with conflicting 'voices' in her review of theatre in Wales in *The Arts in Wales, 1950–1975* (1979).

[4] Hart, *The Drama in Modern Wales*, 73.

[5] Dedwydd Jones, *Black Book on the Welsh Theatre* (London and Lausanne: Bozo and Iolo, 1980, reprinted in 1985).

[6] Ibid., 126.

[7] Ibid., 128.

[8] Carl Tighe, 'Theatre (or not) in Wales', in Tony Curtis (ed.), *Wales: The Imagined Nation* (Bridgend: Poetry Wales Press, 1986), 249.

[9] For an excellent account of J. O. Francis et al., see M. Wynn Thomas, *Internal Difference: Twentieth-Century Writing in Wales* (Cardiff: University of Wales Press, 1992).

[10] Hart, *The Drama in Modern Wales*, 78–9.

[11] Ibid., 81–8.

[12] Ibid., 86.

[13] Jeni Williams, 'Art and stuff', *NWR*, 52 (2001), 59.

[14] Jeni Williams, 'Grown-up theatre?', *NWR*, 51 (2000/2001), 66.

[15] Paul Taylor, 'Against the current', *Independent* (2 January 2002).

[16] Theatre in Wales website, 13 April 2000.

[17] *The Guardian* (2 February 1998).

[18] *NWR*, 27 (1994/5), 67–71.

[19] David Hughes, 'The Welsh national theatre: the avant-garde in the diaspora', in Theodore Shank (ed.), *Contemporary British Theatre* (Basingstoke: Macmillan, 1996), xvii.

[20] Ibid., 139.

[21] Ibid., 142.

[22] Ibid., 143.

[23] Ibid., 147.

[24] *Guardian* (26 September 1989).

[25] Review of *L.O.V.E.*, 14 December 1992.

[26] Review of *Manifesto*, 26 January 1993.

[27] *NWR*, 50 (2000), 62–4.

[28] *NWR*, 36 (1997), 67.

[29] 20 February 1997.

[30] 2 June 2000.

[31] G. Zaslavzki, *Moskovski Nablyudatel*, 5–6 (Moscow, 1996), 81. I am indebted to Dr David Allen for drawing my attention to this review and for its translation.

[32] *NWR*, 32 (1996), 90.

[33] See *NWR*, 35 (1996/7), 75.

34 Ibid., 67.
35 See *NWR*, 43 (1998/9), 70.
36 Hughes, in *Contemporary British Theatre*, 150.
37 Heike Roms, 'A new chapter in theatre', *Planet*, 121 (1997), 80.
38 See, for example, Heike Roms, *Planet*, 134 (1999).
39 Jeni Williams, 'Grown-up theatre?', *NWR*, 51 (2000/2001), 66.
40 Raymond Williams, *The Politics of Modernism: Against the New Conformists* (London: Verso, 1989) 93–4.
41 Raymond Williams, *Culture* (Glasgow: Fontana, 1986), 205.
42 Raymond Williams, *Marxism and Literature* (Oxford: Oxford University Press, 1992), 123.
43 Raymond Williams, *Politics and Letters: Interviews with New Left Review* (London: Verso, 1981), 219.
44 Raymond Williams, *Drama in Performance* (Harmondsworth: Pelican Books, 1972), 184.
45 In an open letter to ACW, 22 January 2000.
46 Gill Ogden, 'A history of theatre in education in Wales', in Anna-Marie Taylor (ed.), *Staging Wales: Welsh Theatre 1979–1997* (Cardiff: University of Wales Press, 1997), 47.
47 Ibid., 57.
48 Hughes, in *Contemporary British Theatre*, 140.
49 Mike Pearson, *Y Llyfyr Glas* (Cardiff: Brith Gof, 1995), 8.
50 Greg Cullen, 'The graveyard of ambition?', in *Staging Wales*, 151.
51 Charles Way, 'A journey of exploration', in discussion with Hazel Walford Davies, *NWR*, 33 (1996), 79.
52 Website, 'Please help Gwent theatre', 3 November 1999.
53 Cullen, in *Staging Wales*, 132–3.
54 Ibid., 136.
55 Ibid., 152.
56 Charles Way, 'Dead man's hat', in Hazel Walford Davies (ed.), *State of Play* (Llandysul: Gomer, 1998), 256.
57 Jeni Williams, 'Art and stuff', *NWR*, 52 (2001), 62–3.
58 Steve Davis, Website, 'Community theatre: Terry Hands', 18 April 2000.
59 *Western Mail* (27 December 1999).
60 Roy Bohana, letter to *Western Mail* (8 December 1999).
61 *ACW* press release, 4 November 1999.
62 For an account of Alexander's work, see *Staging Wales*, 76–84.
63 Ibid., 82.
64 Ibid., 81.
65 Paul Davies, 'In deep waters', *NWR*, 51 (2000/2001), 71.
66 http://www.theatre-wales.co.uk/index.asp
67 Gill Ogden and Keith Morris (eds), *Welsh Theatre Handbook* (Aberystwyth: Aberystwyth Arts Centre, 2002).
68 Janek Alexander, 'Talking turkey', 28 March 2000.
69 'Disillusioned', 8 June 2000.
70 Message headed 'Arts Council', Theatre in Wales website, 17 April 2000.
71 David Adams, 'New Wales's missing ingredient', *NWR*, 50 (2000), 65.

72 Ibid., 66.
73 Edward Said, *Orientalism* (Harmondsworth: Penguin, 1991), 3.
74 Edward Said, *Culture and Imperialism* (London: Chatto & Windus, 1993), xiii.
75 Stanley Leary, 'NYTW – Hamlet', 30 September 2001.
76 Jeni Williams, 1 October 2001.
77 Hart, 'The drama in modern Wales', 79.
78 Paul Davies, 'In deep waters', *NWR*, 51 (2000/2001), 71.
79 'Taff but not naff', *Guardian* (14 March 2001).
80 Raymond Williams, *Keywords: A Vocabulary of Culture and Society* (London: Flamingo, 1983), 40–2.
81 Terry Eagleton, *The Ideology of the Aesthetic* (Oxford: Basil Blackwell, 1990), 9.
82 *NWR*, 51 (2000/2001), 71.
83 Owen Kelly, *Community, Art and the State* (London: Comedia, 1984), 124–31.

CHAPTER 5

1 Figures obtained by relating the 1992 population figures for England and Wales (England: 48.3m; Wales: 2.8m) to the total sums spent on Drama by ACE and ACW in 1994–5, as documented in their respective Annual Reports. England spent £26.7m and Wales £3m.
2 Figures obtained by estimating the number of theatre companies directly subsidized by ACE and ACW in 1994–5, and include producing theatres as well as touring theatre companies. England: 71; Wales: 34.
3 Raymond Williams, *Marxism and Literature* (Oxford: Oxford University Press, 1992), 118.
4 Figures based on the ACW Contacts List of January 2001.
5 Edward Thomas, *House of America*, in *Three Plays* (Bridgend: Seren, 1994), 46–7.
6 Bertolt Brecht, from his play *Galileo*.
7 See Harri Webb's poem, 'Synopsis of the Great Welsh Novel' in *The Green Desert* (Llandysul: Gwasg Gomer, 1969), 34, for a witty exposition of 'suspect' subject matter.
8 Dai Smith, *Aneurin Bevan and the World of South Wales* (Cardiff: University of Wales Press, 1994), 264.
9 Mark Jenkins, 'Virtual reality Wales', *NWR*, 29/viii (1995), 76.
10 ACW, *Opportunity, Innovation, Quality: Annual Report 1997/98*.
11 VAM, *Cwmaman Public Hall and Institute*, ed. Angela Tillcock (Aberdare: VAM, 1995), 8.
12 Cecil Price, *The Professional Theatre in Wales* (Swansea: University College Swansea, 1984), 1–16.
13 Baz Kershaw, *The Politics of Performance* (London: Routledge, 1992), 249.
14 Charles Landry, Lesley Greene, François Matarasso and Franco Bianchini, *The Art of Regeneration: Urban Renewal through Cultural Activity* (Stroud: Comedia, 1996), 5.
15 Ibid., 2.

[16]   Howard Webber and Tim Challans, *A Creative Future* (London: ACGB, 1993), 28.

[17]   Owen Kelly, *Community, Art and the State* (London: Comedia, 1984), 89.

Glossary

ACGB

The Arts Council of Great Britain. The Labour government assumed financial responsibility for the arts in 1945. ACGB's first meeting was in 1945 and it was granted a Royal Charter in 1946. Funding was direct from the Treasury. ACGB's Charter was redrawn in 1967 and funding switched to the Department of Education and Science. Regional Arts Boards (RABs) for England were established in 1991. ACGB disbanded in 1994. In England, the arts body became the Arts Council of England (ACE), accountable to the Secretary of State for National Heritage (later, Culture, Media and Sport).

ACW

The Arts Council of Wales. Formed as an autonomous body in April 1994 it was funded through the Welsh Office. Took over the roles previously assumed by WAC and the three Regional Arts Associations. (Three Regional Arts Boards replaced the Associations.) A registered charity, it was set up by Royal Charter. The Council consisted in 1994 of eighteen unpaid members appointed by the Secretary of State for Wales. Theatre was handled by an art-form team for drama. In 1997/98, theatre was moved to the Artform Development Division. In the late 1990s, ACW received a series of standstill budgets. From 1999, it was responsible to the National Assembly for Wales through the Minister for Culture, Sport and the Welsh Language. Between 1999 and 2002, ACW was involved in a complex process which led to restructuring.

CEMA

The Council for the Encouragement of Music and the Arts. Formed in 1940 under the aegis of the Board of Education. It had a tendency towards classical, 'up-market' theatre. It sponsored theatre tours to the south Wales Valleys during the Second World War. A regional office for Wales, the CEMA Welsh Office, based in Cardiff was started in 1944. CEMA ended in 1945, when it became the ACGB.

ENSA
The Entertainments National Service Association (also nicknamed 'Every Night Something Atrocious'). Established in 1938 as a voluntary association, its main purpose was to entertain the troops and civilian workers during the Second World War. During the war, there was some tension between it and CEMA (ENSA developed out of the commercial theatre): ENSA had a bigger budget than CEMA and specialized in popular performances. Ended in 1945.

Familiar congregation
Audiences which are connected by geography, class, history, shared experiences, cultural practices, traditions or other significant elements. This principle also extends to mixed audiences where the familiarity relates to their actually 'knowing' each other, or recognizing faces, or, even, acknowledging 'kinship' through subtle signs to do with class and self-presentation. Hence, audiences are able to discern a connection between themselves. This is different from audiences who are connected only by the fact of their attending a theatre production on the same night and in the same place.

Incorporation
The power of the Arts Council to create disciplinary procedures, through rules, training and the classification of types of theatre which limit and constrain theatre practitioners into producing 'normalized' theatre. Theatre companies cooperate with incorporation because they need financial subsidy. Incorporation functions as a form of surveillance to pressurize theatre practitioners into developing theatre in accordance with a clearly defined set of standards.

Orature
Described by Kwesi Owusu in *The Struggle for Black Arts in Britain* (1986), it refers to a tradition of African arts practice which utilizes social cooperation, combines different art-forms (dance, storytelling, music, song, design, physical action), takes place in a circle in a centre of the living space, which would also be used for a wide variety of other social activities, transforms the local environment and its resources, incorporates the 'amateur' and the 'professional' in a non-hierarchical structure, and acknowledges the interdependence of members of communities. It does not separate creative expression from the local, lived experience. Orature does not imply exclusion: neither play-texts nor formal events need necessarily be ruled out of orature practices.

Referential power

The means by which plays and productions achieve critical acclaim (after Edward Said). Plays which have referential power – for example, Shakespeare's – are deemed to set the standard of excellence. Plays with referential power can also be described as 'canonical'.

Strategic formation

The processes of constructing an exemplary theatre provision – how the Arts Council, theatre critics and academics, for example, 'hype' playwrights, plays and theatre companies to the extent that their work becomes a standard used to evaluate the worth of other forms of theatre.

Validated theatre

Theatre which has been legitimized by the Arts Council through subsidy: the larger and more permanent the subsidy, the more highly validated the theatre company.

WAC

The Welsh Arts Council. Established in 1967 as an 'independent' sub-committee of ACGB when ACGB's Charter was revised. In 1967/68, its budget was £430K. The Drama Committee was started in 1969. WAC formed three regional Welsh Associations for the Arts between 1968 and 1973. In 1979, the Drama Committee began to establish a Community/Theatre-in-Education group in each county in Wales. WAC ceased in 1994.

The Welsh Committee

Started in June 1945 to serve as an advisory body to ACGB. The Committee was not allowed to control expenditure until 1953, when it was given its first annual budget of £30K. Between 1945 and 1968, the Welsh Committee grew from seven to sixteen members.

Chronology of Significant Events and Documents 1992–2003

1992
March–May: WAC, *Drama Strategy Consultation Paper.*

1993
WAC, National Arts and Media Strategy, *Drama in Wales.*
WAC, *Blueprint for the Nineties.*

1994
John Osmond (ed.), 'The cultural health of the nation', in *A Parliament for Wales.*
April: Separation of WAC from ACGB; WAC becomes ACW.

1995
Bogdanov/Clark, *Consultation Paper on a National Theatre for Wales.*

1996
June: ACW, 'Planning for the millennium' – discussion documents.
June: ACW, 'Taking part: developing participation in arts activity in Wales' – a consultative paper.
December: ACW, *The Way Forward: Consultation on Future Decision-Making, Advisory and Partnership Structures.*

1997
ACW, *Corporate Plan 1997–2000.*

1998
June: ACW, consultation paper, 'Building a creative society' (the largest ever consultation exercise).

Summer: ACW convenes a group of representatives from arts umbrella bodies in Wales.

Autumn: Institute of Welsh Affairs, David Clarke, *State of the Arts* (The Gregynog Papers).

December: ACW, *The Economic Impact of the Arts and Cultural Industries in Wales*.

1999

January: ACW, *Draft Drama Strategy* (includes plans for the five new franchises for TYP).

March: ACW produces some advocacy documents to make the case for the arts in Wales.

May: Establishment of the National Assembly for Wales.

June: ACW, *Drama Strategy*.

June: ACW, *Corporate Plan 1999–2002*.

From July: ACW responsible to the Welsh Assembly (previously to the Secretary of State for Wales). Accountable to Parliament through the Secretary of State for Culture, Media and Sport.

October: ACW, announcement of recipients of TYP franchises.

November: National Assembly for Wales, Post-16 Education and Training Committee, *Arts and Culture Policy Review*.

December: NAW advertises for an 'expert adviser' to the Policy Review.

December: Bogdanov/Clark, *Towards the Provision of a National Theatre for Wales: A Federal System*.

2000

January: ACW decides to retain eight TYP companies rather than cut back to five.

January: ACW, Corporate Plan, *Developing the Arts in Wales 2000–2003*.

January: Ceri Sherlock appointed as 'expert adviser' by NAW.

January: There are calls for the proposal to create Sgript Cymru to be rescinded (but Dalier Sylw and Simon Harris are appointed to run it).

August: NAW, the *Wallace Report*.

August: PricewaterhouseCoopers' audit on TYP strategy.

September: NAW, *Arts and Culture Review*.

September: Joanna Weston resigns as chief executive of ACW.

November: NAW, *A Culture in Common* (a review of ACW which recommends restructuring).

November: NAW, Ceri Sherlock's *Commentary on Culture and the Arts in Wales*.

November: Centre for Visual Arts closes in Cardiff.

December: ACW responds to *A Culture in Common*.

December: ACW releases an initiative: 'What do you think?' (prior to appointing Anthony Everitt as its consultant).

2001

February: Wales Association of Performing Arts makes a response.

March: ACW, *Action Plan* for restructuring the ACW (produced by Everitt and Twine).

October: NAW (Jenny Randerson), *A Platform for Fulfilment*.

October: ACW appoints new chief executive, Peter Tyndall.

October: NAW/Cymru'n Creu, 'Report on performance spaces across Wales'.

November: A report criticizes ACW for its actions over the Centre for Visual Arts.

November: ACW invites responses to its future strategy and funding schemes.

November: Michael Baker leaves ACW.

2002

January: Voluntary Arts Wales makes a response to Everitt and Twine.

January: NAW, *Creative Future: Cymru Greadigol* – a ten-year plan; NAW announces 23% increase in funding to the arts.

April: ACW, *Five Year Arts Development Strategy 2002–2007* (Everitt and Twine).

April: ACW releases a user's guide to the Arts Council of Wales's New Schemes for Funding.

October: A new culture fund is initiated by the National Assembly for Wales, with funding set at £46.8 million for 2003–4, rising to £62.3 million in 2005–6. The arts budget is increased by 16.5 per cent.

December: The Culture Minister of the National Assembly announces that almost £1.2 million is to be made available to ACW for TiE between 2002 and 2005.

2003

March: ACW publishes *Supporting Creativity: The Five Year Arts Development Strategy of the Arts Council of Wales 2002–2007*.

April: The post of ACW chair becomes a salaried position. The new chair, appointed following open competition by the Welsh Assembly Government for a three-year term, is to be Geraint Talfan Davies. He succeeds Sybil Crouch. Talfan Davies was formerly Controller of BBC

Wales, is a former chair of Welsh National Opera and of Cardiff Bay Arts Trust, and a former Board member of the Wales Millennium Centre.

May: Following the elections for a new Assembly, Alun Pugh AM is appointed the new Minister for Culture, Sport and the Welsh Language. Pugh states that *Creative Future* will provide the framework for the arts in Wales for the next few years.

May: ACW holds its first ever annual conference, in Swansea.

June: Cardiff is not selected as European Capital of Culture for 2008. Sir Jeremy Isaacs, leader of the judging panel, comments that Cardiff's proposals were unsuccessful partly because they did not include the Valleys enough in the plans.

July: Following a decrease in funding from the National Lottery to ACW, the Arts Council of Wales announces the closure of many of its mid- and west Wales Lottery-based grant schemes.

Selected Bibliography

Adams, David, *Stage Welsh – Nation, Nationalism and Theatre: The Search for Cultural Identity* (Llandysul: Gomer Press, 1996).

Adams, Gilly, 'The cultural health of the nation: the arts and a Welsh parliament', in John Osmond (ed.), *A Parliament for Wales* (Llandysul: Gomer Press, 1994).

Adamson, David, and Stuart Jones, *The South Wales Valleys: Continuity and Change, Paper 1, Occasional Papers in the Regional Research Programme* (Trefforest: University of Glamorgan, 1996).

Alexander, Janek (ed.), *Export Wales 1991/92* (Cardiff: Chapter Arts Centre, 1992).

Allen, Graham, 'Speechless in two languages', *New Welsh Review*, 29/xiii (Llandysul: Gomer, 1995).

Arts Council of England, *Consultative Green Paper on Drama in England* (London: ACE, 1995).

—— *The Policy for Drama of the English Arts Funding System* (London: ACE, 1996).

—— *Artstat: Digest of Arts Statistics and Trends in the UK 1986/87–1997/98* (London: ACE, 2000).

Arts Council of Great Britain, *First Annual Report 1945–1946* (London: ACGB, 1946).

—— *Extracts from 1991 RSGB Omnibus Survey: Report on a Survey of Arts and Cultural Activities in Great Britain* (London: ACGB, 1991).

Arts Council of Wales, *Planning for the Millennium*, a series of discussion documents (Cardiff: ACW, 1996).

—— *New Lottery Directions: Consultative Document* (Cardiff: ACW, 1996).

—— *Taking Part: Developing Participation in Arts Activity in Wales, a Consultative Paper* (Cardiff: ACW, 1996).

—— *Corporate Plan 1997–2000* (Cardiff: ACW, 1996).

—— *The Way Forward: Consultation on Future Decision-Making, Advisory and Partnership Structures* (Cardiff: ACW, 1996).

—— *Building a Creative Society: A Consultation Paper on a Strategy for the Arts in Wales* (Cardiff: ACW, 1998).

—— *The Economic Impact of the Arts and Cultural Industries in Wales, a Briefing Paper* (Cardiff: ACW, 1998).

—— Artform Development Division, *Draft Drama Strategy for Wales: Consultation Paper* (Cardiff: ACW, January 1999).

—— Artform Development Division, *Drama Strategy for Wales* (Cardiff: ACW, June 1999).

—— *Five Year Arts Development Strategy 2002–2007* (Cardiff: ACW, 2002).

—— *A User's Guide to the Arts Council of Wales' New Schemes Including Advice on Making an Application for Funding* (Cardiff: ACW, 2002).

Bennett, Katy, Huw Beynon and Ray Hudson, *Coalfields Regeneration: Dealing with the Consequences of Industrial Decline* (Bristol: Policy Press and Joseph Rowntree Foundation, 2000).

Bottomore, Tom, Lawrence Harris, V. G. Kiernan and Ralph Milliband (eds), *A Dictionary of Marxist Thought* (Oxford: Basil Blackwell, 1988).

British Council, with the Arts Council of Wales, *Arts From Wales* (Cardiff: Wales Arts International, 1998).

Carless, Richard, and Patricia Brewster, *Patronage and the Arts* (London: Conservative Political Centre on behalf of the Bow Group, 1959).

Central Statistical Office, *Digest of Welsh Statistics, 38* (Cardiff: Welsh Office/HMSO, 1992).

—— *Social Trends, 23* (London: Government Statistical Service/HMSO, 1993).

—— *Digest of Welsh Statistics, 40* (Pontypool: Welsh Office/HMSO, 1994).

Church, Jenny (ed.), *Regional Trends, 31* (London: HMSO, 1996).

Clarke, David, *State of the Arts*, The Gregynog Papers, 2/1 (Cardiff: Institute of Welsh Affairs, 1998).

Closs Stephens, Elan, 'Drama', in Meic Stephens (ed.), *The Arts in Wales* (Cardiff: Welsh Arts Council, 1979).

Coole, Diana, 'Is class a difference that makes a difference?', *Radical Philosophy*, 77 (Nottingham: Russell Press, 1996).

Council for the Encouragement of Music and the Arts, *The Fifth CEMA Report 1944–1945* (London: CEMA, 1945).

Curtis, Tony (ed.), *Wales: The Imagined Nation, Studies in Cultural and National Identity* (Bridgend: Poetry Wales Press, 1986).

Cynon Valley History Society, *Old Aberdare*, vol. 5 (Mountain Ash: D. J. Pryse, 1988).

—— *Aberdare: Pictures from the Past*, vol. 2 (Cardiff: D. Brown & Sons, 1992).

—— *Old Aberdare*, vol. 8 (Neath: Gwasg Morgannwg, 1997).

Davies, D. L., *A History of Cwmaman Institute, 1868–1993* (Mountain Ash: D. J. Pryse & Son, 1994).

Davies, D. R., *The Minute Book of the Trecynon and District Miners' Welfare Association and the Coliseum*, 18 February 1948 to 9 March 1955 (Aberdare Central Reference Library: Cat. No. WH6).

Davies, Hazel Walford (ed.), *State of Play: Four Playwrights of Wales* (Llandysul: Gomer Press, 1998).

Dunlop, Rachel, Dominic Moody, Adrienne Muir and Catherine Shaw (eds), *Cultural Trends in the '90s, Part 2* (London: Policy Studies Institute, 1997).

Dwelly, Tim, *Creative Regeneration: Lessons from Ten Community Arts Projects* (York: Joseph Rowntree Foundation, 2001).

Eagleton, Terry, *The Ideology of the Aesthetic* (Oxford: Basil Blackwell, 1990).

Ebor, William (ed.), *Men without Work: A Report Made to the Pilgrim Trust* (London: Cambridge University Press, 1938).

Edwards, Dic, 'Theatre as forum', an interview with Hazel Walford Davies, *New Welsh Review*, 31/viii (Llandysul: Gomer, 1995).

—— in Brian Mitchell (ed.), *The Shakespeare Factory, Moon River: The Deal and David* (Bridgend: Seren, 1998).

Edwards, Hywel Teifi, *The Eisteddfod* (Cardiff: University of Wales Press and the Welsh Arts Council, 1990).

Edwards, John, *Talk Tidy: The Art of Speaking Wenglish* (Cowbridge: D. Brown & Sons, 1985).

Egan, David, *Coal Society: A History of the South Wales Mining Valleys 1840–1980* (Llandysul: Gomer Press, 1987).

Ellis, E. L., *T.J.: A Life of Dr Thomas Jones, CH* (Cardiff: University of Wales Press, 1992).

Evans, E. Eynon, *Cold Coal: A Drama of Welsh Life* (London: Samuel French, 1939).

Evans, Geoffrey, 'The amusement of the people: popular entertainment in Aberdare before moving pictures', in Cynon Valley History Society, *Old Aberdare*, vol. 7 (Cardiff: Chas Hunt & Co., 1993).

Foucault, Michel, *Discipline and Punish: The Birth of the Prison*, trans. A. Sheridan (Harmondsworth: Penguin, 1991).

Gordon, Colin (ed.), *Michel Foucault: Power/Knowledge, Selected Interviews and Other Writings 1972–1977* (Brighton: Harvester Wheatsheaf, 1980).

Gwyndaf, Robin, *Welsh Folk Tales* (Cardiff: National Museum of Wales, 1989).

Harland, John, and Kay Kinder (eds), *Crossing the Line: Extending Young People's Access to Cultural Venues* (London: Calouste Gulbenkian Foundation, 1999).

Harris, John S., *Government Patronage of the Arts in Britain* (Chicago: University of Chicago Press, 1970).

Hart, Olive Ely, *The Drama in Modern Wales: A Brief History of Welsh Playwriting from 1900 to the Present Day. A Thesis* (Philadelphia: [privately published], 1928).

Hebditch, Richard (ed.), *Theatre in Education: Ten Years of Change* (London: National Campaign for the Arts, 1997).

Hewison, Robert, *Culture and Consensus: England, Art and Politics since 1940* (London: Methuen, 1995).

Horup, Brigitta, *Arts Attendance and Participation in Wales, June 1993–November 1997* (Aberdare: Valleys Arts Marketing, 1997).

House of Commons, 'The Minutes of the Committee on Welsh Affairs', Session 1981–1982. *Minutes of Evidence: Welsh Arts Council, Wednesday 19 May 1982* (London: OHMS, 1982).

Hughes, David, 'The Welsh national theatre: the avant-garde in the diaspora', in Theodore Shank (ed.), *Contemporary British Theatre* (Basingstoke: Macmillan, 1996).

Humphreys, Emyr, *The Taliesin Tradition: A Quest for the Welsh Identity* (Bridgend: Seren, 1989).

Hutchison, Robert, *The Politics of the Arts Council* (London: Sinclair Browne, 1982).

Institute for Welsh Affairs, *Wales: The Arts of the Possible* (Cardiff: Institute for Welsh Affairs, 1990).

Itzin, Catherine (ed.), *British Alternative Theatre Directory* (Eastbourne: John Offord, 1979).

Jenkins, Mark, 'Virtual reality Wales', *New Welsh Review*, 29/viii (Llandysul: Gomer, 1995).

Jones, Dedwydd, *Black Book on the Welsh Theatre* (London and Lausanne: Bozo/Iolo, 1985).

Jones, Patrick, *Fuse: New and Selected Works* (Cardiff: Parthian Books, 2001).

Jordan, Glenn, and Chris Weedon, 'Whose culture? Funding the arts in Wales', in *Cultural Politics: Class, Gender, Race and the Postmodern World* (Oxford: Basil Blackwell, 1995).

Jowell, Roger, John Curtice, Lindsay Brook and Daphne Arendt (eds), *British Social Attitudes, the 11th Report* (Aldershot: Dartmouth, 1994).

Kelly, Owen, *Community, Art and the State: Storming the Citadels* (London: Comedia, 1984).

Kershaw, Baz, *The Politics of Performance: Radical Theatre as Cultural Intervention* (London: Routledge, 1992).

—— 'Building an unstable pyramid: the fragmentation of alternative theatre', *New Theatre Quarterly*, 36/ix (Cambridge: Cambridge University Press, 1993).

Landry, Charles, Lesley Greene, François Matarasso and Franco Bianchini, *The Art of Regeneration: Urban Renewal through Cultural Activity* (Stroud: Comedia, 1996).

Leonard, Deke, *Maybe I Should've Stayed in Bed?* (Bordon: Northdown, 2000).

—— *Rhinos, Winos and Lunatics* (Bordon: Northdown, 1996).

McGillivray, David (ed.), *McGillivray's Theatre Guide 1996–1997* (London: Rebecca Books, 1996).

McGrath, John, *A Good Night Out — Popular Theatre: Audience, Class and Form* (London: Methuen Drama, 1989).

—— *The Bone won't Break: On Theatre and Hope in Hard Times* (London: Methuen Drama, 1990).

Marshall, Gordon, *Repositioning Class: Social Inequality in Industrial Societies* (London: Sage, 1997).

Matovina, Dan, *Without You: The Tragic Story of Badfinger* (San Mateo, CA: Frances Glover Books, 1997).

Morgan, Peter, 'Theatre in Wales: noises off', *New Welsh Review*, 29 (Llandysul: Gomer Press, 1995).

National Assembly for Wales, *A Culture in Common* (Cardiff: Welsh Assembly, 2000).

Norris, Christopher, *Truth and the Ethics of Criticism* (Manchester: Manchester University Press, 1994).

O'Connor, Danny, *Stereophonics: Just Enough Evidence to Print* (London: Virgin, 2001).

Office for National Statistics, *1991 Census Extract* (Cardiff: Welsh Office Statistical Directorate, 1998).

Ogden, Gill and Morris, Keith (eds), *Welsh Theatre Handbook* (Aberystwyth: Aberystwyth Arts Centre, 2002).

Owusu, Kwesi, *The Struggle for Black Arts in Britain: What can we Consider Better than Freedom* (London: Comedia, 1986).

Pearson, Mike, 'Welsh heterotopias', *New Welsh Review*, 21/vi (Llandysul, Gomer, 1993).

—— *Y Llyfr Glas* (Cardiff: Brith Gof, 1995).

Pick, John, *The Arts in a State: A Study of Government Arts Policies from Ancient Greece to the Present* (Bristol: Bristol Classical Press, 1988).

Price, Cecil, *The Professional Theatre in Wales* (Swansea: University College Swansea, 1984).

Pullinger, John (ed.), *Regional Trends, 32* (London: Stationery Office, 1997).

Rabey, David Ian, and Charmian C. Savill, 'Welsh theatre: inventing new myths', in *Euromaske* (Ljubljana: Euromaske, 1991).

Rabinow, Paul (ed.), *The Foucault Reader: An Introduction to Foucault's Thought* (London: Penguin, 1991).

Redcliffe-Maud, Lord, *Support for the Arts in England and Wales* (London: Calouste Gulbenkian Foundation, 1976).

Ros, Nic, 'Big changes in funding are inevitable', *New Welsh Review*, 36/ix(iv) (Llandysul: Gomer, 1997).

Said, Edward, *Orientalism* (Harmondsworth: Penguin, 1991).

—— *Culture and Imperialism* (London: Chatto & Windus, 1993).

Shade, Ruth, 'The march of progress: the Arts Council of Wales and its drama strategy', *Planet: The Welsh Internationalist*, 139 (Aberystwyth: Berw Cyf, 2000).

—— 'Revisiting the Athens of Wales: Aberdare, theatre and disenfranchisement', *Planet*, 141 (2000).

—— 'Direct activists: the roots of Welsh rock', *Planet*, 145 (2001).

—— 'Valley girls: theatre's Welsh "mams" and "slags"', *Planet*, 146 (2001).

Showstack Sassoon, Anne (ed.), *Approaches to Gramsci* (London: Writers and Readers Publishing Cooperative Society, 1982).

Sinclair, Andrew, *Arts and Cultures: The History of the Fifty Years of the Arts Council of Great Britain* (London: Sinclair-Stevenson, 1995).

Smith, Dai, *Aneurin Bevan and the World of South Wales* (Cardiff: University of Wales Press, 1994).

—— *Wales: A Question for History* (Bridgend: Seren, 1999).

Stephens, Meic (ed.), *The Oxford Companion to the Literature of Wales* (Oxford: Oxford University Press, 1990).

Stephens, Russell, *Emlyn Williams: The Making of a Dramatist* (Bridgend: Seren, 2000).

Taylor, Anna-Marie (ed.), *Staging Wales: Welsh Theatre 1979–1997* (Cardiff: University of Wales Press, 1997).

—— 'Mapping the future', *Planet: The Welsh Internationalist*, 126 (Aberystwyth: Berw Cyf, 1998).

Thomas, Edward, *House of America*, in *Three Plays* (Bridgend: Seren, 1994).

Thomas, M. Wynn, *Internal Difference: Twentieth-Century Writing in Wales* (Cardiff: University of Wales Press, 1992).

Tomlinson, Roger (ed.), *The Initial Report on the Beaufort Research Results* (Cardiff: Welsh Arts Council, 1993).

Valleys Arts Marketing, *Audience Research Survey Report, The Coliseum Aberdare, Product Type: Theatre* (Blackwood, VAM, 1993).

—— *The Coliseum, Aberdare: Three Year Plan 1995/6–1997/8*, draft, not for publication. (Aberdare: VAM, 1995).

—— *Cwmaman Public Hall and Institute: Study to Examine Potential for Development of Cinema and Theatre Programme*, ed. Angela Tillcock (Aberdare: VAM, 1995).

—— *Databox Analysis 1997/98: The Coliseum Theatre, Aberdare*, ed. Lynfa Protheroe (Aberdare: VAM, 1997).

—— *Valleys Area Profile Report: Coliseum Theatre, Aberdare* (Aberdare: VAM, 1998).

Vickery, Frank, *Trivial Pursuits* (London: Samuel French, 1990).

Way, Charles, in interview with Hazel Walford Davies, 'A journey of exploration', *New Welsh Review*, 33/ix (Llandysul: Gomer, 1996).

Waugh, Evelyn, *Decline and Fall* (Harmondsworth: Penguin, 1928).

Webber, Howard, and Tim Challans, *A Creative Future: The Way Forward for the Arts, Crafts and Media in England* (London: Arts Council of Great Britain, 1993).

Welsh Arts Council, *Drama Strategy Consultation Paper* (Cardiff: WAC, 1992).

—— *Blueprint for the Nineties* (Cardiff: WAC, 1993).

—— *National Arts and Media Strategy: Drama Strategy for Wales* (Cardiff: WAC, 1993).

Welsh Assembly Government, *Creative Future: A Culture Strategy for Wales* (Cardiff: Welsh Assembly, 2002).

Welsh Office, *Departmental Report 1995: The Government's Expenditure Plans 1995–96 and 1997–98* (London: HMSO, 1995).

White, Eric W., *The Arts Council of Great Britain* (London: Davis-Poynter, 1975).

Williams, Gwyn A., *When was Wales?* (London: Penguin, 1991).

Williams, Raymond, *Drama in Performance* (Harmondsworth: Pelican Books, 1972).

—— *Drama in a Dramatised Society* (Cambridge: Cambridge University Press, 1975).

—— 'The Arts Council', *Political Quarterly*, 50/2 (April–June 1979).

—— *Politics and Letters: Interviews with New Left Review* (London: Verso, 1981).

—— 'Politics and policies: the case of the Arts Council' (1981), in *The Politics of Modernism. Against the New Conformists* (London: Verso, 1989).

—— *Towards 2000* (London: Chatto & Windus/ The Hogarth Press, 1983).

   Culture (Glasgow: Fontana, 1986)

—— *Problems in Materialism and Culture* (London: Verso, 1989).

—— *What I Came to Say* (London: Hutchinson Radius, 1990).

   Marxism and Literature (Oxford: Oxford University Press, 1992).

Witts, Richard, *Artist Unknown: An Alternative History of the Arts Council* (London: Little, Brown, 1998).

Woodruff, Graham, 'Community, class, and control: a view of community plays', *New Theatre Quarterly*, 5/20 (Cambridge: Cambridge University Press, 1989).

Index